CULTURE IS A

MANY SPLENDORED THING.

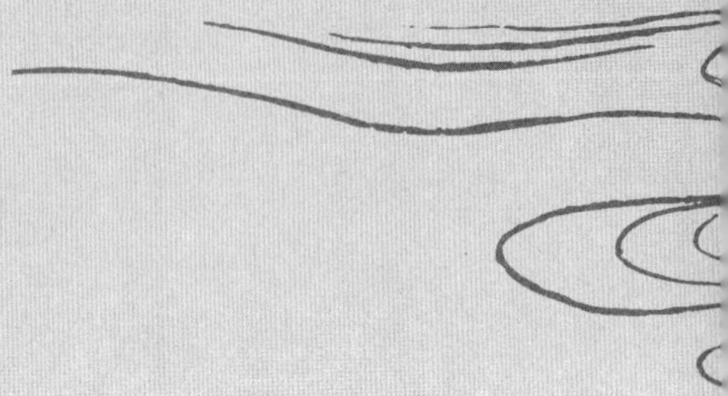

中华文化趣谈

A Kaleidoscope of Chinese Culture

Compiled by: **Zhang Yajun**

Translated by: **Guo Hui**

华语教学出版社
SINOLINGUA

First Edition 2008
Second Edition 2009

ISBN 978-7-80200-400-9

Published by Sinolingua
24 Baiwanzhuang Road, Beijing 100037, China
Tel: (86)10-68320585
Fax: (86)10-68326333
http://www.sinolingua.com.cn
E-mail: hyjx@sinolingua.com.cn
Printed by Beijing Foreign Languages Printing House
Distributed by China International Book Trading Corporation
35 Chegongzhuang Xilu, P.O. Box 399
Beijing 100044, China

Printed in the People's Republic of China

前　言

《中华文化趣谈》是为有一定汉语基础的读者学习汉语言和汉文化而编写的读物。近年来，越来越多的人学习汉语，人们也希望更多地了解中国和中国文化。所以，出版一本能够把语言学习和文化学习结合起来的读物，就显得十分必要。本书正是为了满足这种需求而编写的。

中国是一个历史悠久的国家，中华文化博大而精深，不可能一下子讲全，本书希望通过十几个专题的讲解，带领人们进入中华文化的广大天地，初步了解中华文化的点点滴滴。同时，本人作为一名从事对外汉语教学几十年的教师，也希望能够把自己多年的教学心得和经验融入此书中，力求作到趣味性、知识性和实用性相结合，使人们在轻松愉悦中阅读。

本书采取中英文对照的形式，每篇文章后附有生词解释、重点语法注释、超级链接，旨在帮助读者更好地理解文意。

本书在编写过程中，参阅了一些文献资料，现将书名附录于后，并向作者致以谢意。同时非常感谢华语教学出版社的大力支持，对负责本书翻译工作的郭辉女士和负责本书编辑工作的任蕾女士一并致以诚挚的谢意。

张亚军

2008年5月于美国奥城

Preface

A Kaleidoscope of Chinese Culture is intended for readers who have already developed some understanding of Chinese language and culture. Over recent years there have been increasing numbers of people learning Chinese as a second language, and as such interest in China and Chinese culture has been growing. A book that combines the study of language and culture is necessary to meet the needs of these readers.

Chinese culture is vast, ancient, and deeply fascinating. A single book cannot do justice to its enormity, but it is my hope that the discussions of different topics in this book will introduce readers to some fundamentals of Chinese culture. I have been teaching Chinese as a second language for several decades, and through this book I wish to share my experiences and make the learning and understanding of the Chinese language great fun.

To facilitate readers' comprehension, English translations are provided, not only for texts, but also for sections such as New Words, Notes and Examples, and Questions as attached to the end of each chapter.

I owe my thanks to authors of the books and articles I have referred to. These are listed in the bibliography. I would also like to thank my publisher, Sinolingua, for assistance and professional guidance in preparing this book for publication. My special thanks go to Guo Hui for translating the texts and notes, to Rhys Wesley for polishing the English, and to Ren Lei for editing this book.

Zhang Yajun

May 2008, Oklahoma City

目录

CONTENTS

奇妙的东方魔块

Magical Oriental Cubes

A Kaleidoscope of Chinese Culture

汉字是中国人用来记录语言的文字，它是现在世界上使用人口最多，历史最为悠久的文字。它既似变幻无穷的魔块，又像是精美无比的艺术品。许多人穷其一生揣摩它、研究它、痴迷于它，在遣使文字的快乐中寻找人生的快乐。

因为汉字是一字一块，每个汉字都有三个基本要素，即：形、音、义，比如："日"字，它的字形是在一个方框内有一个"一"字；它的字音是"rì"；它的字义是"太阳"。

所以人们就在这三个不同的方面，利用汉字的特点，做出妙趣横生的文章来。下面我们看看汉字字形的变化。

汉字的最小单位是笔画。有的汉字只有一画,如"一"、"乙"等，有的多达四十画。汉字基本笔画有八种：横、竖、点、撇、捺、挑、钩、折。如果一个汉字是由简单几种笔画构成的，叫做独体字，如：日、月、人、口。由两个以上汉字组成的汉字叫合体字，两个字的叫二合字，三个字的叫三合字等，如：明、朋、从、唱、谢。根据汉字的这一特点，中国人充分发挥着自己的才华，在字形的变换上做着各式各样的文章。有这样一个故事：

从前，有个相国小姐，才貌双全，人品出众。有多少阔家子弟登门求婚，都被小姐拒绝了。她对父亲说："我现在出一上联，不论贫富，谁能对出下联，我就与他成婚。"父亲答应了她的要求。小姐的上联是：

寸土为寺，寺旁言诗，诗曰："明月送僧归古寺。"

这个上联之所以难对，是因为第一句讲了一个二合字，第二句讲了一个三合字，第三句中的第二个字是从句中第一个二合字中拆出来的一个字，而且最后一个二合字与第一句的二合字相同，所以一年过去了，没有人对上。第二年过去了，还是无人对上。到了第三年，有一位姓林的书生，来京赶考，看见了这个上联，他提笔写出了下联，是：

双木成林，林下示禁，禁云：“斧斤以时入山林。”

这个下联对得工整贴切，达到了上述各项要求，小姐十分高兴，于是他们喜结良缘。

人们不仅利用汉字字形大做文章，也利用汉字的字音展示才华。汉字不但表意，也表音，属于音意文字，也就是词符和音节并用的文字。由于汉语音节少，造成汉语中有许多同音字。汉语共有1600多个音节，要表达复杂事物是远远不够的，所以在口语中像“数目”和“树木”、“夕阳”和“西洋”、“中心”和“忠心”在发音上是没有差别的，但一写汉字，人们便明白了它的意思。在古代中国，有这样一种奇特的现象：子女为了表示对长辈的尊重，不会轻易直呼长辈的名字，甚至有些子女为了表示孝心，在日常生活中不仅不说长辈名字中出现的字，而且连长辈名字的同音字都不讲。有这样一个小故事：

有一个老汉叫阿九，他有一个既聪明又贤惠的儿媳妇。因为公公叫阿九，所以儿媳讲话时从来不说“九”字，而且连“九”的同音字也不说。阿九非常高兴，常在人前夸奖儿媳的贤惠。有两个老朋友听了，心中很不服气，说：“我们就不相信她不说‘九’”于是九月九日这一天，他俩一个人怀里抱着一把韭菜，一个人手里提着个酒葫芦，去阿九家。恰巧阿九不在家，儿媳问他们：“两位老伯，找我家公公有什么事吗？”他们说：“阿九回来后，你告诉他，东村有个李老九，西村有个张老九，一个抱着苔下韭，一个提着老烧酒，今天本是九月九，来请阿九去喝酒。”他们想，要把这条信息传达清楚，避开“九”音是不可能的。二人得意洋洋地走了。不久，阿九回来了，儿媳对他说：“东村有个李三六，西村有个张四五，一个抱着扁叶葱，一个提着圆葫芦，今天本是重阳节，来请公公喝一壶。”聪明的儿媳既表达了对公公的尊敬，又轻松化解了朋友的刁难。

汉语和英语一样，都有词义转换的特点，所以中国古代的一些文人学者也很善于利用汉字的这个特点来展示才华。清代（1616-1911）第一才子纪晓岚就曾利用汉语词义转换，巧妙地用“坏”词说好事，做出妙趣横生的文章，成就一番千古佳话：

有一天，纪晓岚到一位朋友家做客，正赶上这位朋友在给高堂老母祝寿，家里是高朋满座，喜气洋洋。大家一看纪晓岚大驾光临，真是蓬荜生辉，于是恭而敬之，尊为上宾。主人更是乐不可支，捧来文房四宝，想请纪晓岚为母亲写一幅寿幛。纪晓岚也不推辞，他略加思索，挥笔写下：“这个女人不是人”。满座皆惊，大家不明白纪学士何出此言。纪晓岚接着写出：“九天仙女降凡尘”，众人破疑为笑，赞叹唏嘘。纪晓岚又写出第三句：“生了儿子是个贼”，人们又吃惊起来，纪晓岚不慌不忙写出最后一句：“偷得仙桃献母亲”。众人抚掌大笑，称赞不已。人们被纪晓岚敏捷的文思、跌宕的文笔所折服。

纪晓岚的这幅寿幛，一落笔就写出了“不是人”三个字，这是一个已经固定化了的词组——惯用语，它有字面义和引申义。它的引申义是一句骂人话，指一个人没有好品质，像畜牲一样。纪晓岚提笔写出来，人们怎能不吃惊呢？这不是明明在骂人嘛！可他写出下半句话“九天仙女降凡尘”时，实际上是使用了“不是人”这三个字的字面义，是在赞颂朋友的母亲是仙女，而不是凡人；下联先写到：“生了儿子是个贼”，将自己的朋友说成了小偷，自然引来众人的诧异，可他笔锋一转，又在“偷”的对象和目的上作了说明。他偷的是“仙桃”，目的是“献母亲”。纪学士在诙谐幽默中，赞扬了朋友对母亲的孝心，真是大巧若拙，风趣超俗。

因为汉字是一个个独立的音义结合的个体，所以它有极强的构词灵活性，而且汉语又是一种非形态语言，它是通过词序和虚词来展示语法意义的，这些又为人们提供了展示才华的新天地。我们来看这样一个有趣的故事：

于右任先生是中国近现代著名的书法家，他的字不仅在今天十分珍贵，就是当年于先生在世时，也是难以求得的。有一次，于先生随人住在一个很偏僻的小地方，居住条件很不好，于先生住的院子的角落处，常常有人随地便溺，于先生对这种既不文明又不卫生的现象很不高兴，于是提笔写了“不可随处小便”几个字，让秘书贴到墙角处。秘书拿着这几个字走出了门，心想这是于先生的墨宝，不忍心把它贴在墙角，很想留为己有，可是这几个字虽写得苍劲潇洒，但这句话实在难登大雅之堂，挂在客厅、书房都不合适。聪明的秘书想到了一个好办法，他用剪刀将这几个字全都剪开，重新排列了一下，交给了装裱店。过了几天字画裱好了，送了回来。秘书拿着它来到于先生面前说：“先生，我想请您在给我写的字画上落款盖印。”于先生很是吃惊，说：“我什么时候给你写过字？”秘书说：“前几天您写了几个字，让我贴在墙角处，我没有贴，现在装裱好了，请您过目。”于先生打开字画一看，原来的六个字“不可随处小便”变成了“小处不可随便”。一句本来不登大雅之堂的话，现在成了一句很有哲理的警言。于先生为这位秘书的聪明感到非常高兴，他欣然题名盖印。从这个故事中，我们可以看到汉字构词的灵活性。

Chinese is the most widely used and ancient language sytem in the world. Chinese characters are something akin to an art form or a magic cubic puzzle. Over the course of history and right up to the present day, people have devoted themselves to improving their knowledge of this system for pleasure and to better express their feelings.

Chinese characters are known as square characters, because each is independent. Each Chinese character is made up of three basic elements: form, sound and meaning. For example, the form of the character 日 is a square with 一 in it, its sound is *ri*, and its meaning is the sun.

There are many interesting combinations and changes of these three elements. In terms of writing formation, the smallest unit of characters is a stroke. Some characters have one stroke, such as 一 and 乙, whereas the more complex characters are made up of as many as 40 strokes. There are eight basic strokes for characters: horizontal, vertical, dot, curve left, curve right, vertical plus right tick, vertical plus left tick, and horizontal plus vertical. There is a group of characters known as one-part characters that includes 日, 月, 人, and 口. However, most characters are compound characters and are composed of two or more parts, such as 明, 朋, 从, 唱, 谢 and many more.

This unique feature has made it much easier to alter pre-existing characters slightly to incorporate different meanings into the language. There are many stories that showcase people's skills and talents in using Chinese characters.

Once there was a daughter of a high-ranking court official, who was not only fair and pretty, but also very intelligent and talented. Many noble and affluent young men wanted to marry her. However, the young lady told her father, "I do not care whether the man I am going to marry is rich or poor, but I need him to match the first line of my antithetical couplet with a second line." Her father agreed. The first line of her couplet went like this:

寸土为寺，寺旁言诗，诗曰：“明月送僧归古寺”

寸土为寺 is about a two-part character, 寺 (temple), which is formed by 寸 and 土; 寺旁言诗 is about a three-part character, 诗 (poem), which is formed by the radical standing for 言 and the two-part character of 寺. The rest of the first line, 诗曰: "明月送僧归古寺", not only uses 诗 at the beginning, but also uses 月 (moon), part of 明 (bright), a new two-part character. And finally, the last character of the whole line is the same as the very first two-part character that has appeared, 寺.

It is not only a most clever deployment of these characters, but also contains a line of poetry, which says, the bright moon accompanies the monk back to his old temple.

This was indeed very difficult to match. The rule for matching a couplet requires that the second line must correspond stylistically to the first line. In this case, the whole line also needed to be meaningful, and some combinations of character needed to be in the right place.

One year passed, and yet another year passed, but no one ever came up with a second line. By the third year, a young scholar named Lin (林) came to the capital to take the imperial examination. He produced the matching line:

双木成林，林下示禁，禁云：“斧斤以时入山林”

Similar to the first line, 双木成林 is about a two-part character, 林 (woods), which is formed by two 木; 林下示禁 is about a three-part character, 禁 (forbidding sign), which is formed by 示 (showing) and the two-part character of 林. The rest of it, 禁云：“斧斤以时入山林”, uses 禁 at the beginning, and also uses 斤 (blade), part of 斧 (axe), a new two-part character. Finally, the last character of the whole line is the same as the very first two-part character that has appeared, 林. Is there any meaning in it? Yes, there is. The second line means, the forbidding sign shows that axes can only be carried into the woods at specific times (to chop down trees).

This well-matched line helped win the heart of the young lady, and happily she married the young scholar at last.

Due to the fact characters are both phonographic and ideographic, logograms and syllables both play important roles in the language. Despite their complexity, Chinese characters represent the relatively small amount of 1,600 syllables. As a result, many characters share the same pronunciation. For example, in spoken Chinese 数目 (*shumu*, number) sounds exactly the same as 树木 (tree), 夕阳 (*xiyang*, setting sun) sounds the same as 西洋 (western), and 中心 (*zhongxin*, center) sounds the same as 忠心 (loyal). When written, however, they are quite different. On occasion, people enjoy playing with the pronunciations of characters in order to demonstrate their mastery of the language, just as they do with the forms of characters.

In times past, it was deemed disrespectful to speak the names of the elderly people in one's family. In fact, people went so far as to avoid words or characters that were pronounced in the same way as the name. The following is an interesting story regarding this practice.

An old man named A Jiu (阿九) had a smart and dutiful daughter-in-law. Since his name had the character 九 (*jiu*, nine) in it, the daughter-in-law never mentioned this character or any other characters pronounced in the same way. Old man A Jiu was very proud of his filial daughter-in-law and spoke highly of her to his friends. Two of them, however, decided to take it upon themselves to challenge her. They did not really believe that she would never use any words pronounced *jiu*.

One day, they went to A Jiu's home. One took a bunch of Chinese chives, (pronounced *jiucai*), and the other took a gourd-shaped bottle containing liquor (pronounced *jiuhulu*). As it happened, A Jiu was not there, but his daughter-in-law received the guests and asked if they wanted to leave a message. They said, "Please let your father know, Li Lao Jiu from the East Village and Zhang Lao Jiu from the West Village come to visit, one with some *jiucai* (Chinese chives), the other with a *jiuhulu* (liquor gourd). And today is *jiuyuejiu* (the 9th day in the 9th month), we come to invite him to drink *jiu* (liquor)." Because each sentence contained a character pronounced *jiu*, they felt assured the daughter-in-law would not be able to give the message successfully without mentioning that sound.

However, their plan was to be thwarted. When the old man arrived home, his daughter-in-law passed on the message in this way: "Li three plus six from the East Village and Zhang four plus five from the West Village came, one with some flat-leaf *cong*, (standing for Chinese chives, but with the modifier flat-leaf, the noun 葱 *cong*, instead of 韭 *jiu*, is used), the other with a round gourd bottle. And since today is the Double Yang Festival (another name for the 9th day in the 9th month, as nine was regarded as Yang in the theory of Yin Yang), they came to invite you for a drink." Thus the quick-witted daughter-in-law was able to pass on the message without being disrespectful toward her father-in-law.

Over the course of history, there have been numerous masters of both Chinese characters and the spoken language. Ji Xiaolan, regarded as the most talented scholar of the Qing Dynasty (1616-1911), is one such master. He was renowned for using the converse meanings of some "bad" words to describe things that were good and was therefore adept at making witty comments.

One day, Ji Xiaolan and many others went to celebrate the birthday of a mutual friend's elderly mother. Due to his status, the appearance of Ji Xiaolan was appreciated by all guests at this happy occasion. To help celebrate, some of the friends gave him a brush and asked him to write something for the old lady on a birthday banner. After giving it some thought, Ji Xiaolan wrote "This lady is not a human being." Everybody was shocked, because in Chinese this phrase means a person without any virtue. Why would a respected man such as Ji Xiaolan write such a thing? A moment later, he wrote the second line: "She is a heavenly fairy who has come down to earth." The relief of understanding in the room was palpable, but it did not last long, because Ji Xiaolan wrote the next line: "She gave birth to a thief." However, the wily Ji Xiaolun again managed to impress everybody with his last line: "He stole a peach of longevity for his mother." All present could not help but admire Ji Xiaolan's quick-mindedness and intelligence in praising the old lady and her dutiful son.

Each Chinese character is an independent unit with its combination of meaning and sound, and words and sentences can be easily formed by characters in fairly flexible ways. In addition, Chinese does not have tense morphology, so word orders and functional words play an important grammatical role. These particular features also make it possible to showcase some great skills with language, as a more recent story tells.

Mr. Yu Youren was a renowned statesman and great calligrapher from the time of Sun Yatsen. During his lifetime, it was considered a great honor to receive one of his works of calligraphy, and nowadays they are considered to be highly valuable.

For a period in his life, Mr. Yu lived in a remote and destitute place. The living and sanitation conditions were poor and people sometimes urinated in the corner of his courtyard. To stop this, he wrote a sign with his brush: 不可随处小便 (do not urinate in inappropriate areas), and asked his secretary to post it in the corner of the courtyard. But the secretary thought the characters were too beautifully written to be placed in such a position. Instead, he carefully cut and separated each character, and took them to a specialized mounting shop. In a few days, he came back to Mr. Yu with the finely mounted piece of work – but with the order of the characters rearranged to 小处不可随便 (behave oneself even over trivial matters). The secretary explained that he had reorganized the six characters to turn the sign of discouraging impolite behavior into advice with a more general application. Mr. Yu appreciated his secretary's flexibility and intelligence and signed and stamped his name on the piece. This story provides a fitting example of the flexibility in forming words and sentences by characters.

生词 New Words

1.变幻	biànhuàn	to change irregularly; to fluctuate
2.精美	jīngměi	exquisite, elegant
3.艺术品	yìshùpǐn	work of art
4.揣摩	chuǎimó	to try to fathom; to try to figure out
5.要素	yàosù	essential factor; key element
6.笔画	bǐhuà	strokes of a Chinese character
7.才貌双全	cáimào-shuāngquán	to be endowed with both beauty and talent

8.人品	rénpǐn	moral standing; moral quality character
9.出众	chūzhòng	to be out of the ordinary; to be outstanding
10.阔家	kuòjiā	rich family
11.子弟	zǐdì	children, juniors
12.登门	dēng mén	to call at sb.'s house
13.求婚	qiú hūn	to make an offer of marriage; to propose
14.赶考	gǎn kǎo	to take the imperial examination
15.贴切	tiēqiè	suitable, appropriate
16.喜结良缘	xǐjié-liángyuán	to make a good match
17.展示	zhǎnshì	to show, to reveal; to lay bare
18.长辈	zhǎngbèi	elder member of a family
19.贤惠	xiánhuì	(of a women) virtuous; genial and prudent
20.韭菜	jiǔcài	fragrant-flowered garlic; Chinese chives
21.刁难	diāonàn	to create difficulties; to make things difficult
22.佳话	jiāhuà	a story on everybody's lips; a much-told tale
23.高堂	gāotáng	one's parents
24.祝寿	zhùshòu	to congratulate (an elderly person) on his or her birthday
25.高朋满座	gāopéng-mǎnzuò	a great gathering of distinguished guests
26.喜气洋洋	xǐqì-yángyáng	full of joy; jubilant
27.光临	guānglín	(of a guest or visitor) to honor sb. with one's presence
28.蓬荜生辉	péngbì-shēnghuī	luster lent to a humble house (said in thanks for a visitor)
29.乐不可支	lèbùkězhī	overwhelmed with joy; overjoyed
30.文房四宝	wénfáng-sìbǎo	the four treasures of the study (writing brush, ink stick, ink slab and paper)

31.寿幛	shòuzhàng	birthday banner (with a congratulatory message)
32.挥笔	huī bǐ	to wield the brush
33.跌宕	diēdàng	free and easy; hold and unconstrained
34.书法家	shūfǎjiā	calligrapher, calligraphist
35.便溺	biànniào	to urinate or defecate; to relieve oneself
36.墨宝	mòbǎo	treasured scroll of calligraphy or painting; beautiful handwriting
37.难登大雅之堂	nán dēng dàyǎ zhī táng	too low to enter polite company; vulgar
38.深奥	shēn'ào	abstruse, profound
39.哲理	zhélǐ	philosophy
40.警言	jǐngyán	aphorism, epigram
41.欣然	xīnrán	joyfully; with pleasure

语法聚焦 Notes and Examples

一、它既似变幻无穷的魔块，又像是精美无比的艺术品

"既……又……"是连词。它连接两个并列成分，表示具有两个方面的情况或性质。

既…又… is a conjunction and links two parallel components to indicate two aspects of what is mentioned. For example:

1. 他既会英语又会法语。
2. 坐飞机既快又舒服。
3. 我们既要批评他的缺点，又不要伤了和气。

二、汉字不但表意，也表音

"不但"是连词，用在表示递进关系的复句中，后面常与"而且"、"并且"、"也"等词搭配。"不但……也"一方面表示前后两层意思是并存的，同时也把

后一层意思推进了一步。

不但 is used with other conjunctions such as 而且, 并且, or 也 in sentences with progressive implication, meaning not only... but also.... For example:

1. 这不但符合我们的利益，也符合你们的利益。
2. 这个孩子不但语文成绩好，数学成绩也好。
3. 马先生不但会工作，也很会生活。

三、正赶上这位朋友在给高堂老母祝寿

"正"是副词，表示巧合、刚好、恰好的意思。

正 is an adverb meaning just, exactly, or almost exactly at this or that moment. For example:

1. 你的想法正合我意。
2. 昨天我们去逛商店，正赶上商品大减价。
3. 这双鞋你穿正合适。

四、大家不明白纪学士何出此言

"何"是文言词，在现代书面语中还用。它作为疑问代词，有"什么"、"怎么"、"为什么"的意思。

The interrogative pronoun 何 is a classic Chinese word still used in modern Chinese, meaning what, how, why, depending on the context. For example:

1. 他是何人?
2. 你有何事?
3. 此事何不求教韩先生?

五、众人抚掌大笑，称赞不已

"不已"是不停继续的意思。书面语，用于双音节动词后面，作补语。

不已 is used as an supplement after a disyllabic verb in written language, meaning non-stop or continuously. For example:

1. 这首诗令人赞叹不已。
2. 孩子们的杂技表演，令观众惊叹不已。
3. 他被气得双手颤抖不已。

六、我们来看这样一个有趣的故事

这里的“来”是动词，但它已失去了原来的意义，并不表示具体动作，而是表示将要做某事。它后面的动词所表示的动作不能是过去的或已完成的。

来 here is a verb used immediately before another verb, meaning going to do something. For example:

1. 大家来想办法，这个问题怎么解决。
2. 你来宣布董事会的决定。
3. 我来帮你写。

七、但这句话实在难登大雅之堂

“实在”是副词，强调某种情况的真实性，表示“真的”、“的确”。

Adverb 实在 emphasizes what is mentioned is true, meaning indeed, really. For example:

1. 这里的气候实在让人受不了。
2. 今天我实在太累了。
3. 这篇英文稿，我实在看不懂。

想一想 Questions

1. 每一个汉字有哪三个基本要素?
   What are the three basic elements of a Chinese character?
2. 从字形角度看，汉字最小的单位是什么?
   What is the most basic unit of a Chinese character in terms of its form?
3. 汉字的基本笔画有哪些?
   What are the basic strokes of the Chinese characters?
4. 什么是独体字? 什么是合体字?
   What is a one-part character, and what is a compound character?

超级链接Super Links

回文诗欣赏

汉字既有构词的灵活性，又是一字一音，一字一词或一语素，人们综合利用汉字的这些特点，就写出了顺念倒念皆能成文的回文对或回文诗。现在我们抄录宋朝李禺的一首回文诗，使大家看一看汉字之奇妙。这首诗从上往下正读是夫忆妻，从下往上逆读是妻忆夫：

正读是：

枯眼望遥山隔水
往来曾见几心知
壶空怕酌一杯酒
笔下难成和韵诗
途路阻人离别久
讯音无雁寄回迟
孤灯夜守长寥寂
夫忆妻兮父忆儿

倒读是：

儿忆父兮妻忆夫
寂寥长守夜灯孤
迟回寄雁无音讯
久别离人阻路途
诗韵和成难下笔
酒杯一酌怕空壶
知心几见曾来往
水隔山遥望眼枯

再谈汉字

More on Chinese Characters

2

A Kaleidoscope of Chinese Culture

世界上最古老的文字有三种：一种是苏美尔人的楔形文字，它产生于公元前3000年左右，后来巴比伦人、亚述人、赫梯人和波斯人都使用过，到公元前330年，随着波斯王国的灭亡而消亡了；另外一种是古埃及的象形文字，它产生于4100年以前，历经岁月沧桑后也消亡了；再就是中国的方块字，已有5000多年的历史了，今天还在被人们使用着。汉字之所以能如此被华夏民族的子孙推崇，与汉字本身的特点息息相关。

一、众所周知，文字是记录语言的符号，它负载着特定的信息，人们用它表达思想，传播文化。世界文字有表音文字和表意文字之分，汉字作为以表意为主的文字，其最大的优点在于其具有跨越历史、超越方言的能力。

从时间上看，汉语在历史发展中，古今语音变化很大，但是由于汉字字形和所代表的字义基本稳定，因此，现代人仍然可以很方便地阅读古籍资料。汉字之所以有这样稳定的字形，是要归功于古人科学的造字方法。汉字的造字方法归结起来有六种，这就是所谓的“六书”。东汉（25-220）郑众说：“六书，象形、会意、转注、处事、假借、谐声也。”所以我们今天在读两千年前的古书时，还明白“于乎皇考，永世克孝”是什么意思。如果这句话是用表音符号记录下来的，那么随着语音的变迁，我们今天就不一定能读懂了。

从空间上看，汉字可以跨越方言进行交际。中国地域广大，南北方语音有很大差别，甚至在同一个地方，尚有“十里不同音”之说，但无论字音多么千差万别，字义却基本相同，人们在交流时没有障碍。有一个北京人到上海出差，想找一个叫“外白渡桥” 的地方，他用纯正的普通话问一位上海老者：“外白渡桥怎么走？”可他说了数遍，老人只是摇头不懂，于是，他拿出纸笔写下“外白渡桥”几个字，老人一见脱口而说“瓦帮焦”（上海话发音），老人完全明白了这个人的意思。

有日本学者认为，中国之所以能创造出千古不变的汉字，与中国人的民族性和文明价值标准有关，中国人追求的文明是“以经得起时间考验的文明价值为标准”的。他举例来说，中国人常说：希望中日两国世世代代、子子孙孙友好下去。“子子孙孙”这句话早在中国青铜器时代就是常用语。中国人把字铸在青铜器物上，铭文的结尾总是说“子孙其永宝用”。所以中国人认为，真正有价值的东西，是能超越时代而永久保存下去的东西，而不是只图眼前的方便。

二、汉字与汉语相适应。汉语是一种非形态语，汉语的词没有严格意义的形态变化。与英语相比，英语是形态语，英语词有形态变化，比如动词是根据时态而变化的，像“eat”，它有“ate, eaten, eating”的不同。汉语的“吃”，不管在什么时候，它都不会有任何变化。汉语不需要有表示形态变化的音素符号，只要有音节符号就可以了，一个汉字就是一个音节(但汉字不是音节文字)，所以我们常听到这样的话：“这个人说话咬字真清楚，一字一板的。”汉语“字”这个概念，在英语中很难找到相对应的词，所以有人翻译为“character”，也有人翻译成“word”、“writing”等。所以一个汉字一般代表一个词或一个语素。一个汉字又是语音符号又是语素符号，用起来十分方便。这也是汉字能够长期存在的一个重要原因。

三、汉字数量听起来虽多，但常用字不多。如果人们翻开几本从古到今的汉字字典，就会发现，记录3000多年前汉字的字典《甲骨文编》，收字4672个；东汉许慎编的记录2000多年汉字字典《说文解字》，收字9353个；清代陈敬廷等人编纂的《康熙字典》，收字47035个；1915年编辑的《中华大字典》，收字48000多个；20世纪90年代出版的《汉语大字典》，收字56000个左右。乍一听来，十分吓人，仔细一看，原来这是把几千年出现的汉字集合在一起的总和，其中绝大多数古字，早已不用了。那么，在现代汉语中，汉字的使用情况是怎样呢？最近，人们用计算机进行了统计，现在常用的汉字有6300多个，可分为五级。一级：使用频率占80.02%以上的有560个。二级有807个。一、二级合起来，使用频率占95.03%。三级常用字1033个。这三个级别字合起来，使用频率就占99%。也就是说，掌握了560个汉字就可以进行一定的日常对话，掌握2400个汉字就可较为顺畅地阅读书刊报纸了。

四、记、写汉字有法可循。对于一个没有接触过汉语、不了解汉字的外国人来说，一想到要学那么多汉字便望而生畏。其实不然，大多数汉字是表意的，也就是说，我们可以见字知意。而且汉字是有一定笔顺和一套偏旁部首构字部件的，前面我们曾谈到，有相当多的汉字是合体字，只要注重不同构字部件的比例和位置，书写起来也并不是一件难事。事实上，外国人通过一段时间的学习，很快便能掌握汉字，并不觉得学习汉字是一件难得不得了的事情。

The three most ancient systems of writing in the world are Sumerian cuneiform, Egyptian hieroglyphs, and Chinese characters. Cuneiform was created in about 3,000 BC, and later used by Babylonians, Assyrians, Hittites and Persians. The use of cuneiform disappeared with the withering away of the Persian Kingdom in about 330 BC. The ancient Egyptians developed a system of pictographs around 4,100 years ago, but this system has also long disappeared. The final system, that of Chinese characters, was first invented about 5,000 years ago. However, unlike the other two systems, the Chinese one did not die out. Due to certain unique features, Chinese characters remain a powerful system of writing.

1. Written language is a representation of spoken language. It transmits specific information and disseminates culture and knowledge. Humans are thought to use two broad types of written language, namely ideographs and phonographs. Chinese characters are basically ideographic. This has the advantage of overcoming historical and geographical differences.

In fact, over time modern Chinese characters have had many changes in phonetics when compared to their ancient predecessors. However, the composition and meaning of the characters have remained strikingly constant. There are six basic ways of composing characters. Zheng Zhong, a scholar of Confucian and other classic works in the Eastern Han Dynasty (25-220), noted "The six categories of Chinese characters are pictographic, ideographic, mutually explanatory, indicative, or are phonetic loans and homophones."

As the result, even today many Chinese can read ancient texts with a minimum of difficulty. For example, an educated person would understand the meaning of 于乎皇考, 永世克孝 (to devote filial piety to the late emperor and to ancestors), even though it was uttered by an emperor and recorded in a book more than 2,000 years ago! In contrast, if the same phrase was written in a phonographic script a contemporary reader would have no idea of its meaning.

Chinese characters can also be used to overcome mutual incomprehension of other dialects within the borders of the country. Characters may be pronounced differently in as short a distance as ten miles, but the meanings of the characters are largely the same. There is a good example for this.

Several years ago, a man from Beijing went to Shanghai on a business trip. However, he was having trouble finding his way around town and stopped to ask an old man, in Mandarin, where "外白渡桥" (*Waibaiduqiao*) would be. However, the old man simply could not understand what he was saying. So the man from Beijing wrote the characters out on a piece of paper. The old man immediately replied, "Oh, *wabangjiao*" in Shanghai dialect, and showed him the way. *Waibaiduqiao* was pronounced *wabangjiao* in the dialect, but the characters helped in clarifying.

A Japanese scholar has an interesting insight into how Chinese characters have been able to stand the test of time. He believes it is linked to the cultural values of the Chinese and the pursuit of establishing a civilization able to last far into the future. He notes that when talking about Sino-Japanese relations, the Chinese often say "We hope that our friendship continues generation after generation." Amazingly, this very expression was recorded in an inscription as far back as the Bronze Age. On a piece of bronze ware were the words "to be used forever, by generation after generation." Chinese culture values continuation through the generations very highly. It is not just concerned about what is convenient for the moment.

2. Unlike English, Chinese does not have tense morphology. Due to the different tenses found in English, verbs change their forms depending on, for example, whether they are in the past, present, or future. As such, the verb "eat" has three different forms, "ate, eaten, eating". The Chinese character for eat, 吃, remains the same regardless of the time the action took place. There is no phoneme to indicate tenses in Chinese, and as a result, when spoken clearly every character is a syllable. A Chinese character may stand for a word or a morpheme, and it is both a phonetic and a morphemic element that can be used quite conveniently. This is one of the reasons that Chinese characters have endured over several millennia.

3. Although there are a great number of characters, the number of commonly used ones is limited. As time goes by more and more characters are created. In fact, there were already 4,672 oracle bone script characters in existence, according to the dictionary *Oracle Bone Scripts*. According to Eastern Han Dynasty scholar Xu Shen, writing in *Explanations of Scripts and Elucidation of Characters*, there were 9,353 characters in existence at that time. Cheng Jingting's *Kangxi Dictionary*, from the Qing Dynasty, however, recorded 47,035 characters. In 1915, the *Chinese Dictionary* recorded over 48,000 characters. And finally, a recent edition of a dictionary collected some 56,000 characters.

Despite the large number of characters, only a relatively small amount are often used. According to computer-based statistics, there are over 6,300 commonly used characters, which can be divided into five categories. Category one, which consists of 560 characters, has a frequency of use over 80.02% in daily life. Category two is made up of 807 characters. In total the first two categories have a frequency of use of over 95.03%. Category three consists of 1,033 characters. Altogether, the first three categories have a frequency of use of 99%. In other words, a person can manage with daily conversations when he or she masters 560 characters, and easily read books or papers when he or she masters 2,400 characters.

4. Chinese characters appear to be difficult to both write and remember, actually there are many rules to follow. Due to the fact many foreign learners come from a background of reading words from a selection of twenty to thirty letters, they find Chinese study a formidable task. But as we know, Chinese characters are ideographic, getting to know the meaning of different radicals and parts helps greatly in understanding and remembering characters. As mentioned, many characters are compound ones, if the positions or sizes of the components are made clear, writing will become easier. As a matter of fact, many foreign students learning Chinese become skilled at writing Chinese characters over a short period of time, and they do not regard it extremely difficult.

生词 New Words

1.楔形文字	xiēxíng wénzì	cuneiform characters
2.消亡	xiāowáng	to wither away; to die out
3.象形文字	xiàngxíng wénzì	pictographic characters
4.方块字	fāngkuàizì	square-shaped Chinese characters
5.华夏	huáxià	archaic name for China
6.众所周知	zhòngsuǒzhōuzhī	as everyone knows; as is known to all
7.符号	fúhào	symbol, mark
8.负载	fùzài	to load
9.信息	xìnxī	information, message
10.表意	biǎoyì	ideograph
11.方言	fāngyán	dialect

12.六书	liùshū	the six scripts – the six categories of Chinese characters
13.地域	dìyù	region, district
14.脱口而说	tuōkǒu'érshuō	to say sth. unwittingly; to blurt out
15.价值标准	jiàzhí biāozhǔn	standard of value
16.青铜器时代	qīngtóngqì shídài	the Bronze Age
17.形态	xíngtài	morphology
18.时态	shítài	tense
19.音节	yīnjié	syllable
20.甲骨文	jiǎgǔwén	inscriptions on bones or tortoise shells of the Shang Dynasty (1600 BC-1046 BC)
21.乍	zhà	first; for the first time
22.吓人	xiàrén	frightening
23.总和	zǒnghé	sum, total
24.频率	pínlǜ	frequency; rate of recurrence
25.掌握	zhǎngwò	to grasp, to master
26.顺畅	shùnchàng	smooth and easy
27.望而生畏	wàng'érshēngwèi	to be terrified (or awed) by the sight of sb. or sth.
28.笔顺	bǐshùn	order of strokes observed in calligraphy
29.不得了	bùdéliǎo	extremely, exceedingly

语法聚焦 Notes and Examples

一、汉字之所以能如此被华夏民族的子孙推崇，与汉字本身的特点息息相关。

“之”是助词，“所以”是连词，“之所以”结构放在主语之后，谓语之前，提出有待说明的事实、结果，后面常跟着“是因为”来说明原因。
之 is an auxiliary word, 所以 is a conjunction. The structure of 之所以 is used after the subject and before the predicate to raise a fact or result yet to be explained. 是因为 often follows to further explain the reason. For example:

1. 这次试验之所以成功，与全体工作人员的努力分不开。
2. 她之所以有这么好的成绩，是因为平日刻苦钻研的结果。
3. 吴先生之所以不讲话，是因为他心中有顾忌。

二、汉字作为以表意为主的文字……在于其具有跨越历史、超越方言的能力

“在于”是动词，用来指出事物内容或本质的关键所在。多作谓语，后面带有宾语。
Verb 在于 indicates the content, the nature or the key of something. It is mostly used as the predicate followed by an object. For example:

1. 一年之计在于春，一日之计在于晨。
2. 这本小说能够获奖，就在于它的题材新颖。
3. 事情能不能成功，全在于用人是否得当。

三、但是由于汉字字形和所代表的字义基本稳定

“由于”是介词，表示原因或理由，意思和“因为”差不多。
Preposition 由于 has almost the same meaning of 因为 to indicate the reason or cause. For example:

1. 由于大家的帮助，所以我们才克服了这么大的困难。
2. 对这件事，由于我不了解情况，所以不能发表意见。
3. 由于时间的关系，第三个问题我们明天再讲。
4. 由于情况变了，我们的计划也必须变。

四、汉字与汉语相适应

“相”是副词。它表示两个或两个以上主体发出同样的动作、行为，并且交互于对方。
Adverb 相 indicates that an action or a behavior is done by two or more subjects, mutually and reciprocally. For example:

1. 朱先生与林小姐二人相爱已经三年多了。
2. 这个故事，就是人们口口相传，流传至今。
3. 你的教学内容必须与孩子们的智力水平相适应。

五、一个汉字又是语音符号又是语素符号

“又……又……”这种格式表示几种情况、动作同时存在。它所连接的成分，在意思上是同类或相近，在结构上一般相同。

The pattern 又…又… connects components of the same structure and of similar nature, indicating the co-existence of situations or actions. For example:

1. 田小姐又大方又稳重。
2. 白教授又是我的老师又是我的朋友。
3. 在晚会上，大家又是唱歌，又是跳舞，真是高兴极了。

六、用起来十分方便

“十分”是副词，表示达到充分的程度，相当于“非常”。

Adverb 十分 indicates the highest degree, meaning completely or very much. For example:

1. 今天参加贵公司挂牌盛典，敝人感到十分荣幸。
2. 经理对我们的工作感到十分满意。
3. 化验工作要十分小心，不能出一点点差错。

七、对于一个没有接触过汉语，不了解汉字的外国人来说

“过”是动态助词。它放在动词后边，表示某种动作在过去发生。常用来强调有过某种经历。

Verbal auxiliary 过 follows a verb to indicate an action once took place. It emphasizes a past experience. For example:

1. 沈博士以前来过这里。
2. 我还没吃过法国饭。
3. 这个电影只有两个学生看过。
4. 从来没有人研究过这个问题。

想一想 Questions

1. 世界上最古老的文字有几种?
   What are the most ancient writing systems?
2. 记录文字的方式一般有哪两种?
   What are the two broad types of written language that we use?
3. 汉字的特点是什么?
   What kind of features do Chinese characters have?
4. 常用汉字有多少个?
   How many Chinese characters are commonly used?

超级链接 Super Links

(一) 象形字欣赏

古代中国人以人本身、动物和自然界中的事物为描绘对象，造出了很多象形文字。下面，我们来欣赏一些古老的象形字。

描绘人本身的象形字
人 目 面 眉 口 心 女 耳 齒 手 子
描绘动物的象形字
鳥 鱼 馬 牛 羊 象 鹿 燕 犬 龍 龜
描绘自然界事物的象形字
雨 雲 土 生 舟 車 貝 瓜 鼎 壺 果

(二) 有趣的会意字

1 看
2 見
3 令
4 寒
5 冠
6 孕
7 孫
8 焚
9 莫
10 災
11 安
12 宿
13 昏
14 賓
15 保
16 祭

1. 看：手放在眼的上方，遮住阳光远望。

2. 见：画出人体，突出人的眼睛，表示看见了什么东西。

3. 令：上面是发令人的口，下面弯曲的身体表示接受命令的人。

4. 寒：一个人在屋子里，地上有冰，人钻在草中，使人想到寒冷。

5. 冠：“冠”就是帽子。一只手正把帽子(冂)往人的头上戴。

6. 孕：人的肚子很大，里边有个小孩。

7. 孙：子的旁边有丝，表示连续不断。

8. 焚：下面的火把上面的树木烧着了。

9. 莫：这是最早的“暮”字。太阳落在草丛中，表示太阳落山了，天快要黑了。

10. 灾：屋里着火了。

11. 安：女人在屋里，使人联想到安全舒适。

12. 宿：在一间屋子里，有人在草席上睡觉。

13. 昏：太阳落下去，位置比人还低，表示黄昏时刻。

14. 宾：一个人走进屋里，表示客人到了。

15. 保：一个大人抱着婴儿，本义是养育、抚养，引申为保护、保佑等义。

16. 祭：一只手拿着肉，放在祭台上进行拜祭。

引自韩鉴堂《中国文化》

中国的谐音文化

Homophones

3

A Kaleidoscope of Chinese Culture

汉语因为音节少，所以同音字多。从《普通话声韵拼合总表》上看，汉语只有400多个音节，加上四声和儿化韵，也只有1600多个，而英语则有10,000多个，这就出现了若干个字共为一个音节的现象。比如，《现代汉语词典》里，“xī”这个音节，就有“西、希、奚、昔……”等77个字，它们发音一样，写法不一样，意义也不一样，这就在汉语中，出现了一种谐音修辞法。

这种谐音修辞就是利用某一个词的音，联想到与它发音相同或相近的另外一个词，从而采取这个词的意义，这不仅仅是一种语言现象，也形成了独特的民俗文化和文化心理。下面我们从几个方面加以介绍：

一、讨吉利的谐音文化。祈求幸福吉祥，平安顺利，这是人们共同的心愿，于是人们就利用这种“谐音”的办法，来达到心理上的满足，民间称之为“讨口彩”。比如，中国人普遍喜欢葫芦，因其与“福禄”两字谐音，且藤枝蔓延，结果甚多，而被国人视为多子多孙的吉祥物；再如，中国传统新年的节庆风俗更包含着许多谐音文化：过年时家家要贴“福”字，有的人故意将“福”字倒着贴，因为“倒”与“到”谐音，从而得到“福到（倒）了”这一吉祥效应；人们还要吃一种用黏米做的“年（黏）糕”，“年糕”与“年高”又是谐音，因而得到“年年增高”的意义；在传统习俗中，过年这一天家家还要贴年画，过去在杨柳青年画中，画着一个大白胖小子抱着一条大鲤鱼，旁边还有一朵大莲花，这样的画最受人们欢迎，因为它以莲花和鱼的谐音寓意“连年有余”，表达了人们希望生活富裕的愿望。

除此之外，人们还画蝙蝠，用“蝠”来表现“福”，体现出“五福临门”、“洪福齐天”等意愿。画喜鹊鸟站立在梅枝上，表现出“喜上眉梢”的意思。还有在日常生活中，人们也十分注意利用生活中一些具体事物的名字，来谐音取义，表现出祈求美好幸福的意愿。著名京剧艺术大师梅兰芳先生家中院子里，种了两棵柿子树和一棵苹果树，寓意是“事事平安”。也有的人家把槐树和苹果树种在一起，取意是“怀抱平安”。有一年，台湾在正月十五元宵节灯会上，用彩灯拼成几个大字“灯丰照吉”，就是借用了“登峰造极”的谐音。

二、民风民俗中的谐音文化。民俗是历史和文化的精髓，是中国传统文化的重要载体。在日常结婚、送礼、祝寿等活动中，更是处处都能见到利用谐音表现民俗意义的现象，尤其是在传统的婚礼上。比如，新娘下轿以后，不能马上进屋，要迈过一个火盆，为的是取这个“火”字，将来的日子“红红火火”。新娘还要跨过一个马鞍，咬一口苹果，意思是“平平安安”。在洞房的被褥底下，放一些红枣、栗子、花生、核桃、桂圆等，是为了取这些物品的音。红枣和栗子谐“早立子”；花生谐“花着生”，不要都是男孩，也不要都是女孩，儿女双全。核桃谐“和和美美”；桂圆谐“祥贵团圆”。放这些东西的老太太还要一边撒一边念叨：“一把栗子，一把枣，小的跟着大的跑”。你看，孩子还要成帮成串，表现了人们多子多孙的愿望。

尽管中国幅员广大，各地区有着不同的风俗习惯，但总是体现着这种谐音文化。比如，在安徽有些地区，新娘子进洞房，要脱掉自己的鞋，穿上新郎的鞋，取意是“夫妻同偕”。在北京，新娘坐帐要吃子孙饺子，人们故意不煮熟，问新娘子：“生不生呀？”新娘要回答：“生。”意思是能早生孩子。

三、忌讳的谐音。所谓忌讳的谐音，就是人们对生活中不好的事，或与这些事谐音的词，采取回避或换一种说法。比如：在结婚或年节等喜庆的日子里，人们忌说“死、输、完、散、倒霉”等不吉利词语。这时送礼也不要送伞，因为“伞”与“散”谐音。也不要送钟，因为“送钟”与“送终”同音。夫妻不能分吃一个梨，因为“分梨”与“分离”也是谐音，这些都会使人产生不愉快的文化心理。新年时，人们认为打碎器皿是不吉利的，如果小孩子不小心打碎了一个杯子，妈妈会说：“没关系，岁岁（碎碎）平安。”人们用这种谐音办法，把自己从坏心情中解脱出来。坏事变成了吉祥语。

另外，中国有很多方言，因为发音不同，也有不同的禁忌。比如，广东人把“猪舌”叫“猪俐”，因为广东话，“舌”与“蚀”、“折”同音，是亏本的意思。北方有很多人忌说“蛋”，因为有很多骂人话中有“蛋”。如：坏蛋、混蛋、笨蛋、王八蛋。所以有人把“鸡蛋”叫“鸡子儿”，“鸡蛋汤”叫“木须汤”，“摊鸡蛋”叫“摊黄菜”。还有像吃饭时，不要问别人“你还要饭吗？”，“你吃不吃醋？”因为“要饭”、“吃醋”都会使人产生不好的联想。有的地方干脆把“醋”字改叫“忌讳”，问：“你要忌讳吗？”

这种谐音文化，形成了中国人的独特文化心理。人们通过谐音力求趋吉避凶。20世纪初，袁世凯当了大总统，后来又当了皇帝。他下令，正月十五一律不许说吃“元宵”，把“元宵”改为“汤圆”，因为“元宵”与“袁消”谐音。虽然人们不敢再说“元宵”了，但他还是“消”了，这不是因为这种球形食品的名字，是因为他逆历史潮流而动。

四、诙谐幽默的谐音。我们在日常谈话时，也常常使用谐音这种修辞手段，以增加语言的幽默感。比如，一个人说：“老李得了气管炎，整天是床头柜。”乍一听，好像老李呼吸道出了问题，实际上，“气管炎”是“妻管严”的谐音，“床头柜”是“床头跪”的谐音。这里是说老李的妻子管他很严，每月工资如数上交，每日活动如实报告，每天还要在床头跪着。这就十分风趣地在挖苦老李惧内。

在汉语中还有许多谐音歇后语，用在说话中，更是妙趣横生，比如，娶媳妇坐抬筐——缺觉（轿）；和尚打伞——无法（发）无天；电线杆上绑鸡毛——好大胆（掸）子。

这种诙谐幽默的谐音，常常被演员用在节目表演中，取得了非常好的喜剧效果。有一次，相声演员马季到香港与台湾演员合作演出。马季一上台就说："香港马季刚过，北京马季就来了。"他说的香港马季，是指赛马季节，巧妙地把两个"马季"联在一起，引起了人们哄堂大笑。接着他问合作的台湾演员："你从哪里来？"回答是："我从台北来。"马季说："我从台南来。"观众有些不解，马季接着说："我是从舞台南边上来的。"于是又抖响了一个"包袱"，观众报以热烈掌声和笑声。演员这种即兴表演，熟练运用汉语谐音的能力，是他们智慧的表现。

五、人名、地名中的谐音。谐音也常常被用在人名和地名中。人们总是希望自己的名字能给自己带来好运，也都希望把一些不够高雅的地名赋予一些高雅内涵，于是也借助于谐音。比如，有人的名字叫郝蕴琦，就是谐音"好运气"，于得水谐音"鱼得水"。在北京，以前有一个母猪胡同，现改名"墨竹胡同"。狗尾巴胡同改名"高义伯胡同"，大墙缝胡同，改名"大翔凤胡同"。台湾基隆，原名鸡笼，1883年改为基隆。这么一改发音不变，意义却高雅多了。

六、谐音是记忆的窍门。在记忆过程中，我们可以把某些零散的、枯燥的、无意义的难记材料进行谐音处理，形成了新奇有趣、富有意义的语句，这样就容易记住了。从前有个爱喝酒的教书先生，一天他给学生们布置了一道题目，要把圆周率背到小数点后30位，并宣布放学前考试，背不出不得回家，说罢就走了。学生们眼睁睁地望着这一长串数字3.141592653589793238462643383279，个个愁眉苦脸。一些学生摇头晃脑地背起来，还有一些顽皮的学生揣好题单，溜出私塾，跑上后山去玩。忽然，他们发现先生正与一个和尚在山顶的凉亭里饮酒作乐，就扮着鬼脸，钻进了林子。夕阳西下，老师酒足饭饱，回来考学生。那些死记硬背的学生结结巴巴、张冠李戴，而那些顽皮的学生却背得清脆圆顺，弄得老师莫名其妙。原来，在林子里玩耍时，有个聪明的学生把要背诵的数字编成了谐音咒语："山巅一寺一壶酒，尔乐苦煞吾，把酒吃，酒杀尔，杀不死，遛尔遛死，扇扇刮，扇耳吃酒。"一边念，一边还指着山顶做喝酒、摔死、遛弯、扇耳光的动作，念叨了几遍，很轻松的记住了如此复杂的数字。

谐音作为一种语言现象，普遍存在于各种语言之中，而汉语中的谐音现象尤其多。这主要是跟中华民族的文化传统和民族心理相关。中国人从远古以来，在特殊的地理环境和经济生活方式的氛围中养成了宏观看待世界的方式。这使得中国人习惯以感性直观的方式感悟人与世界的内在联系，他们重直觉，崇尚观物取象，立象得意。同时，这也形成了中国式思维具有穿透语言本身、领略语言背后意蕴的特点。从文化本身而言，中国文化是一种含蓄而不直露的文化，表意明确而手段多样、隐蔽，含蓄雅洁向来为中国文化所崇尚。因此，谐音是中国文化的内在要素。它的生成植根于中国文化这个大环境中，其理解和接受更是与中华民族的文化心理息息相关。

Chinese language has not many syllables, and as a result many words have the same pronunciation. A standard text known as *The Table of Sound Combinations in Mandarin* shows there are only just over 400 different sounding syllables in Mandarin Chinese. If the four tones and the non-syllabic *-er* (a diminutive suffix) are counted as syllables, the number of syllables is still just over 1,600. In comparison, English has 10,000 plus different sounding syllables.

As a result, many Chinese words that sound the same have totally different meanings. Although this may seem confusing, the beauty of Chinese is that these homophones use different characters. Take the syllable *xi* as an example. In *The Contemporary Chinese Dictionary*, there are 77 characters for this syllable, including, 西, 希, 奚, 昔.... This feature of Chinese allows speakers to use homophones quite ingeniously in riddles, humor and rhetoric.

Homophone rhetoric in Chinese is to relate a word that is pronounced the same or similar as another word, and to use the meaning of the other word. In Chinese it is more than a language phenomenon that has unique customary and cultural implications. There are quite a few different types of homophone rhetoric.

1. **Homophones for auspiciousness.** In Chinese culture, symbols and expressions of auspiciousness and happiness take special precedence. Due to this, people use homophones as "auspicious remarks" to address their psychological needs. For example, Chinese people have special regard for the fruit of the bottle gourd vine, known as 葫芦 (*hulu*), because it sounds similar to 福禄 (*fulu*), happiness and wealth. In addition, the bottle gourd is a vigorous, climbing vine with large leaves and a lush appearance. It grows fast and bears a lot of fruit. Chinese like these implications of bounty and fertility.

More homophone rhetoric can be found in the celebrations around the Chinese New Year period. It is very common for Chinese people to paste the character *fu* (福, good fortune) on walls and doors. Some people take this a step further and paste it upside down, because *dao* (倒, upside down) sounds the same as another *dao* (到, advent). Thus, by placing *fu* (福, good fortune) upside down they are inviting the advent of good fortune into their household.

A New Year cake made of glutinous rice called 黏糕 (*niangao*) is also a popular subject for homophone rhetoric because it sounds the same as 年高, which implies each year is better than the last.

It is also customary in many places to display New Year pictures. A common theme from Yangliuqing near Tianjin is of a plump baby boy holding a big carp in his arms, with a lotus next to him. This seems quite odd to foreign eyes but in fact is another clever example of homophone rhetoric. Fish, which is pronounced *yu* (鱼), has the same pronunciation as 余, which means surplus. Even better, lotus, (莲, *lian*) has the same pronunciation as 连 in 连年有余 (*liannian youyu*), an idiom literally meaning surplus year after year.

Chinese paintings are another rich source of homophone rhetoric. Due to the fact bat (蝠, *fu*) sounds exactly like 福 (good fortune), bats are traditionally considered harbingers of good fortune. A magpie perched in a plum tree somewhat surprisingly implies radiant with happiness. This example of homophone rhetoric comes from another idiom, 喜上眉梢 (literally joy on the eyebrow meaning radiant with happiness). In Chinese a magpie is 喜鹊 (literally joyful bird), and a plum tree is 梅 (*mei*) which has the same pronunciation as eyebrow (眉). So magpie on plum tree sounds the same as joy on the eyebrow.

Homophone rhetoric can also be found in daily life. Mei Lanfang, a Peking Opera master singer, planted two persimmon trees and one apple tree in his courtyard to invite an obstacle-free future. This example is once again related to an idiom, in this case 事事平安 (*shishi ping'an*, literally affairs safe and sound). In Chinese persimmon 柿 and thing 事 are both pronounced *shi*, and since there are two uses of 事 in the idiom, he planted two persimmon trees. Furthermore, one syllable of apple is pronounced like the 平 (*ping*) in 平安 (*ping'an,* meaning peaceful).

Apple trees are also planted beside Chinese scholar trees as a wish for embracing peace and security, as Chinese scholar trees 槐 sounds like 怀 (*huai*, in one's arms).

One year in the traditional Lantern Festival celebration in Taiwan, lanterns were patterned into four large characters: 灯 (*deng*) 丰 (*feng*) 照 (*zhao*) 吉 (*ji*), meaning brilliant and plenty lanterns lighting for auspiciousness, homophone of an idiom 登峰造极 meaning being supreme.

2. Homophone rhetoric used in folk customs. Chinese folk customs are rich and varied, and homophone rhetoric is often used on occasions such as birthdays, gift-giving, and particularly weddings. In a traditional wedding, the bride is first carried to the groom's house on a sedan, and must then step over a fire pan, because fire represents flourishing, which is obviously a good omen for the newly weds.

The next step is over a saddle and followed by a bite of an apple. We have already discussed apples, but in addition saddle (鞍) enhances the invitation to peace and security because it sounds like 安 (*an*, peaceful and secure).

Jujubes, chestnuts, peanuts, walnuts and longans are put underneath the newly weds' bed. The names of all these nuts and fruits sound similar to wishing the couple will soon have children. The older women who prepare the chamber for the newly-married couple would chant a rhyme that translates to English as "chestnuts and jujubes, babies soon follow."

Although China is geographically massive and culturally quite diverse, homophone rhetoric is a common linguistic feature. In Anhui Province, a bride will take off her shoes and put on her husband's shoes when she is led into the bridal chamber, because 鞋 (*xie*, shoe) and 偕 (harmony) are homophones. In Beijing, the bride is ceremonially served with half-cooked dumplings and asked "Are the dumplings cooked or not?" She answers "Uncooked". The same character, 生 (*sheng*) means give birth to. This is done in the hope that she will conceive soon after marriage.

3. **Homophones for certain taboos.** People all over the world avoid using certain words that may be considered impolite or distressing to the person with whom they are speaking. At Chinese weddings, for example, the words such as dead, lost, ended, over, and unlucky are prohibited, for obvious reasons. However the Chinese take this a step further and also often avoid using homophones of these words.

Likewise, umbrellas and clocks can not be given as gifts, because umbrella (伞, *san*) sounds like coming loose or being scattered (散), and giving a clock (送钟, *songzhong*) sounds like attending to a dying person (送终). Couples should not share a pear, because 分梨 (*fen li*) sounds exactly like splitting up (分离).

During the New Year holiday, people deem it unlucky to break anything. If a child breaks a glass, his or her mom will quickly say, "Never mind. Safe and lucky year after year!" 碎碎 (*suisui*, broken) is taken to mean its homophone 岁岁 (year after year). Therefore, instead of being affected by the unlucky action of breaking things, people turn it into an auspicious blessing.

Due to the fact there are many dialects in China, different taboo homonyms appear in different regions. In Cantonese, pig's tongue 猪舌 (*zhushe*), a popular ingredient for soup, is called 猪俐 (*zhuli*) instead, because in Cantonese *she* sounds like *shi*, which is a homophone of loss 蚀.

In North China, many people avoid saying 蛋 (*dan*), meaning egg, because this word is the second half of common insults, including *huaidan* 坏蛋, meaning scoundrel, and *bendan* 笨蛋, meaning fool. For this reason, people also avoid using the word "egg" in cooking. Thus egg soup is known as osmanthus soup, and scrambled eggs as scrambled yellow dish.

The culture embodied in the use of homophones reflects the bent in Chinese psychology of seeking the fortunate and auspicious and attempting to avoid the unlucky. A more extreme example of this was implemented by Yuan Shikai, who in 1912 declared himself the President of the Republic of China, and subsequently Emperor of the Chinese Empire. He ordered that a certain Lantern Festival food have its name changed from 元宵 (*yuanxiao*) to 汤圆 (*tangyuan*), because the original name sounds like the disappearance of Yuan (袁消).

4. Humorous homophones. Homophones are often used in daily talks for humorous effect. For example, talking about a Mr. Li, one might say, "Li gets tracheitis and he is a nightstand." This is actually saying in a humorous way that Mr. Li's wife rules the family to the extent that he kneels beside her bed! 气管炎 (*qiguanyan*), meaning tracheitis, and 妻管严, meaning the wife rules strictly, sound alike. Furthermore, 床头柜 (*chuangtougui*), meaning nightstand, and 床头跪, meaning kneel beside the bed, also sound the same.

Homophones are common to the second part of the two-part allegorical (post-pause) expressions that are unique to Chinese. These expressions are especially effective at making written expressions more vivid. Although in English it sounds a little odd, it is still possible to appreciate these examples.

Carrying the bride in a basket – there lacks a sedan. Lacking a sedan in Chinese is 缺轿 (*que jiao*), a homophone of 缺觉, which means lack of sleep.

Monk holding an umbrella – he has no hair and is shielded from the sky. This expression sounds the same as an idiom 无法无天, which means, doing things with no regard of their superiors or the law. Hair (发) and law (法) are homophones.

Chicken feathers tied to a power pole – what a giant duster. Here, duster 掸子 sounds exactly like 胆子 (*danzi*), meaning having a lot of nerve. Thus the second part of this expression is saying something like "How dare you?!"

Humorous use of homophones are often used in performances and a traditional kind of stand-up comedy known as cross-talk. This involves two performers telling sarcastically funny stories. A Beijing master of cross-talk, Ma Ji, once performed with a Taiwanese counterpart in Hong Kong. He began by saying "Ma Ji from Beijing came to Hong Kong soon after the horse-racing season was over." This clever remark evoked a lot of laughters from the audience, due to the fact that Ma Ji is a homophone of horse racing season.

Ma Ji then asked his co-performer "Where are you from?" He answered "I come from Taipei." Ma Ji then claimed "I come from Tainan." The crowd was very confused. However, this was brilliant play on homophones, for several reasons. First of all, Taipei literally means north Tai whereas Tainan literally means south Tai, with the same character of Tai in the word Taiwan. But Tai has yet another meaning, which is stage or platform. Thus what Ma Ji was saying was technically true, he came on to the stage (*tai*, 台) from the south (*nan*, 南). Although not even the Chinese speaking audience immediately understood the subtlety of this joke, when he explained it they were mightily impressed.

5. Homophones of people and place names. Homophones are chosen carefully with regards to names of people and places in order to sound auspicious and lucky. For example, a person surnamed 郝 (*hao*) may be given the name 蕴琦 (*yun qi*), because this is a homophone of 好运气 (*hao yunqi*), meaning good luck (remember in Chinese the family name is mentioned first). Likewise a person named 于得水, Yu Deshui, is lucky because this is a homophone of 鱼得水 (*yu de shui*), meaning a fish with plenty of water.

With hindsight, place names may be changed at times to something that sounds similar but is more appropriate. In Beijing there was a hutong named 母猪胡同 (*muzhu*, bitch), which was changed to 墨竹胡同 (*mozhu*, dark green bamboo). One has to agree this was definitely for the better! Similarly, 狗尾巴胡同 (*gouyiba*, Dog Tail Hutong) was changed to 高义伯胡同 (*gao yi bo*), a much more classy-sounding name, though with no particular meaning. In the same way, the somewhat dull 大墙缝胡同 (*da qiangfeng*, Big Wall Cranny Hutong) was renamed 大翔凤胡同 (*da xiangfeng*, Big Flying Phoenix Hutong). Keelung of Taiwan (*Jilong*, 基隆) kept its original name 鸡笼 (meaning chicken's cage) until 1883, however a mere change of characters with the same pronunciation lifted the name to one with more elegance, 基隆.

6. Homophones as a memory aid. In Chinese homophones are also used when trying to memorize dry or non-logical information, which may turn into novel or funny expressions with odd meanings. Once there was a teacher from an old-fashioned private school who left his students the task of memorizing pi to 30 digits before he went away drinking for the afternoon. When he returned in the afternoon, they would have to recite it to him before they would be allowed to go home. Staring at the long string of 3.1 41592653589793238462643383279, the students were devastated. Some students tried their best to memorize the information, and others ran up the hill behind the school, although they did take the numbers with them. Before long, they saw their teacher drinking and chatting with a monk in a pavilion on top of the hill.

As the sun was going down, the teacher made his way back to the school to test the students. Somewhat surprisingly, the students who were usually badly behaved (and who, unbeknown to him had been playing on the hill all afternoon) did an excellent job of memorizing. The reason for this was that one of these boys had made up a long rhythmic line based on homophones that helped them remember the numbers. The line was 山巅一寺一壶酒，尔乐苦煞吾，把酒吃，酒杀尔，杀不死，遛尔遛死，扇扇刮，扇耳吃酒，which means something like "At the top of the hill, there is a temple. You happily drink alcohol, we are sadly burdened. If the alcohol does not kill you, we will slap you in your face." They not only completed the task, but in their clever use of homophones also managed to criticize the teacher for his unprofessional behavior.

As a phenomenon, homophones are common to all languages, but Chinese has substantially richer possibilities than many other languages for homophone rhetoric due to the relatively small amount of sounds in the spoken word. Over a long period of time, the use of this rhetoric has maintained a close relationship with Chinese cultural traditions and psychology. The Chinese world view, especially speaking in a historical sense, extracts meaning from phenomena observed around them and this has made a deep impression on the language. In addition Chinese is a language of rare subtlety, where the listener must grasp the subtext of the spoken or written word. As the culture is outwardly reserved, although the meaning of language may be quite specific, the way in which it is delivered may not. As we have discussed, homophones are in this way an intrinsic part of Chinese language. But more than that, a non-native Chinese speaker must know something of Chinese culture as well as the language to be able to fully appreciate and understand the nuances implicit in the use of homophones.

生词 New Words

1.儿化韵	érhuàyùn	suffixation of a non-syllabic *er* to nouns and sometimes verbs or adjectives, causing a retroflexion of the preceding vowel, typical of the pronunciation of standard Chinese and of some dialects
2.若干	ruògān	a certain number or amount
3.相同	xiāngtóng	identical; the same; alike
4.相近	xiāngjìn	similar, close; about the same
5.民俗	mínsú	folk custom; folkways
6.祈求	qíqiú	to earnestly hope; to pray for
7.平安	píng'ān	safe and sound; well
8.顺利	shùnlì	smooth, successful; without a hitch
9.心愿	xīnyuàn	wish; cherished desire
10.满足	mǎnzú	satisfied, content; to meet
11.故意	gùyì	intentionally, willfully; on purpose
12.黏米	niánmǐ	glutinous rice
13.增高	zēnggāo	to get higher; to rise, to increase
14.年糕	niángāo	New Year cake
15.年画	niánhuà	New Year (or Spring Festival) pictures
16.小子	xiǎozi	boy
17.鲤鱼	lǐyú	carp
18.莲花	liánhuā	lotus flower
19.寓意	yùyì	implied meaning
20.蝙蝠	biānfú	bat (an animal)
21.京剧	jīngjù	Peking Opera

22.大师	dàshī	great master
23.柿子树	shìzishù	persimmon tree
24.苹果树	píngguǒshù	apple tree
25.槐树	huáishù	Chinese scholar tree
26.婚礼	hūnlǐ	wedding ceremony
27.轿	jiào	sedan (chair)
28.火盆	huǒpén	fire pan
29.跨	kuà	to step over; to stride
30.马鞍	mǎ'ān	saddle
31.洞房	dòngfáng	bridal (or nuptial) chamber
32.红枣	hóngzǎo	jujube, (Chinese) date
33.栗子	lìzi	chestnut
34.花生	huāshēng	peanut
35.核桃	hétao	walnut
36.桂圆	guìyuán	longan
37.风俗	fēngsú	custom
38.忌讳	jìhui	taboo; to avoid as taboo
39.回避	huíbì	to evade, to avoid
40.送终	sòngzhōng	to attend upon a dying parent or other senior member of one's family; to bury a parent
41.吃醋	chīcù	to be jealous (usu. of a rival in love)
42.总统	zǒngtǒng	president
43.诙谐	huīxié	humorous, jocular
44.气管炎	qìguǎnyán	tracheitis
45.床头柜	chuángtóuguì	bedside cupboard; nightstand
46.惧内	jùnèi	henpecked

47.不解	bùjiě	not to understand
48.巧妙	qiǎomiào	ingenious, clever
49.即兴	jíxìng	impromptu
50.窍门	qiàomén	key (to a problem)
51.枯燥	kūzào	dry and dull
52.圆周率	yuánzhōulǜ	ratio of the circumference of a circle to its diameter
53.愁眉苦脸	chóuméi-kǔliǎn	to wear a worried look; to pull a long face
54.顽皮	wánpí	naughty
55.鬼脸	guǐliǎn	funny face; wry face
56.酒足饭饱	jiǔzú-fànbǎo	have drunk and eaten to one's heart's content
57.张冠李戴	zhāngguān-lǐdài	to put Zhang's hat on Li's head; to attribute sth. to the wrong person or confuse one thing with another
58.宏观	hóngguān	macroscopic
59.感悟	gǎnwù	to come to realize
60.含蓄	hánxù	reserved
61.息息相关	xīxī-xiāngguān	to be closely linked; to be closely bound up

语法聚焦 Notes and Examples

一、汉语因为音节少，所以同音字多

“因为……所以……”是连词，用于表示因果关系的复句里。

Conjunctions 因为... 所以... are used in a compound sentence indicating cause and effect. For example:

1. 因为工作关系，所以他常常和保险公司打交道。
2. 因为他努力学习，所以成绩优秀。
3. 因为我另有约会，所以明天不能参加这个会。

二、从而采取这个词的意义

“从而”是连词，用于同一主语的复句中，引出表示结果的副句。

从而 is a conjunction used to connect two clauses with one subject, with the latter as a result of the former. For example:

1. 这个工厂进行了彻底改革，引进了先进技术和经验，从而大大提高了产品的竞争能力。
2. 袁先生和徐小姐多年来在一起学习和工作，从而产生了感情，他们终于喜结良缘。
3. 由于公司把劳资关系处理得非常好，从而激发了广大员工的工作积极性。

三、老太太还要一边撒一边念叨

“一边……一边”这个格式用来表示两个以上动作同时发生或进行。这些动作可以是同一主语。

The pattern 一边...一边 indicates two actions happen at the same time. The subject of the two actions can be the same or different. For example:

1. 小杜一边走一边唱歌。
2. 史秘书一边打字，一边接电话。
3. 我们一边把计划往上报，你们就一边做好各项准备工作。

四、尽管中国幅员广大，各地区有着不同的风俗习惯，但总是体现着这种谐音文化

“尽管”是表示让步关系的连词。用法和“虽然”一样，但让步的语气更重些。

尽管 as a conjunction indicates concession, but with a higher degree than 虽然. For example:

1. 尽管天气这么冷，还下着大雨，李大爷还是来了。
2. 尽管有人说闲话，他还是把这个孤儿接到家里抚养。
3. 尽管这个研究课题非常难，但是大家有信心，一定能完成。
4. 他尽管工作非常忙，还是抽出一定时间锻炼身体。

五、如果小孩子不小心打碎了一个杯子，妈妈会说……

“如果”是连词，表示假设。用在主从复合句中的副句中，常与“就”、“还”、“那么”、“那”等词连用。

如果 as a conjunction indicates assumption and is used in the secondary clause of a compound sentence. Word such as 就, 还, 那么 or 那 is usually used in sentences with 如果. For example:

1. 如果价钱合理，我就多买一些。
2. 如果大家都赞成，那么就这样办了。
3. 你如果需要帮忙，请告诉我一下。
4. 如果经理不同意我们的意见，那怎么办?

六、马季一上台就说……

“一……就……”格式表示两件事紧接着发生。有时前一分句表示条件，后一分句表示结果。

The 一…就… structure indicates two actions happening one after the other. Sometimes, the first part refers to conditions, and the second part the result. For example:

1. 莉莉同学一下课就去图书馆了。
2. 一到冬天，白大娘的咳嗽病就犯了。
3. 老师一讲，同学们就明白了。
4. 王刚一喝酒，脸就红。

想一想 Questions

1. 中国人春节时为什么把“福”字倒着贴?
   Why is *fu* pasted upside down in the Chinese New Year?
2. 在过去中国人结婚时，他们要做哪些事情? 为什么?
   What kind of customs does a traditional Chinese wedding have? And why?
3. 中国人忌讳做哪些事情? 为什么?
   What are considered taboos for the Chinese? Why?
4. 你能说出几个谐音歇后语吗?
   Do you have any examples of two-part allegorical expressions with homophone rhetoric?

超级链接 Super Links

半空中挂口袋——装疯（风）

这是一个谐音的歇后语。在半空中挂上一个大口袋，能用来干什么呢？只能用来装风。“疯”与“风”同音，“装风”就变成“装疯”。“装疯”指一个人故意装做疯癫痴呆的样子。（含贬义）

打破沙锅——问（璺）到底

这是一个谐音歇后语。“璺”（wèn）是陶瓷、玻璃等器具上的裂痕。沙锅一打破，裂痕就从上面直到底部，“璺到底”了。“问”和“璺”同音，“璺到底”变成“问到底”。这个歇后语用来比喻追问一件事情，寻根刨（páo）底，非要弄清楚不可。

和尚的脑壳——没法（发）

这是一个谐音的歇后语。和尚不留头发，所以是“没发”。“法”与“发”同音（不同音调），“没发”变成“没法”。“没法”的意思是没有办法，没有门路。

孔夫子搬家——净是输（书）

这是一个谐音歇后语。孔夫子是中国儒家学说的创始人。人们认为他最有学问，家中的书当然很多了。孔夫子搬家，搬的都是书。“输”与“书”同音，“净是书”变成了“净是输”。这个歇后语用来比喻总是失败。

外甥打灯笼——照旧（舅）

这是一个谐音的歇后语。“舅”和“外甥”是亲戚称呼。一个孩子，称他母亲的哥哥或弟弟为“舅”，舅舅则把他叫“外甥”。外甥打着灯笼给舅舅照明引路。由于“旧”与“舅”同音，“照舅”变成“照旧”。“照旧”的意思是：仍旧保持从前的样子，没有一点儿变化。

小葱拌豆腐——一清（青）二白

这是一个谐音歇后语。小葱是青青的，豆腐是白白的。用小葱拌豆腐，做成一道菜，有青又有白，好看又好吃。“清”与“青”同音，“一青二白”成了“一清二白”。“一清二白”也是个成语，有两个意思：（1）清清楚楚，毫不含糊；（2）一个人很纯洁，没有污点。（含褒义）

引自华语教学出版社《歇后语100》

汉语禁忌语与委婉语

Taboos and Euphemism in Chinese

4

A Kaleidoscope of Chinese Culture

禁忌是存在于各民族中的一种普遍文化现象。它的学术名词是taboo，是来自南太平洋玻利尼西亚汤加岛上的土语，18世纪由英国航海家库克船长带到了欧洲。禁忌是人们对自然现象的本质还不能理解时，在心理上产生了对某些事物的崇拜、对危险事物的畏惧和对不洁事物的憎恶，因而在言行上规定的不能说、不能做的事情。形成禁忌的原因不同，有的产生于宗教，有的来自世俗习惯。

中国人自古就很重视禁忌。《礼记》中说："入竟（境）而问禁，入国而问俗，入门而问讳。"《周礼》中也说："掌道方慝，以诏辟忌，以知地俗。"可见古人是何等重视禁忌习俗。而且中国古代也存在着各种各样的禁忌，其中有很多与崇拜有密切关系，例如：古时候，人们对水十分崇拜，所以有不准在井上磨刀的禁忌，以免使井中的水神有一种杀机感，因而招致灾祸；由于古人崇拜鬼魂，所以在丧礼中有很多禁忌，如果邻家在办丧事，自家是禁止舂米的，因为这可能把鬼魂引入自家。另外，由于人们对日、月、星辰的崇拜，所以产生了对日食和晦日的一些禁忌。古人特别把晦日看做一个非常不吉利的日子，军队不能出兵打仗，官员不能上班办事，夜里不能唱歌，夫妇不能同房等，唯恐会招致灾难。其他还有对色彩、数字、动物、器皿等事物的崇拜和禁忌，所以形成了内容丰富的中国禁忌文化。

语言禁忌是人们对语言的迷信和崇拜，认为语言与事物之间有着某种神秘的联系，不吉祥的话语能招致不吉祥的事情发生，这就使人们对不好事情的禁忌心理转化成了对语言的回避。比如，人们都不喜欢"死、亡、丧、败、破"等不好的事情，所以这些字词在中国古代较为忌讳，特别是在逢年过节、婚姻嫁娶、修屋建房等重要喜庆活动时，更是十分注意回避这些不吉利的字词，而代之以"喜、吉、顺、发"等吉祥词，所以在中国旧时的婚礼上或建房上梁时，总是有人来念"喜歌"，以满足人们求平安吉祥的心理需求。在小说《济公全传》中，有这样一个故事：

有一天，济公在路上走，看见路旁有很多人在建造一所大房，正要上横梁。做活的工匠们看见济公和尚走过来了，便提议请他在上梁时念一个“喜歌”，以讨个吉利。主人同意了，于是把济公叫了过来，请他念喜歌。济公说我要喝完酒、吃完肉才能念，主人赶忙拿来酒肉。济公吃完以后开始念到：“今日上红梁，愿出千口丧，父在子先死，妻在夫先亡。”说完便立刻走了。众人一听十分吃惊，这又是死，又是亡，又是丧，哪里是“喜歌”，简直是一个“丧歌”。主人心中更是不悦，命人去把济公和尚捉回来，可为时已晚。过了一会，有一个人忽然悟出了这几句话的道理，对大家说：“这个和尚说的句句都是吉利话。你们想，要从这个屋子里出千口丧，这个屋子该是多么坚固，它最少要挺立几百年。父亲死在儿子之前，是说这个屋内没有孤鳏老人，妻子死在丈夫之前，是说这个屋内没有寡妇，这不是最吉利的事情吗？”大家听了恍然大悟，主人也转怒为喜。

这个故事写出了济公的聪明诙谐，他利用人们的禁忌心理在和大家开玩笑。同时，我们从中也可看出中国禁忌文化现象的一二。

人们除了认为不吉利的语言能给人带来灾祸以外，同时认为有些语言能表现出对神圣事物的不恭敬和亵渎，因此在禁忌语中出现了对名字的避讳现象。孔夫子是中国古代大教育家，在旧时被人们尊为“圣人”，因此过去的读书人每当遇到他的名字“孔丘”时，要改变“丘”的写法，少写一竖，并且把读音也改为“mǒu”，否则被视为不恭敬。中国封建社会的帝王更是威严无比，为了显示他的“九五之尊”，皇帝的名字是要避讳的，比如，秦始皇姓嬴，名政，于是“政”字不能说，与“政”同音的字也不能说，所以人们把“正月”（zhèngyuè）读成zhēngyuè。汉高祖刘邦因他的名字叫“邦”，所以汉朝（前206–公元220）时将“邦家”一词改为“国家”，此词也一直沿用至今。此种现象在几千年的中国封建社会里一直存在，例如，清朝康熙皇帝名玄烨，“玄”字避讳时缺末笔；雍正皇帝名胤禛，“胤”字避讳时缺末笔，同时雍正皇帝还命他的兄弟将“胤”字改作“允”字。这种君讳现象的背后，是与权力紧密联系着的，如果有人触犯了禁忌会受到刑罚的处置。

中国古代这种讳名现象，不仅仅限于帝王，就是在下面官吏或士大夫文人中也同样存在。宋朝（960–1279）时有一位地方官，名字叫田登，因为忌讳，他不准别人说“登”字，连“灯”字也不许说，把“灯”改为“火”。正月十五元宵节放灯，他写的告示是：“本州依例放火三日”。由此便留下了“只许州官放火，不许百姓点灯”的俗语。

古时候一些文人、士大夫也有家讳，如果去他家做客，要先问清他家避讳哪些字，这叫做“入门而问讳”。起码主人父亲的名字是不能说的。《世说新语》记载了这样一个故事，有一个人叫王忱，他到朋友桓玄家做客，桓玄置酒款待。王忱说，我因为服五石散，不能喝冷酒，请拿温酒来，不料桓玄听了，泪流满面地哭了起来。因为王忱犯了他的家讳，桓玄的父亲叫桓温，这使他想起了已经过世的父亲，让王忱非常尴尬。实际上，古代文人的这种避讳，多半是有附庸风雅的成分在内。

中国古代社会的禁忌与封建君王的政治统治有关，当人们推翻封建君主后，禁忌语逐渐远离了政治，像古代的君讳、家讳已经消失，禁忌的内容也越来越少，现在保留下来的禁忌语多与民俗有关，作用也逐渐变成了满足人们祈求平安、幸福、吉祥的心理需求。

在中国农村，有些地方每到春节时，父母亲唯恐孩子小，不懂事，在春节期间说出一些禁忌的话来，于是在屋内贴上一张字条，上面写着：“童言无忌”，以此防范不吉利的话变成现实。另外，不同行业的人有不同的禁忌语，比如：商人自己不说、也不愿听人说“关门”，因为这意味着倒闭；船夫不说“翻”、“沉”，因为怕出海时，招来事故；戏剧演出团忌说“伞”，因为“伞”与“散”同音，害怕演出团散伙。就连新加坡、日本也有类似的禁忌。在新加坡有一个地方书店非常多，称得上“书城”，可此地偏偏叫做“黄金城”，这是因为“书”与“输”谐音，人们有意避开不好字，代之以吉祥词。另外，日本大阪地铁的所有招牌，都将“铁”字写成繁体字“鐵”，而不是简体字“铁”（在日本两字并用），因为简体“铁”字是由“失”、“金”二字组合而成，如果地铁“失金”，不就意味公司赔本嘛。从以上几例，我们不难看出汉语禁忌文化对亚洲文化的影响。

既然有语言的禁忌，那么委婉语的产生就很自然了。所谓委婉语，就是用典雅、含蓄、好听、有礼的话，来代替那些禁忌、粗鲁、刺耳的词语。比如前面谈到“死”这个大家都不喜欢的词，在汉语中，“死”的委婉语就有100种之多，如：去世、谢世、逝世、不在了、长眠、安息、寿终、归天、殉职、阵亡、捐躯、牺牲、就义、撒手人寰等。这种现象在英语中也同样存在。有人统计，英语中关于死亡的委婉语就有60多种。

委婉语还常常用于不能说或不想说的话语中，像妇女来月经，本是正常的生理现象，可不管中国、外国，人们都不愿直说出来，而是使用委婉语，汉语常说，“来例假了”、“倒霉了”、“来红”、“身体不适”等；妇女怀孕常说“有了”、“有喜了”、“要当妈妈了”等；人们要去厕所则说“方便一下”、“去1号”、“去洗手间”、“我出去一下”等，古代人还说“出恭”、“更衣”、“宽衣”等等。另外，对一些生理缺陷，人们也尽量用委婉语，比如，不说耳朵聋，而说“耳背”、“失聪”、“耳朵有点不好”或“重听”；不说腿瘸，而说“腿脚不好”等。

近年来，委婉语更是作为一种修辞手段，被人们在社交活动，政治事务、商贸合作中广泛使用，而且不断产生出一些新的委婉语。比如，英语中不说poor nation，而说developing nation；增税不说tax increase，而是revenue enhancement；二手汽车不说second-hand cars，而说pre-owned cars；售货员说成customer's representative；殡仪工说成funeral director等。汉语也同样出现了一些新的委婉语，比如不说被单位解雇，而说“下岗”；不说“失业”，而说“待业”；青少年犯罪，不称“犯罪青年”，而称“失足青年”；把“涨价”说成“调价”；“高价商品”说成“议价商品”。

由此可见，禁忌语和委婉语是一种语言现象，也是一种文化现象和社会现象，我们了解和认识它，是很有意义的。

Taboo can be defined as a prohibition that excludes something from use, approach, or mention. This may be on the grounds it is considered sacred, has the ability to inspire fear, or is thought to be disgusting or disagreeable. It is not a word indigenous to English. In fact, it comes from the language of the South Pacific island of Tonga, and was introduced to English by the famous 18th century navigator Captain James Cook.

Chinese culture has, even from ancient times, incorporated a large number of taboos. In *The Book of Rites* it was noted that when one visits another state or kingdom, it is wise to be aware of the local taboos. *The Book of Rites of the Zhou Dynasty* also mentioned the fact that educating oneself on what people in a particular location disliked could help in avoiding taboos and understanding local customs.

Many ancient taboos were related to religion and worship. At one point in time, water was thought to be a sacred and powerful spirit. People were not permitted to sharpen knives by a well for fear that the God of Water may take revenge and inflict disaster. Ancient people also had a well-developed fear of ghosts, and as such there were many taboos surrounding funerals. For example, if a neighboring household was holding a funeral, it was considered best not to husk rice in case the ghost would be attracted to one's own home.

Other taboos were related to the solar eclipse and the last day of the month in the Chinese lunar calendar. These taboos originated in people's worship of the sun, moon and stars. The last day of the month was considered particularly unlucky. Activities that were prohibited included troops being dispatched to fight, officials going to work, evening singing, and sexual relations. It was thought that these acts would bring disaster. There were still more taboos – associated with animals, colors, numbers, and even certain utensils. Chinese culture has historically been very rich in terms of taboos.

The ancient Chinese people also believed that language had a mystical inherent power that could influence certain things to happen, for example, unlucky words could encourage unlucky things to happen. To avoid mishaps, certain words were avoided. Some of these were obvious – "death", "bad luck", "loss", "defeat", "damage", or "being broken". It was especially important to avoid these kinds of words on celebratory occasions such as holidays, weddings, or the building of a new house. At these times it was better to say words like "happy", "auspicious", "smooth", and "prosperous". At weddings or when a house was completed, happy songs were sung to satisfy the cultural craving for auspiciousness.

The Full Story of Jigong the Monk is a classic novel that portrays an interesting example of Chinese taboos, expectations, and humor. One day, the eccentric monk Jigong was passing by a newly completed house. One of the more quick-witted workmen inside noticed that he was passing and invited him in to sing a song of happiness while they were applying the finishing touches to the new abode.

Before he began, Jigong allowed himself to be treated to some alcohol and meat. Upon satisfying these important needs, Jigong uttered four lines:

On the day of completing your new house,
I wish you would have a thousand family members die in it.
Father dies before his sons,
Wife dies before her husband.

Then he walked away. Everybody was dumbfounded. How could Jigong utter such horribly inauspicious words? The owner of the house was so furious he sent out some of his workmen to catch Jigong and bring him back. However, Jigong had vanished like a puff of smoke.

A more thoughtful man, who had been considering the words for a while, stepped forward and said, "In fact, Jigong did indeed speak words of auspiciousness. Your house must be a most strong one and will stand for several hundred years, otherwise it is not possible for a thousand people to die in it. And if father dies before his sons, there will be no old man left uncared for in your family. If wife dies before her husband, there will be no miserable widow in your family. Isn't this the very best luck?" This explanation satisfied everybody, including the owner, who was then very happy.

Jigong was indeed a quick-witted and linguistically gifted person. He also had a deep understanding of taboos and how people reacted to them. This story is good for the modern reader, too, because it helps us understand what taboos people had and how one could circumvent them.

Historically, people believed that not only did some words show disrespect to the sacred, but also went so far as to bring about disaster. Fascinatingly, they also avoided speaking or writing the given names of highly respected people. In particular, the great sage Confucius and feudal emperors were often not mentioned by name.

To demonstrate their reverence for the sage, when scholars wrote the characters for Confucius they deliberately omitted the second vertical stroke of his given name, 丘. When reading his name out aloud, they would change the pronunciation of his given name to "*mou*" from the original "*qiu*".

Emperors had absolute authority and due to this their names were not written or spoken. The first emperor in the Qin Dynasty (221 BC-206 BC) had the given name 政 (*zheng*). During this period, the character 政 could not be used by anybody else, and even characters with the same pronunciation were avoided. 正月, the first lunar month was altered to a different tone, *zhengyue*, and the new pronunciation has persisted to the current day. The Emperor Gao of the Han Dynasty (206 BC-220 AD) had the given name 邦 (*bang*). As a result, the word 邦家, meaning country, was changed into 国家 during his reign. This new word also has persisted to the modern day.

For several thousand years, it was a feudal tradition to alter the emperor's name. In the Qing Dynasty, 玄, the first character in the given name of Emperor Kangxi, 玄烨, was written without the last stroke. 胤, the first character in the given name of Emperor Yongzheng, 胤禛, was written without the last stroke, too. At the same time, Emperor Yongzheng ordered his brothers to change the shared 胤 in their own names into 允. This particular language phenomenon is known as "sovereign taboo", which was closely linked to the sovereign power, and anyone who ever broke the rule would be seen as disrespectful and would be punished.

In fact, not only was mentioning the given name of the emperor prohibited, but the given names of scholars and officials were also sometimes avoided as a way to show respect. One local official in the Song Dynasty (960-1279) went even further. The official's family name was 田, and his given name was 登. So prideful was he that he did not allow his given name or homophones of his given name to be spoken. Thus people could not say words like lantern or lamp, which are pronounced *deng*, the same as his given name. However the Lantern Festival presented him with a problem of homophones, which he got around by proclaiming "The holiday is to be celebrated by setting fire for three days." By this he meant lighting up lanterns was permitted. This event gave rise to a saying "The officials can set fire, the common people can not light up lanterns", meaning that officials enjoy special rights, but common people do not.

Although scholars did not enjoy the prestige of the officials, some of them felt it befitting their rank to avoid using certain characters. One example of this is the story of Wang Chen, who visited his friend Huan Xuan. Being a dutiful host, Huan Xuan offered his friend food and wine, but because Wang Chen was ill at the time he did not want to accept cold wine. He asked Huan Xuan to warm up the wine for him, but unexpectedly, Huan Xuan burst into tears. At that moment, Wang Chen was extremely embarrassed because he realized that warming wine, 温酒 (*wenjiu*), reminded Huan Yuan of his deceased father, 桓温 (Huan Wen), for there was a shared character 温.

Historically speaking, many taboos were related to the nobility wishing to maintain their control over the symbols associated with power. More recently, taboos such as mentioning the name of the emperor or one's ancestors have gradually disappeared. As a result there are now many less taboos. Those remaining are mostly customary and reflect the cultural hankering for auspiciousness and happiness.

The Spring Festival is supposed to be a time of auspiciousness. People try to stay clear of saying things that might invite bad fortune on the family in the coming year. To be extra careful, some rural families will post notes in the house that say, "Words of children mean no harm", to ensure unthinking children do not bring bad fortune into the household.

Different trades also have their own taboo words. Merchants dislike the word "close" for fear it could lead to bankruptcy. Sailors avoid "sink" and "turn over" because they may lead to accidents at sea. At the beginning of a season, actors avoid saying "umbrella" because in Chinese "umbrella", *san*, is a homophone of a word that means "scattered" or "dismissed".

Singapore and Japan both have some similar taboos. The Singaporean book-selling district is called "gold city" rather than "book city" because "book", *shu,* is a homophone of "loss". In Osaka, all signs for the subway use the traditional 鐵, which means (rail)way. There is a simpler character, 铁 which could be used, but the two radicals mean "gold" and "loss". These are not auspicious characters to be used by a subway company. These two examples illustrate how far-ranging the influence of Chinese taboo culture is.

Where there is taboo, there is its polite cousin, euphemism. Euphemism refers to the use of a more agreeable term in the place of one that may offend the listener. As has previously been mentioned, the word "die" is considered inauspicious, there are more than 100 ways to convey the fact that someone has died, such as 去世，谢世，逝世，不在了，长眠，安息，寿终，归天，殉职，阵亡，捐躯，牺牲，就义, and 撒手人寰. Similarly, in English there are over 60 euphemisms for "die".

Euphemisms are useful for getting around situations where things are not generally directly mentioned. Menstruation is considered a delicate topic in many cultures, and so many euphemisms have evolved to refer to it in a polite way, including "period", "be unlucky", "red comes", or plain old "feeling unwell". Pregnancy is also often talked around, including "She has it", "She has something happy", or "She is going to be a mother". When going to the toilet, people might say "relieving nature", "going to do a No. 1", "going to wash my hands", or merely "Please excuse me for a while". In former times, people were even more circumspect, saying "changing clothes". Euphemisms are also used for some physical disabilities, including "hard of hearing" for deafness, or "has difficulty walking" for "lameness".

Euphemisms are also used in social, political and economic terms. In English, developing nation is used to describe a poor nation. A tax increase becomes revenue enhancement. Second-hand cars are known as pre-owned cars....

In Chinese, a fired employee is said to be "laid-off". Unemployed people are said to be "waiting to be employed". When discussing juvenile delinquency, a young person is not said to have committed a crime, but said to have "lost his/her way". Price rises are said to be price "adjustments" and overpriced goods are said to be "negotiable".

生词 New Words

1.委婉语	wěiwǎnyǔ	euphemism
2.土语	tǔyǔ	local, colloquial expression
3.航海	hánghǎi	navigation
4.本质	běnzhì	essence, nature
5.憎恶	zēngwù	to abhor, to loathe
6.重视	zhòngshì	to attach importance to; to pay attention to
7.杀机	shājī	murderous intention
8.鬼魂	guǐhún	ghost, spirit, apparition
9.日食	rìshí	solar eclipse
10.晦日	huìrì	the last day of a month
11.同房	tóngfáng	(of husband and wife) to sleep together; to have sexual intercourse
12.转化	zhuǎnhuà	to transform to change
13.回避	huíbì	to evade, to dodge, to avoid
14.丧	sāng	unlucky; out of luck
15.败	bài	defeated, lost
16.破	pò	broken, damaged

17.逢年过节	féngnián-guòjié	on New Year's day or other festivals
18.婚姻嫁娶	hūnyīn jiàqǔ	marriage
19.喜庆	xǐqìng	joyous, jubilant; a happy event or occasion
20.顺	shùn	smooth, successful
21.上梁	shàng liáng	to put the beams in place (in building a house)
22.坚固	jiāngù	firm, solid, strong
23.孤	gū	lonely, solitary
24.鳏	guān	wifeless; widower
25.寡妇	guǎfu	widow
26.恭敬	gōngjìng	respectful
27.亵渎	xièdú	blaspheme; to profane, to pollute
28.圣人	shèngrén	the Sage
29.威严	wēiyán	dignified, majestic
30.沿用	yányòng	to continue to use
31.触犯	chùfàn	to offend, to violate; to go against
32.服	fú	to take (medicine)
33.泪流满面	lèiliú-mǎnmiàn	a face bathed in tears
34.过世	guòshì	to die; to pass away
35.附庸风雅	fùyōng-fēngyǎ	to mingle with men of letters and pose as a lover of culture
36.行业	hángyè	trade, profession
37.招牌	zhāopái	shop sign; sign board
38.赔本	péiběn	to sustain losses in business; to run a business at a loss
39.含蓄	hánxù	implicit, reserved
40.好听	hǎotīng	pleasant to hear
41.粗鲁	cūlǔ	rough, rude

42.刺耳	cì'ěr	harsh words
43.月经	yuèjīng	menses, menstruation
44.生理	shēnglǐ	physiology
45.怀孕	huáiyùn	to be pregnant
46.缺陷	quēxiàn	defect, drawback; handicapped

语法聚焦 Notes and Examples

一、有的产生于宗教，有的来自世俗习惯

"有的"是代词，表示分别述说一个集体里的各种情况。

Pronoun 有的 is used to state varied situations respectively. For example:

1. 我学了很多生词，有的记住了，有的没记住。
2. 昨天晚会上的节目，有的很精彩，有的不太好。
3. 学生常常问我一些汉语语法问题，有的我想都没想过。
4. 来这里锻炼身体的人很多，有的是工人，有的是学生，也有的是教师。

二、以免使井中的水神有一种杀机感

"以免"是连词，用在复句中第二分句的开头，表示前面所说的目的使下文所说的结果不至于发生。

Conjunction 以免 is used at the beginning of the second clause of a complex sentence, meaning in order not to. For example:

1. 请不要把手伸出车窗外边，以免发生危险。
2. 车不要停在这里，以免堵塞交通。
3. 取菜时要用公筷，以免传染疾病。
4. 支票上的字一定要写清楚，以免产生误会。

三、因为这可能把鬼魂引入自家

"可能"是副词，放在动词前，作状语，表示"也许"、"或许"的意思。

Adverb 可能 is used before a verb and functions as an adverbial meaning perhaps or probably. For example:

1. 明年夏天，我可能去中国旅游。
2. 他不在家，可能去图书馆了。
3. 系领导可能同意他的要求。
4. 小李可能知道这件事，你去问问他。

四、这就使人们对不好事情的禁忌心理转化成了对语言的回避

“成”是动词，这里是放在别的动词之后作结果补语，意思是“成为”、“变成”，后面一定要带宾语。

Verb 成 used after another verb as a resultative complement means become or change to. An object always follows 成. For example:

1. 我要把五百美元换成人民币。
2. 我们要养成好的生活习惯。
3. 会议改成四点半召开。
4. 这件事造成了很不好的影响。

五、这个和尚说的句句都是吉利话

“句”是名量词，这里是名量词的重叠用法，表示“由个体组成的全体”、“毫无例外”的意思。

句 is a nominal measure word and is reduplicated here to show all are included, and there is no exception. For example:

1. 条条道路通罗马。
2. 这个科研室的职工，个个都是好样的。
3. 在学习上，我们班人人都争第一名。

六、这个屋子该是多么坚固

“多么”是副词，用在感叹句里，表示程度很高，常常有较强的主观夸张色彩。

Adverb 多么 is used in exclamatory sentences to show a high degree. It is more often an exaggeration. For example:

1. 要是妈妈看到这个孩子，她该多么高兴啊！
2. 你好像没事似的，不知道我是多么急呀！
3. 瞧，这些郁金香多么漂亮！
4. 这孩子多么可爱啊！

七、中国封建社会的帝王更是威严无比

"无比"是副词，它的意思是"没有别的能够相比"，多用于褒义，在句子中作状语或补语。

Adverb 无比, often commendatory, means nothing can be compared to, and is used as adverbial or complement in a sentence. For example:

1. 我们的力量无比强大。
2. 战士们一个个英勇无比。
3. 桂林山水美丽无比。

八、起码主人父亲的名字是不能说的

"起码"是副词，表示最低限度的意思。

Adverb 起码 means the lower limit, the minimum. For example:

1. 从这里到市中心，开车起码也得四十分钟。
2. 这幅画起码也值三万元。
3. 想通过这种语言考试，起码要掌握五千词。
4. 这活最起码也得干五天。

九、就连新加坡、日本也有类似的禁忌

"连"是介词，有"甚至"的意思，后面常与副词"也"或"都"连用，表示强调。

Preposition 连 means even. It is often followed by adverb 也 or 都 to show emphasis. For example:

1. 这样的谜语连小孩子也能猜得到。
2. 大家干得非常起劲，连吃饭都忘了。
3. 参加今天长跑的人非常多，连七十岁的郑大爷也来参加了。
4. 我现在兜里连一分钱也没有。

十、既然有语言的禁忌，那么委婉语的产生就很自然的了

"既然"是连词，用在因果关系复句中的副句，提出原因，后面主句中常常带"就"、"便"等词，说出由此推出的结果。

Conjunction 既然 is used in the secondary clause in a cause and effect compound sentence to raise the cause, and the main clause shows the result, usually followed by word such as 就 or 便. For example:

1. 既然领导已经批了，我照办就是了。
2. 既然大家都不同意，那这件事就算了吧。
3. 既然生米已经做成了熟饭，那就顺水推舟送个人情吧。

想一想 Questions

1. 世界上为什么有禁忌现象?
   Why are there taboos in different cultures?
2. 你能说出一些行业禁忌语吗?
   What kinds of taboos are there in different trades?
3. 中国封建社会的皇帝有哪些禁忌?
   What kinds of taboos did emperors in the feudal society of China have?
4. 你能说出一些委婉语吗?
   Can you give some examples of euphemism?

超级链接 Super Links

英语中的委婉语

1. 怀孕

anticipating	(本义) 期待的
awkward	(本义) 行动不便
eating for two	(本义) 吃双份饭
expecting	(本义) 期待
fragrant	(本义) 香喷喷的
full of heir	(本义) 怀有继承人

in a particular condition	(本义) 处于特殊状态
in anticipating	(本义) 期望得子
lady-in-waiting	(本义) 有期待的女人
to swallow a watermelon seed	(本义) 吞了颗西瓜子
waiting for the patter of little feet	(本义) 等待小脚丫声

2. 如厕

the call of nature	(本义) 自然的需要
to cash (write) a check	(本义) 开张支票
to do a job for oneself	(本义) 做点私事
to do one's business	(本义) 干自己的活
to find a haven of rest	(本义) 寻找安息所
to fix one's face	(本义) 化装
to freshen up	(本义) 梳妆打扮
to get some fresh air	(本义) 去呼吸一点新鲜空气
to give oneself ease	(本义) 自己舒服一下
to relieve oneself	(本义) 轻松一下

3. 死亡

to be asleep in the arms of God	(本义) 安睡在上帝的怀里
to be at peace	(本义) 平静了
to be at rest	(本义) 休息了
to be called to God	(本义) 被召唤到神那里去了
to be called to home	(本义) 被召回家
to rest in peace	(本义) 安息
to return to dust	(本义) 归土
to sleep	(本义) 长眠
to go off	(本义) 离去
to go one's last	(本义) 走到了自己的终点
to go to one's place	(本义) 回老家
to go to one's resting place	(本义) 到休息的地方去了
to pass away	(本义) 去世了
to take one's rest	(本义) 休息了

引自赵宝斌《英语中一些委婉的说法》

中国的数字文化

Numbers

5

A Kaleidoscope of Chinese Culture

世界上每个民族都有数量概念，所以任何一种语言都有数词。这小小的普通数字，除了向人们传达数量信息以外，它还与各民族的哲学理念、历史背景、吉凶事件、谐音文化等紧密相连，形成了丰富的文化内容，所以它既是数量符号也是神秘符号。人们觉得它似乎有一种超自然的力量，有些数字能给人带来福气和好运，而有些数字却能招灾引祸。这就使人对数字产生了或喜爱或厌恶的不同感情，以及或崇敬或禁忌的民俗心理。不同的民族有不同的禁忌，因此出现了不同的数字文化。下面我们对几个数字略加分析，看一看它们所包含的文化内涵。

数字文化是中国文化的一个重要内容。中国人对数字有独特的文化理念和好恶感情。在过去，由于人们受到了中国阴阳五行观念的影响，把从一到九的几个数字分为两大类：一类是1、3、5、7、9奇数，为阳；一类是2、4、6、8偶数，为阴，它像乾坤、刚柔、夫妇一样，阴阳相对，相生相克，形成了中国人的数字阴阳观。总的看来，中国人对偶数有些偏爱，但对奇数也不厌恶，这大概与中国人求对称、求和谐、求平、求稳的心理相适应。

“一”是最小的自然数。中国人自古就很尊崇“一”，认为它是万数之始，万物之祖，万事之源。《老子》说：“道生一，一生二，二生三，三生万物。”朱熹说：“一分为二，二分为四，四分为八。”可见“一”在人们心目中的位置。“一”在汉语中，除了作数词以外，它还与其他字组成许多词语。在汉语中，以“一”开头的词，至少有260多个；“一”开头的成语，最少有420多个。人们喜爱它，也赋予了它许多意义，比如：一心一意、一心向往、一往无前，这里“一”字是“专一”的意思；一刻千金、一针一线、一草一木，“一”字是“每一”的意思；一身是胆、一身是病、一天星斗，这里“一”是指“全、满”的意思。其他还有，一丝不苟、一掷千金、一元复始、一言九鼎、一笑置之等。由此可见，由“一”构成的词语非常之多，人们对“一”十分重视。

“三”字受到东西方许多国家人们的尊重，被看做一个吉祥数字。古希腊哲学家毕达哥拉斯认为，“三”是一个有头有尾有腹的完全数。古埃及人认为，它代表父、母、子。基督教认为，神是圣父、圣子、圣灵三位一体。在中国，人们对“三”也十分崇敬，中国道教称玉清、太清、上清为三清。《史记》中说：“数始于一，终十，成于三。”《周易》六十四卦，每卦六爻，阴爻称六，阳爻称九，都是三的倍数。在汉语中用“三”表示的事物和组成的词语非常之多，例如：古有“三皇”（伏羲氏、燧人氏、神农氏），自然有“三光”（日、月、星），宗教有“三教”（儒、释、道），祭祀有“三牲”（牛、羊、猪），礼教有“三纲”（君为臣纲、父为子纲、夫为妇纲），植物有岁寒“三友”（松、竹、梅），节令有“三伏”（初伏、中伏、末伏），佛教有“三世”（前世、今世、来世），宇宙有“三才”（天、地、人）等。其他由“三”组成的词语还有：三心二意，三教九流，三思而后行，三长两短，三个臭皮匠、顶个诸葛亮等。

“四”是一个很特殊的数字。它是一个偶数，是二的倍数，它能体现成双成对，所以被中国人所钟爱。在汉语中，用“四”来表示的事物非常多，生活中的方方面面几乎都有用“四”来概括的词语，如：古书有“四书”（论语、孟子、中庸、大学），礼教有“四维”（礼、义、廉、耻），空间有“四方”（东、南、西、北），一年有“四季”（春、夏、秋、冬），佛教有“四大佛山”（五台山、九华山、峨眉山、普陀山），国画有“四君子”（竹、兰、梅、菊），书法有“四体”（真、草、隶、篆），京剧有“四大名旦”（梅兰芳、程砚秋、尚小云、荀慧生），中医有“四诊”（望、闻、问、切）等。

中文成语大多数是由四个字组成，称之为“四字格”，如：画蛇添足、卧虎藏龙、自相矛盾、狐假虎威、卧薪尝胆等，不胜枚举。但是，由于“四”与“死”在一些方言中谐音，因而人们在汽车牌号、电话号码中，十分忌讳“四”字。

“六”对中国人来说，是个非常吉利的数字，俗语说：“六六大顺”。人们喜欢66、666、6666等号码，它象征顺顺利利、万事顺利。所以有很多事物冠之以“六”，例如：宇宙有“六合”（上、下、东、西、南、北），自然有“六气”（阴、阳、风、雨、晦、明），人有“六情”（喜、怒、哀、乐、爱、恶），牲畜有“六畜”（马、牛、羊、鸡、犬、猪），人际有“六亲”（父、母、兄、弟、妻、子），人体有“六腑”（胆、胃、大肠、小肠、膀胱、三焦），典籍有“六经”（诗经、书经、礼记、乐经、易经、春秋），中医有“六淫”（风、寒、暑、湿、燥、火）等。由“六”构成的词语也很多，如：六畜兴旺、六神无主、六亲不认、人过六十花甲子等。

可是对于西方人来说，“六”是一个很不吉利的数字，是魔鬼的代号。美国前总统里根买了一座别墅，门牌号码是666，因十分厌恶这个数字，南希把门牌号改为668。

“七”被东西方许多国家尊崇为圣数。西方人称它是“lucky seven”。在《圣经》中，与“七”有关的记载真是太多了。神是六天完成创造世界万物的壮举，第七天为安息日；《圣经》中有“七福”；主祷文有“七部分”；法老做梦，有七年丰收年，七年灾年；神向摩西传示，耕耘六年后，第七年为安息年；每七七四十九年，犹太人要庆祝五十年节等。

中国人也很崇敬数字“七”。《周易》中说：“反复其道，七日来复，利有攸往。”所以在汉语中，以“七”构成的词也很多，如：“七窍”（口、眼、耳、鼻之孔），“七色”（红、橙、黄、绿、青、蓝、紫），中医有“七方”（大方、小方、缓方、急方、奇方、偶方、复方）等。

“八”是个偶数。因为它的发音与“发”字谐音，寓意事业蓬勃发展、万事顺利、繁荣富足，所以人们特别喜欢“八”。有些商品标价两元八（谐音“双发”）或八元八（谐音“发发”）。有的电话号码尾数是918（谐音“就要发”）、168（谐音“一路发”）。不仅如此，第29届北京奥运会的开幕式时间就是2008年8月8日晚8点。更令人惊奇的是，在四川，电话号码88888888竟然拍出了233万的天价。由此可见，中国人对数字“八”的喜爱程度。汉语中“八”字组成的词语也很多，佛教有“八宝”，道教有“八仙”，乐器有“八音”，占卜有“八卦”，文章有“八股”，家具有“八仙桌”，食物有“八宝粥”、“八宝酱菜”，中医有“八纲”，婚姻有“八字帖”，成语有：八面威风、八拜之交、八斗之才、八仙过海等。

但也有的地方，把“八”字与“分别”联系起来，所以有“逢八不回家”之说。也有的老人八十多岁，不肯说出真实年龄，也是怕与人世分离。

“九”也是个含义复杂的数。它是基数中最高的数，也是阳数中最大的数。《素问》中说：“天地之至数，始于一，终于九焉。”所以“九”有表示最高最多的意义，也寓意“长久”。它被中国皇帝看中，用在与皇家有关的事物上。例如：故宫三大殿的高度是九丈九尺；宫殿各大、小门上的门钉是横九排、竖九排；宫殿的台阶是九层或九的倍数；北京内城是九个城门，故宫的房间据说有9999间；清乾隆时，建造两个九龙壁，一个在北海天王殿西，一个在故宫宁寿宫。这一切都是向人们显示皇帝的“九五之尊”。

但在中国人的心中，“九”又有主凶的理解。民谚说：“明九、暗九，非病即死。”这是指人的年龄，“明九”是九、十九、二十九、三十九等，“暗九”是十八、二十七、三十六、四十五等，人们认为这些岁数容易生病或死亡，所以这些年龄的人，每逢谈到岁数时，他们都会多说或少说一岁，藉以避开这一不吉利的数字。

这种对数字的禁忌和好恶，是世界上各个民族共同的文化现象，只是文化内容和表现形式不同罢了。

Each and every cultural group on earth has a concept of numbers, and all languages have some numerical forms. Numbers, unlike language, are concrete and closely tied in with the idea of measurement. In addition, numbers are associated with philosophical notions, historical events, or happenings good and bad. In this way, numbers themselves become a part of the culture of a society. More than a symbol of measurement, they are also a symbol of myth. People over the ages have firmly believed that numbers carry with them some kind of supernatural power; some bring good luck and fortune, and others bad luck and disaster. In turn, some numbers are preferred and some distrusted, and some are even worshipped or prohibited. Since this is a culturally specific phenomenon, different cultures all have their own ideas about numbers.

Number culture is an important part of Chinese culture. As influenced by the Theory of Yin Yang and the Five Elements, in the past Chinese divided the digits from 1 to 9 into two groups. Odd numbers of 1, 3, 5, 7, 9 belonged to Yang (masculine) and the even numbers of 2, 4, 6, 8 belonged to Yin. Just like heaven and earth, masculine and feminine, husband and wife, odd and even numbers were seen as two opposing and complementary principles. Overall, Chinese culture is more biased toward even numbers, though they do not dislike odd numbers. This is because of a preference for symmetry, harmony, peace and stability.

One is the smallest natural number. In Chinese history, this number has been highly regarded and taken as both the beginning of all numbers and the origin of all things. The Taoist sage Lao Zi noted that "Tao begets one, one begets two, two begets three, and three begets all things." A great philosopher known as Zhu Xi believed that things are created by the division of one into two, two into four, and four into eight. The character for one has been combined with other characters to create many words. In Chinese there are at least 260 characters and at least 420 idioms beginning with the character for one.

As a favorite number, one has been given different meanings in addition to its measurement function. One means devotion or wholeheartedness in idioms such as 一心一意, 一心向往, 一往无前. In idioms or sayings such as 一刻千金, 一针一线, 一草一木, one means every and each one. In 一身是胆, 一身是病, 一天星斗, it means full, or all over. There are many more fixed expressions such as 一丝不苟, 一掷千金, 一元复始, 一言九鼎, 一笑置之, etc.. The importance of one is easily seen.

The number three is regarded as a lucky number in both the west and east. Pythagoras, the Greek philosopher and mathematician, believed the number three expressed perfection. The ancient Egyptians thought the number three as representing father, mother and son. Christians believe that God is the trinity of the Father, Son and Holy Spirit. Likewise Chinese Taoism regards the Jade Pure, the Upper Pure and the Great Pure as the Three Pure Ones. This trinity represents the three divine natures of all living beings. *The Records of the Historian* by Sima Qian described that "Numbers begin at one, terminate at ten, and are fulfilled at three."

In *Zhou Yi*, or *The Book of Changes*, there are 64 hexagrams. Each hexagram has variables, with the 9 horizontal variables symbolizing Yang and the 6 horizontal variables symbolizing Yin. Both are multiples of the number three. Further examples of the esteem in which Chinese people hold the number three lie in many principles, expressions and institutions formed with three. Some of these include: the three virtuous emperors of ancient China (Fuxi Shi, Suiren Shi, Shennong Shi), the three lights of nature (the sun, the moon and the stars), the three religious schools (Confucianism, Buddhism, Taoism), the three ritual sacrifices (ox, sheep, pig), the three cardinal guides of the ethical pedagogy (ruler guides subject, father guides son, husband guides wife), the three strong plants resisting winter cold (pine, bamboo, plum tree), the first, second and third phase of the "dog days" of summer, the three lives of Buddhism (the former life, the current life and the future life), the three elements of the cosmos (heaven, earth and human beings), etc.. Words or expressions with the character for three include 三心二意, 三教九流, 三思而后行, 三长两短, 三个臭皮匠顶个诸葛亮, etc..

Four holds a curiously ambivalent place in Chinese culture. It's a multiple of the number two, and two by two is a sequence for which Chinese people have a high regard. There are numerous auspicious examples of the use of the number four in Chinese society.

In terms of schools of thought and places of learning, there are the four classic books: *The Analects of Confucius*, *Mencius*, *The Doctrine of the Mean*, *The Great Learning*. There are four essentials of the ritual doctrine, being moral etiquette, righteousness, frugality and humility. On a more elemental level there are the four directions of north, south, east and west, and the four seasons, spring, summer, autumn, and winter. Buddhism has the four holy mountains of Mt Wutai, Mt Jiuhua, Mt E'mei, and Mt Putuo.

In artistic culture, the four plants of bamboo, orchid, plum, and chrysanthemum represent a cultured personality and conduct in Chinese paintings. There are four styles of brush calligraphy, being regular script, cursive script, official script and seal script. In Peking Opera there are four celebrated female roles played by male singers, Mei Lanfang, Cheng Yanqiu, Shang Xiaoyun, and Xun Huisheng.

Even medicine makes an appearance with the four traditional steps to assess health: observe, listen, question and check a patient's pulse. And last but not least, most Chinese idioms are comprised of four characters.

On the other hand, in Chinese, four, pronounced *si*, sounds similar to 死 (*si*, death). As a result, people are reluctant to include four on car number plates or in telephone numbers. This reluctance originated in Guangdong and its surrounding areas, and has now spread to many places in China.

Six is a very lucky number for Chinese people. A popular saying is 六六大顺, which literally means six and six, lucky and smooth. Due to the belief that six is associated with smoothness, 66, 666, 6666 are favorite numbers for Chinese people. Similar to three and four, six denotes various things. The cosmos has six dimensions: the east, the west, the south, the north, the upper and the lower. Nature is thought to have six types of mood: overcast, sunny, windy, rainy, dim and bright. People have six passions: happiness, anger, sadness, joy, love and hatred. There are six farm animals: horse, ox, sheep, chicken, dog and pig.

In terms of family, a person traditionally has six connections, father, mother, older brother, younger brother, wife and son. The human body is thought to have six viscera: small intestine, large intestine, gall bladder, stomach, bladder, as well as upper, middle stomach and upper bladder as one.

In literary terms, the six classics include *The Book of Songs*, *The Book of History*, *The Book of Rites*, *The Book of Music*, *The Book of Changes*, plus *The Spring and Autumn Annals*. Chinese medicine believes there are six excesses shown in syndromes caused by wind, cold, summer heat, dampness, dryness and internal heat. There are also many idioms and expressions with the character for six, such as 六畜兴旺, 六神无主, 六亲不认, 人过六十花甲子.

In western countries, six is related to different cultural ideas and has evil implications. Ronald Reagan's house number was 666 before Nancy changed it to 668. On the contrary, number seven is considered a holy number in the west and seen as lucky seven. In the *Bible*, there are many special sevens: in *Genesis* the world was created in six days, leaving the seventh day for rest. Pharaoh's dream was a prediction of seven good harvest years to be followed by seven years of famine. The Lord told Moses that the field should be sown for six years and the seventh is the Sabbatical year. Every 49 years, seven by seven, the Jews will celebrate the Year of Jubilee.

In Chinese culture, the number seven also features rather prominently in some aspects of life. For example, in *Zhou Yi* it was noted, "He will return and repeat his (proper) course. In seven days comes his return. There will be advantage in whatever direction movement is made." There are also sevens in many things, such as seven holes, mouth, eyes, ears and nostrils; seven colors, red, orange, yellow, green, azure, blue, purple; seven types of prescriptions in Chinese medicine, major, minor, mild, emergency, odd, even and compound.

Eight is an even number and is favored by people, as it sounds similar to 发 (*fa*) which means fortunate and prosperous. Two and eight may mean both are fortunate (双发), double eight may mean more fortunate (发发). Number 918 is homophone of 就要发, destined to fortune and prosperity, number 168 is homophone with 一路发, fortunate all the way. It is interesting to note that the 29th Olympic Games in Beijing opened at 8 p.m. on August 8th, 2008. And astonishingly, the telephone number 88888888 was auctioned off for 2.33 million yuan in Sichuan.

Like some other numbers, there are also many eights in subjects related to Chinese cultural history. Some examples include: the eight treasures of Buddhism, the eight divine beings of Taoism, the eight traditional musical instruments, the eight categories in fortune telling, the essays to be written with eight components in Ming and Qing dynasties at imperial examinations, and an old style piece of furniture known as the eight immortals table.

In regards to food, there is congee with eight delicacies, and the eight pickled delicacies. There are also eight principles of Chinese medicine, and eight characters about one's birth that are used in match-making.

Once again, there are also numerous idioms that incorporate the character for eight, including 八面威风, 八拜之交, 八斗之才, 八仙过海, and many more.

But in some places, eight is connected with "apart". In these places there is a saying, "do not return home on the eighth day." In addition, some senior citizens in their eighties are reluctant to tell their true age because they hate to pass away.

Nine is a number related to sophisticated ideas. It is the biggest cardinal number and the highest Yang number. *Plain Questions of the Yellow Emperor's Classic of Internal Medicine* noted that all numbers start at one and terminate at nine. Nine means the highest and the most, and also means everlasting. Emperors chose it as a symbol of royalty. The three major palaces in the Palace Museum have the height, according to the traditional Chinese measurement system, of nine *zhang* and nine *chi*.

The rows of nails on gates, whether they be large or small, are numbered in nine both horizontally and vertically. The staircases in each palace are made up of either nine steps or multiples of nine. The inner city in Beijing had nine gates, and it is said there are 9,999 rooms in the Palace Museum. In Qianlong's reign during the Qing Dynasty, two Nine Dragon Screens were built, one at Beihai and one at the Forbidden City.

On the other hand, nine sometimes is interpreted as a symbol for disaster. A proverb states, "Implicit or explicit nine, one might be sick or die." Explicit nine here refers to the ages of 9, 19, 29, 39, etc., and implicit nine refers to the ages of 18, 27, 36, 45, etc., which are multiples of nine. It was believed that people at these ages are prone to illness and even death. People at these ages who believe in such a notion will say they are one year younger or older than they actually are, as a way to avoid the number nine.

Favor towards, dislike of, or taboo towards numbers is a common cultural phenomenon to all cultures in the world, though the ideas and meanings are represented in many different ways.

生词 New Words

1.数字	shùzì	numeral, figure
2.概念	gàiniàn	concept, notion
3.传达	chuándá	to pass on; to transmit
4.背景	bèijǐng	background, backdrop
5.吉凶	jíxiōng	good or ill luck
6.符号	fúhào	symbol, mark
7.神秘	shénmì	mysterious, mystical
8.似乎	sìhū	as if; seemingly
9.超自然	chāo zìrán	supernatural
10.福气	fúqì	good luck; good fortune
11.招灾引祸	zhāozāi-yǐnhuò	to court disaster; to invite trouble
12.喜爱	xǐ'ài	to like, to love; to be fond of
13.厌恶	yànwù	to detest, to abhor; to be disgusted
14.影响	yǐngxiǎng	influence, effect; to affect
15.奇数	jīshù	odd number
16.偶数	ǒushù	even number
17.乾坤	qiánkūn	heaven and earth; the cosmos
18.刚柔	gāngróu	hardness and softness
19.夫妇	fūfù	husband and wife

20.相生相克	xiāngshēng xiāngkè	mutual promotion and restraint between the five elements (a concept held by the ancients to explain natural phenomena)
21.偏爱	piān'ài	to have partiality for sth.; to show favoritism to sb.
22.对称	duìchèn	symmetry
23.和谐	héxié	harmonious
24.宗教	zōngjiào	religion
25.祭祀	jìsì	to offer sacrifices to gods or ancestors
26.礼教	lǐjiào	the Confucian or feudal ethical code
27.佛教	fójiào	Buddhism
28.宇宙	yǔzhòu	the universe, the cosmos
29.钟爱	zhōng'ài	to dote on; to cherish
30.空间	kōngjiān	space
31.典籍	diǎnjí	ancient codes and records; ancient books
32.魔鬼	móguǐ	devil, demon, monster
33.代号	dàihào	code name
34.别墅	biéshù	villa
35.法老	fǎlǎo	Pharaoh
36.商品	shāngpǐn	commodity, goods
37.标价	biāojià	to mark a price
38.乐器	yuèqì	musical instrument
39.占卜	zhānbǔ	to practice divination; fortune-telling
40.文章	wénzhāng	essay, article
41.家具	jiājù	furniture
42.中医	zhōngyī	traditional Chinese medical science
43.联系	liánxì	contact, connection
44.分离	fēnlí	to separate, to part

45.复杂	fùzá	complicated, complex
46.基数	jīshù	cardinal number
47.故宫	Gùgōng	the Palace Museum or the Imperial Palace (in Beijing)
48.横	héng	horizontal, transverse
49.竖	shù	vertical, upright
50.台阶	táijiē	steps leading up to a house
51.九五之尊	jiǔwǔzhīzūn	the imperial throne
52.避开	bìkāi	to avoid, to evade

语法聚焦 Notes and Examples

一、而有些数字却能招灾引祸

"却"是副词，表示转折，语气比"但是"、"可是"轻，可以和"但是"或"可是"连用。"却"只能用在主语后，不能用在主语前。

却 is an adverb indicating a contrast with what has already been mentioned and can only be put after the subject. It has a lighter tone than 但是 or 可是, and can be used together with 但是 or 可是. For example:

1. 现在已经是冬天了，天气却不冷。
2. 这里虽然很少下雨，可是地下水却很丰富。
3. 杭州离上海不远，可我在上海住了几十年却一次也没去过。

二、这就使人对数字产生了或喜爱或厌恶的不同感情

"对"是介词，引进对象或有关事物。"对"和它的宾语构成介词词组，在谓语或主语前作状语。

对 as a preposition introduces its object. The prepositional pattern 对+object functions as adverb before the predicate or the subject. For example:

1. 您的话对我很有帮助。
2. 我对物理很感兴趣。
3. 代表团对大家的热情款待表示感谢。
4. 主任有话要对你说。

三、因此出现了不同的数字文化

“因此”是连词，它的意思是“因为这个(这样)所以……”多用在因果复句中表示结果的分句句首，有时跟“由于”连用。

Conjunction 因此 means as a result, which introduces a resultative clause in a cause and effect compound sentence. For example:

1. 大家见你不来，因此就都回去了。
2. 由于我们缺少经验，因此这次试验不够理想。
3. 小强这次考试不及格，我们不能因此说他不聪明。

四、“六”数对中国人来说，是个非常吉利的数字

“对……来说”这个格式表示从某人、某事的角度来看。

The pattern 对…来说 means from the perspective of sb. or sth. For example:

1. 这点钱对你们公司来说是九牛之一毛。
2. 对一个留学生来说，取得这样好成绩真不容易。
3. 这里的气候对种植水稻来说，很不合适。

五、也有的老人八十多岁，不肯说出真实年龄

“出”是动词，此处是放在动词后面作补语，表示向外或显现。

出 is a verb and may be used to function as a complement of an action, meaning outwards or starting to show. For example:

1. 妈妈从衣袋中拿出一百元钱，给了儿子。
2. 这个球被守门员踢出了场外。
3. 市场上呈现出一片繁荣景象。
4. 罗律师对案情提出了质疑。

六、它被中国皇帝看中

“中”是动词，它表示“恰好合上”、“正对上”。这里是放在动词后面作补语。

Verb 中 in this context functions as a complement of the action, indicating exactly or as expected. For example:

1. 王队长在射击比赛中，每枪都打中了靶心。
2. 你的心事我早就猜中了。
3. 香草看中了张大妈的儿子大牛。

七、只是文化内容和表现形式不同罢了

“罢了”是助词，它用在句尾，对句子表示的意思有减轻、冲淡的作用。
罢了 is an auxiliary word used at the end of a clause to give an understated tone. For example:

1. 他只是说说罢了，你何必太认真。
2. 我也只能说个大意罢了，详细情况我也说不清楚。
3. 这点小礼品只是表表心意罢了，请你收下。

想一想 Questions

1. 中国人为什么尊崇“一”？
   Why is the number one favored by the Chinese?
2. 你能说出几个用“四”表示的事物吗?
   Can you name a few things with the number four?
3. 中国人为什么喜欢“八”？
   Why do the Chinese like the number eight?
4. 中国人为什么喜欢“九”？请说几个与皇帝有关的“九”的事物来。
   Why do the Chinese like the number nine? Can you name a few things with the number nine related to emperors?
5. 谈一谈你对数字的爱恶。
   Please talk about your likes and dislikes towards different numbers.

超级链接 Super Links

古时候，有很多人将数字写入诗中，称之为“数字诗”。将一至十依序入诗的，称之为“十数诗”或“十字令”。另外也有许多其他形式的数字诗，使人读起来别有一番趣味。

宋代的邵康节曾经写过这样一首小诗：

一去二三里，
烟村四五家。
亭台六七座，
八九十枝花。

相传，清乾隆进士李调元出任苏州主考时，夜游西湖，写了两首数字诗：

一名大乔二小乔，
三寸金莲四寸腰。
买得五六七色彩，
打扮八九十分娇。
十九月亮八分圆，
七个才子六个癫。
五更四点鸡三唱，
怀抱二月一枕眠。

中国的动物文化

Real and Mythical Animals

6

A Kaleidoscope of Chinese Culture

所谓动物文化，是指一个民族对动物的崇拜、禁忌和赋予动物的某种象征意义，以及在语言中用动物作比喻来表达人类的感情。这种文化现象，中外各国普遍存在，只是文化内容不同而已。

中华民族最崇拜的动物是龙，这大概起源于上古社会的图腾崇拜。在古人的心中，龙是有灵气的吉祥物。古人曾有“山不在高，有仙则名；水不在深，有龙则灵”的名句。由于“龙”蕴涵权威、力量、才华、吉祥等赞美的语义，因此，中国人以“龙的传人”自称，龙也成了中华民族的象征而被华人加以信仰。人们也崇拜凤，所以在中国文化中，逐渐形成了龙凤文化。其实人们所崇拜的龙凤，在现实中是没有的，它是一种“神灵化”、“艺术化”了的动物。它的形态古今有很大不同，我们今天所见到的龙凤形象，大体是在宋朝时定型的。明朝（1368-1644）李时珍在《本草纲目》中记载：“龙其形有九——头似驼，角似鹿，眼似兔，耳似牛，颈似蛇，腹似蜃，鳞似鲤，爪似鹰，掌似虎。”可见这是人们把各种动物的不同特征集中在一起，创造出的一种神化了的形象。至于凤，古人描绘为“鸡头、蛇颈、燕颔、龟背、鱼尾、五彩色，高六尺许”，这也是一种想象。不同的地方，有着不同的创造。安徽凤阳是明代开国皇帝朱元璋的故乡，这里至今还以画凤著称。据当地民间艺人讲，他们最早画凤是为了献给朱元璋的妻子马娘娘，因马娘娘属蛇，故把凤头画成“蛇头”，尾和翅都采用“九”和“九”的倍数。这样做是为了讨马娘娘的欢心。

中华民族认为，龙是神，它腾飞于云水之间，兴云降雨，昂首摆尾，威武雄壮；凤是百鸟之王，声鸣于天，不落无宝之地，于是把它们作为民族的象征加以信仰。到了汉朝，汉高祖刘邦说，他是其母与龙结合而生，所以自此以后，龙就逐渐成了皇帝的代表和皇权的象征，皇帝自称“真龙天子”，皇后也自命“凤仪非凡”，于是凡与皇帝和皇后有关的事物，都加以“龙”、“凤”字样，如：龙体、龙颜、龙袍、龙帐、龙子龙孙、凤衣、凤冠、凤阁、凤辇等。紫禁城内更是一个“龙的世界”，宫殿内外，房上房下，到处都装饰着“龙”。这里到底有多少“龙”，至今没有一个人能说得清。有一个细心人只对太和殿作了一次调查，殿内装饰的龙共有13844条。这仅仅是一个殿，据说故宫有房9999间，龙的数量加起来恐怕是一个天文数字。到了元明清时代，皇宫中所画的龙都是五爪大龙，这是皇家专用品，其他人是绝对不许用的，擅自使用将被满门抄斩。

在民间，龙凤也是吉祥的象征，每逢年节，人们总是舞龙灯加以庆祝。五月端阳节，在中国南方，更要举行龙舟竞渡，以表达人们喜悦、欢乐的心情。

在汉语中，含有“龙”、“凤”的词语很多，如：龙凤呈祥、龙飞凤舞、龙翔凤翥、攀龙附凤、龙腾虎跃、生龙活虎、龙马精神、望子成龙、百鸟朝凤、凤鸣朝阳、凤毛麟角等。

除了龙凤以外，中国人还喜欢喜鹊和燕子。民间传说故事中，喜鹊是成人之美的瑞鸟，民谚说 “喜鹊叫，喜来到”，听到了喜鹊的叫声，意味着喜事将要临门。在年画中，人们常常画喜鹊与梅花，取“喜上眉梢”之意。另外，在中国，还流传着在七夕（农历七月初七）这天，天上的牛郎、织女在银河相会，由喜鹊搭桥的故事，所以“鹊桥相会”是指夫妻或情人久别相聚的意思。中国人认为，燕子也是一种瑞鸟。如果燕子飞到家里，在檐下筑巢做窝，被看做非常吉祥的事情，主人绝不去打扰，他们相信燕子会给他们带来好运。

蝙蝠和鹿，因其发音与“福”、“禄”谐音，所以被用来比喻“福”、“禄”；蝙蝠和桃组成的谐音图案意为“福寿双全”；蝙蝠和鱼构成的图案谐音取其“富裕”之意，表现了人们对美好生活的憧憬。人们又用鹤（传说中是长寿的仙禽）来比喻长寿。在中国人的心目中，“福、禄、寿”是人生再好不过的三件事了。

孔雀也是中国人喜欢的鸟，人们认为它美丽吉祥。相反，英国人却把孔雀看做淫鸟、祸鸟，是自我吹嘘、自我炫耀的象征，英语中有“像孔雀一样骄傲”的比喻。

虎被当成兽中之王，雄壮勇猛。中国人对虎情有独钟，它是中国画中最为常见的主题之一。以“虎”组成的汉语词语非常之多，如：虎踞龙盘、卧虎藏龙、虎虎有生气、将门虎子、虎头虎脑、虎视眈眈、如虎添翼等。相比之下，汉语中“狮”字组成的词语就少得多了。而在西方，很多国家对狮子大加赞扬，有许多以狮子作比喻的词语，如：“狮子般庄严”、“像狮子一样雄伟”等。

另外，中国人不喜欢猫头鹰。虽然猫头鹰在自然界中是一种益鸟，可它在中国文化中却不被人喜欢。俗语说：“夜猫子进宅，无事不来”、“夜猫子抖搂翅，大小有点事”。人们把它看做一种不祥的鸟。由于它常常在夜间活动，并且鸣声凄厉，所以人们常把它的叫声与厄运相联系，避而远之。相反，在一些西方国家，人们认为猫头鹰是智能鸟，英语中有“像猫头鹰一样聪明”的话。

狼、狐狸也是不被中国人所喜欢的动物。狼被看做本性残忍、凶恶，忘恩负义。汉语中带狼的词都是贬义词，如：狼子野心、狼狈为奸、豺狼当道、狼心狗肺、狼奔豕突等。狐狸代表狡猾，人们常常把狡猾诡诈的人叫“老狐狸”，把坏女人叫“狐狸精”。

中国人对狗的态度有些特别。人们知道狗对主人非常忠诚，看家护院忠心耿耿，可在汉语词语中，以狗为比喻的词，全是不好的词，如：走狗、狗腿子、狗崽子、丧家狗、狐朋狗友、狼心狗肺、狗仗人势、狗嘴里吐不出象牙、狗急跳墙等。可见中国人对狗的态度有些复杂。

中国人对动物不仅有自己独特的爱恶，而且还选取了十二种动物用于纪年。它是中国人特有的一种表示出生时间的方式，类似于西方的黄道十二星座。因此，在中国每一个人都有与自己相对应的属相。汉族的十二生肖是：鼠、牛、虎、兔、龙、蛇、 马、羊、猴、鸡、狗、猪。之所以各种动物会按照这个顺序排列，在中国还有一个有趣的传说：当年轩辕黄帝（传说中的华夏始祖之一）要选十二种动物担任宫廷卫士，猫托老鼠报名，老鼠只顾自己，把好朋友猫的事情给忘了，结果猫没有选上，所以猫从此与鼠结成冤家。大象也来参赛，被老鼠钻进鼻子，给赶跑了。其余的动物，原本推牛为首，老鼠却窜到牛背上，快到终点的时候，老鼠一下子跳到了牛的前面，结果老鼠排了第一。虎和龙为争先后斗了起来，动物们赶紧封它们为山中之王和海中之王，使它们甘心排在鼠和牛的后面。兔子又不服了，和龙赛跑，小猪当裁判，小猪不顾众人的反对将兔子排在了龙的前面。狗对此愤愤不平，一气之下咬了兔子，为此被罚在了倒数第二。蛇、马、羊、猴、鸡也经过一番较量，一一排定了位置，而小猪因为不分黑白、私心太重被排到了最后。最后形成了鼠、牛、虎、兔、龙、蛇、马、羊、猴、鸡、狗、猪的顺序。

生肖信仰中非常重要的一部分是中国人本命年的观念。本命年是指：十二年一遇的农历属相所在的年份，俗称属相年。也就是说，一个人出生的那年是农历某年，那么以后每过12年便是此人的本命年。这样依次推出，人的本命年为12岁、24岁、36岁、48岁、60岁……民间认为本命年为凶年，需要趋吉避凶，消灾免祸。汉族北方各地每到本命年时，不论大人小孩都要系红腰带，称为“扎红”，有时还要穿红背心、红裤衩、红袜子。这种习俗到今天仍在各地流行。每逢春节，市场上到处可买到代表吉祥的红绸带，过本命年的人们将之系在腰间、手腕上，以求消灾解祸、化凶为吉。

一种语言有一种语言的文化积淀。汉语中有关动物的词语在中华民族文化中的表现形式是具体而形象的，它承载了丰厚的文化内涵，值得细细玩味。

Similar to other cultures, in China, some animials are given certain symbolism and used in a metaphorical way to express human feelings.

The dragon and phoenix are mythical creatures venerated by the Chinese, and intrinsically linked to their cultural identity. Belief in the dragon can be traced back to primitive society, when certain prehistoric tribes adopted the dragon as their symbol and guardian. Ancient people regarded the dragon as a lucky and miraculous creature, a symbol of power, authority, talent, and auspiciousness. Over time it became recognized as a symbol of the Chinese nation.

A piece of Tang prose claimed "A mountain will become famous if there's deity on it, even if it is a small mountain; a river will become divine if there is a dragon in it, even if it only has shallow water." Different physical attributes were added over time, including the head of a camel, the antlers of a deer, the eyes of a rabbit, the ears of an ox, the neck of a serpent, the scales of a fish, the mane of a horse, the claws of an eagle, and the palms of a tiger. As noted by Li Shizhen in the Ming Dynasty (1368-1644), in his *Compendium of Materia Medica*, the dragon appropriated the distinctive features of many animals to become what it is today.

The phoenix, quixotically, has the head of a chicken, the neck of a serpent, the chin of a swallow, the back of a tortoise, and the tail of a fish. Its skin has five colors and it is over two meters in length. People in different places have their own imaginations of the phoenix. Fengyang in Anhui Province was the birthplace of the first Ming emperor, Zhu Yuanzhang. It is also renowned for its artistic interpretations of the phoenix, but with a local twist. According to artists there, drawings of the phoenix were presented to the wife of Emperor Zhu Yuanzhang. However because her birthday was in the year of the serpent, the head of the phoenix was changed to that of a serpent. Also, because the empress was partial to the number nine, its tails and wings were numbered at nine or multiples of nine.

The Chinese long regarded the dragon as a powerful divine being, who freely roamed high clouds and deep water, and commanded changes in the weather at will. The phoenix was considered the queen of the birds, and made a roaring sound. It never stayed in a place that did not have treasure. The first emperor of the Han Dynasty, Liu Bang, claimed his father was a dragon. Since then the dragon gradually became a symbol of imperial power, and a representative of the emperor. Empresses, on the other hand, were connected to the phoenix. Anything related to the emperor or empress was labeled dragon or phoenix. For example, the emperor's countenance was known as 龙颜, his robe as 龙袍, and his descendents as 龙子龙孙. The empress gown was known as 凤衣, her crown as 凤冠, her chamber as 凤阁, and her carriage as 凤辇.

At the Forbidden City, dragon decorations are everywhere, to the point where nobody knows exactly how many. A survey carried out at the Taihe Palace found that there were 13,844 dragons in that building alone. Bearing in mind there are 9,999 rooms at the Forbidden City as believed, the total number of dragons must be an astronomical figure. During the Yuan, Ming, and Qing dynasties, all dragons in the imperial palaces were depicted with five claws. The five-clawed dragons were used exclusively in the imperial household, and anybody else who dared to use it would, somewhat drastically, have their entire family executed.

In recent times, dragons and phoenixes have also been considered a sign of auspiciousness. The dragon dance has become a part of festival celebrations. On the fifth day of the fifth lunar month, dragon boat races are held in the south of China to celebrate the Dragon Boat Festival.

Many idioms and phrases include mentions of the dragon and the phoenix, such as 龙凤呈祥, 龙飞凤舞, 龙翔凤翥, 攀龙附凤, 龙腾虎跃, 生龙活虎, 龙马精神, 望子成龙, 百鸟朝凤, 凤鸣朝阳, 凤毛麟角. These often refer to a sense of auspiciousness, power, or rarity.

Apart from mythical creatures such as the dragon and phoenix, Chinese people also value other kinds of animals that are thought to help address their cultural need to seek happiness and auspiciousness.

According to folklore, magpie, which in Chinese literally means joyful bird, is a harbinger of good and happy things. "Happiness comes when the magpie sings" is a folk saying. Magpies perched on plum trees are painted in New Year pictures to represent a homophonic metaphor of radiance with happiness. According to legend, on the seventh day of the seventh lunar month the cowherd Niu Lang and his lover, the weaver girl Zhi Nu, go to the Milky Way for their once annual meeting. To assist them in making their way there, a group of magpies form a bridge so they can be reunited. As a result, the idiom 鹊桥相会, meeting at the magpies' bridge, was created to mean the reunion of a couple or lovers after a long separation. For some reason, swallows also enjoy a similarly favorable status in Chinese culture. If swallows nest in the roof of a Chinese family's house, the hosts will never disturb them, because it's believed that it will bring luck to the family.

In Chinese fortune is a homophone for the word bat. Likewise, deer is a homophone of 禄 (*lu*), which means something like official rank and salary. The crane was thought to be divine and represent longevity. In the world view of Chinese tradition, one cannot aim higher in life than to have fortune, high rank, good salary, and a long life.

The peacock is also admired in China, for both its beauty and auspicious implications. By way of contrast, in the UK it was believed to be unlucky to have the feathers of a peacock in one's home. The peacock's beauty and carriage led its name to become synonymous with vanity, and the expression "as proud as a peacock".

The tiger is regarded as the king of wild creatures and symbolizes unlimited power, courage, dignity, and military prowess. It is often depicted in Chinese paintings and idioms, including 虎踞龙盘，卧虎藏龙，虎虎有生气，将门虎子，虎头虎脑，虎视眈眈，and 如虎添翼. Probably due to the fact the lion is not native to China, there are few uses of it in idioms, despite the fact it is an equally powerful animal. In the west, the lion is regarded as the embodiment of courage, strength and nobility, similar to how the tiger is perceived by Chinese people.

By contrast, the owl is considered to be a bad omen by Chinese people. It is a bird to be feared and avoided. When an owl enters a house, people believe something bad is sure to follow. Due to its nocturnal lifestyle and terrifying screeches, it is quite an apt symbol of darkness and bad luck. However, to some western people, the owl is a wise and benevolent creature. "As wise as an owl" is an expression in English.

Other creatures disliked and distrusted by the Chinese are wolves and foxes. The wolf is considered a fierce and ruthless beast devoid of gratitude. Expressions that include the character for wolf are replete with derogatory meanings, including 狼子野心，狼狈为奸，豺狼当道，狼心狗肺，and 狼奔豕突. The fox is considered cunning and plotting. A cunning person is sometimes referred to as an old fox, and an evil woman as a fox demon.

There is an ambivalent attitude toward dogs in Chinese culture. Though they are considered loyal and reliable, most phrases that include dogs have derogatory connotations, such as 走狗 or 狗腿子, which means henchman or jackal, 狗急跳墙, a cornered dog will do something desperate, 狗仗人势, being a bully under the protection of a powerful person, and 狐朋狗友, a gang of scoundrels. Other expressions with derogatory meanings include 狗崽子, 丧家狗, 狼心狗肺, and 狗嘴里吐不出象牙.

There are 12 animals in the Chinese zodiac. In order, they are: rat, ox, tiger, rabbit, dragon, snake, horse, sheep, monkey, rooster, dog and pig. The Chinese zodiac is a 12-year cycle, with each animal representing one year. There are many legends surrounding the conception of these 12 signs. One has it that the Yellow Emperor was to choose 12 animals as palace guards. To make things simpler and faster, he decided that the first animals to register would be given the honor. The cat asked his best friend the rat to apply for him, but the rat forgot and so the cat lost his place. Ever since then, cats and rats have been mortal enemies. The elephant came to register, but the rat snuck into his trunk. The elephant was so shocked he ran away. The ox arrived first, but the rat jumped onto his back and then ahead of him. The tiger and the dragon fought each other for the third place behind the rat and the ox. The tiger, the king of the mountain, won and came in third. As the dragon was about to take his place after the tiger, the rabbit proposed a race with him. The pig acted as the referee and declared the rabbit the victor, even though this was contrary to the actual outcome. The dog, who was an outraged spectator of this fiasco, was so angry he bit the rabbit and was punished by being put in second last place. The last place was reserved for the duplicitous pig. The snake, rooster, horse, sheep and monkey jostled for the remaining places.

According to the Chinese zodiac, your sign is the animal of the year in which you were born. Every 12 years, therefore, your sign comes around once again. This is called your zodiac year, and happens when you turn 12, 24, 36, 48, 60, and so on. Your zodiac year is considered a sensitive and unlucky period. During the year one should practice caution. It is a common practice for people in their zodiac year to wear at least some red, be it a belt, underwear or socks, to protect them from misfortune.

Animals have played an important role in the life and culture of Chinese people from prehistoric times. In a sense, there is no distinction made between real and mythological animals when they are seen as symbols.

生词 New Words

1.普遍	pǔbiàn	universal, general, common
2.神灵	shénlíng	gods, divinities
3.大体	dàtǐ	roughly; more or less
4.定型	dìngxíng	to finalize the design; to fall into a pattern
5.似	sì	similar; like
6.蜃	shèn	clam
7.想象	xiǎngxiàng	imagination; to fancy
8.开国	kāiguó	to found a state
9.娘娘	niángniang	used in speaking to or of an empress or an imperial concubine
10.欢心	huānxīn	favor, love

11.腾飞	téngfēi	to fly swiftly upward; to soar
12.昂首	ángshǒu	to hold one's head high
13.威武雄壮	wēiwǔ-xióngzhuàng	full of power and grandeur
14.皇权	huángquán	imperial power
15.天子	tiānzǐ	the Son of Heaven
16.龙颜	lóngyán	imperial countenance
17.紫禁城	Zǐjìnchéng	the Forbidden City
18.细心人	xìxīnrén	a careful man
19.天文数字	tiānwén shùzì	astronomical figure
20.专用品	zhuānyòngpǐn	things for special use
21.满门抄斩	mǎnmén-chāozhǎn	(in feudal China) execution of the entire family
22.喜鹊	xǐquè	magpie
23.燕子	yànzi	swallow
24.喜上眉梢	xǐshàngméishāo	to be radiant with joy
25.牛郎	Niúláng	cowherd
26.织女	Zhīnǚ	weaver girl
27.七夕	qīxī	the seventh evening of the seventh lunar month
28.银河	yínhé	the Milky Way
29.鹊桥	quèqiáo	Magpies Bridge
30.檐下	yánxià	under the eave
31.打扰	dǎrǎo	to disturb, to bother
32.福	fú	good fortune; blessing, happiness
33.禄	lù	official rank and salary
34.寿	shòu	long life; longevity
35.自我吹嘘	zìwǒ chuīxū	self-glorification
36.炫耀	xuànyào	to make a display of; to show off; to flaunt

37.猫头鹰	māotóuyīng	owl
38.抖搂	dǒulou	to shake off
39.益鸟	yìniǎo	beneficial bird
40.凄厉	qīlì	sad and shrill
41.厄运	èyùn	adversity, misfortune
42.残忍	cánrěn	cruel, ruthless
43.凶恶	xiōng'è	fierce, ferocious, fiendish
44.忘恩负义	wàng'ēn-fùyì	devoid of gratitude; ungrateful
45.看家	kānjiā	to look after the house
46.忠心耿耿	zhōngxīn-gěnggěng	loyal and devoted
47.纪年	jìnián	a way of numbering the years
48.生肖	shēngxiào	any one of the 12 symbolic animals associated with 12-year cycle, used to denote the year of a person's birth
49.宫廷	gōngtíng	palace
50.冤家	yuānjia	enemy, foe
51.裁判	cáipàn	judge
52.愤愤不平	fènfèn-bùpíng	indignant; to feel aggrieved
53.较量	jiàoliàng	to measure one's strength with; to have a contest
54.本命年	běnmìngnián	every 12th year after the year of one's birth
55 凶年	xiōngnián	a famine year; a bad year
56.消灾	xiāozāi	to rid calamities
57.玩味	wánwèi	to ponder, to ruminate

语法聚焦 Notes and Examples

一、所谓动物文化，是指一个民族对动物的崇拜、禁忌和赋予动物的某种象征意义

"所谓" 是形容词，它在句中作定语，意思是"所说的"，由此引出要解释的内容。

所谓 means as said and introduces the contents of an explanation. For example:

1. 所谓科学是指反映自然、社会、思维等客观规律的知识体系。
2. 古人所谓的小学，是指研究文字、训诂、音韵的学问。
3. 所谓人生观，是指对人生的看法。

二、只是文化内容不同而已

"而已"是助词，用在陈述句末尾，有把事情往小里说的意思。它前面常与"不过"、"只是"、"无非"、"仅仅"等词连用。多用于书面语。

Auxiliary word 而已 is put to the end of a declarative sentence for an understated tone. 不过, 只是, 无非, or 仅仅 is often used before it. It is mostly used in written language. For example:

1. 我和胡先生只是一般接触而已，没有更深交往。
2. 这小小的礼物请您收下，只是表示我一点心意而已。
3. 我所能做的，如此而已。
4. 就让孩子到培训班进修两年，无非花一点钱而已。

三、大体是在宋朝时定型的

"大体" 是副词，表示多数情况或主要方面。

大体 is an adverb and means by and large, for the most part or generally. For example:

1. 教学楼大体完工了，还有一些扫尾工作。
2. 这次会议议程大体安排好了。
3. 关于这件事情，我大体知道一些，不是非常清楚。

四、不同的地方，有着不同的创造

动词"有"的后面加动态助词"着"，表示"具有"、"存在着"的意思，主要

用于书面语。它后面的宾语多是抽象名词。

Verb 有 followed by auxiliary 着 indicates existence or possession. Its object is usually abstract nouns. It is mostly used in written language. For example:

1. 这次两国元首互访，对改善双方关系有着深远影响。
2. 我对故乡的一草一木都有着深厚的感情。
3. 这是一座有着悠久历史文化传统的城市。

五、龙也成了中华民族的象征而被华人加以信仰

“加以” 是动词，放在双音节动词前，表示对前面提到的事物施加某种动作。动词后面不能带其他成分。

Verb 加以 before a disyllabic verb means to exert an action to what is mentioned afore. No other element should follow verb after 加以. For example:

1. 对这些设计方案，我们要召开全体大会加以研究。
2. 我们对他们提供的情况，还要进一步加以分析。
3. 卫生部门对这里的卫生状况必须加以全面检查，以免出现问题。

六、“福、禄、寿”是人生再好不过的三件事了

“不过” 是副词，在这里是放在由程度副词修饰的形容词后面，表示一种程度的极限，意思是“再怎么样，也莫过于此”。

Adverb 不过 is put after an adjective modified with a degree adverb to show the highest degree. For example:

1. 我绝对不能和他们做这种事情，顶多不过被他们开除。
2. 要是能把吴小姐这样大明星请来，那是再好不过了。
3. 这些年来，刘先生一直被工作重担压着，现在退休了，真是感到再轻松不过了。

想一想 Questions

1. 中国人最崇拜的动物是什么？
   What is the animal that the Chinese have the highest regard for?

2. 龙为什么成了皇权的象征？
Why did dragon become a symbol of imperial power?

3. 除了龙、凤以外，中国人还喜欢哪些动物？
What are the favorite animals of Chinese people, in addition to dragon and phoenix?

4. 中国人不喜欢哪些动物？
What are the animals that Chinese people do not like?

5. 谈一谈你喜欢和厌恶的动物有哪些。
What are your favorite animals? What are not?

超级链接 Super Links

在中国的一些建筑或器物上，人们能看到似龙又不是龙的装饰物。人们说这是龙的九个儿子。它们样子和脾气各不相同，所做的工作也不一样。关于这九子的情况，有不同的说法，我们选其一种，记录如下：

老大囚牛（qiúniú），形似有鳞角的小龙，好音乐，胡琴上刻的兽头就是它的形象。

老二睚眦（yázì），形似豺，好杀人武斗，被雕刻在古代的刀把上。

老三嘲风（cháofēng），形似剪尾四脚蛇，喜欢站在高处观望，所以宫殿屋脊上的兽头就是它。

老四蒲牢（púláo），形似龙，个子小，好鸣叫，生活在海边，畏惧鲸鱼。寺庙、祠堂铜钟上的兽钮就是它的形象。因为它怕鲸鱼，所以撞钟的长木都雕成鲸鱼状，以使其声音宏大。

老五狻猊（suānní），长得像狮子，好烟火，又好坐，所以佛座香炉上雕的兽头就是它。

老六霸下（bàxià），形似龟，力大好负重，它总驮着一个大石碑，人们说的“乌龟驮石碑”，就是指它。

老七狴犴（bì'àn），喜好诉讼，有威力，监狱门上刻的狮子头就是它的形象。

老八负屃（fùxì），很像一只螺蚌，好静，碑两旁的文龙就是它。

老九螭吻（chīwěn），好吃东西，青铜餐具、鼎盖上的兽头就是它的面孔。

中国的植物文化

Plants Symbolism

7

A Kaleidoscope of Chinese Culture

以花草树木植物为象征，表达人的思想感情，是各民族语言文化中的一种共同现象，中华民族自古便种花、养花、赏花。人们在欣赏花草外在美的同时，也赋予了它们某种特定的意义。特别是历代文人学士、诗人画家，他们通过咏诗赋词、写文作画，把他们内心的感情和审美情趣都寄托于大自然的花草之中，因而使其具有了丰富的文化内容，形成了中华民族的植物文化。反之，这种植物文化又在塑造中华民族文化心理、生活习俗和铸就民族性格等方面发挥了重要的作用。

中国是一个花的国度，据有关数据记载，可供人们观赏的各种花卉有数千种之多。被人们公认的名花就有十种，它们是：牡丹、芍药、山茶花、杜鹃、水仙、菊花、梅花、荷花、海棠、兰花。人们不仅赞赏它们婀娜的形态、艳丽的姿色和醇美的清香，更是“咏物言志”，赋予了它们人的品格和情操。实际上，它们成为了人的某种精神的物化者，所以有了“岁寒三友”（松、竹、梅），“花中四君子”（梅、兰、竹、菊），“花草四雅”（兰花的淡雅、菊花的高雅、水仙的素雅、菖蒲的清雅）等美誉。

松是中国人最为喜欢的植物之一，也是“岁寒三友”之一，因其高昂挺拔，岁寒而不凋，四季常青，被人们用来象征正直坚强，不屈不挠，刚直不阿。孔子说过：“岁寒，然后知松柏之后凋也。”唐代（618–907）大诗人李白在《赠韦侍御黄裳》诗中说：“太华生长松，亭亭凌霜雪。天与百尺高，岂为微飙折。”白居易也在《栽松二首》中写道：“爱君抱晚节，怜君含直文。欲得朝朝见，阶前故种君。知君死则已，不死会凌云。”总之，人们把松视为一种坚贞顽强、处乱世而不改节的精神象征。

另外，因为松的树龄很长，它又象征长寿。画家们常常以松、鹤为题作画，寓意益寿延年。在汉语中有许多以松为比喻写成的贺寿联，如："福如东海长流水，寿比南山不老松"、"元鹤千年寿，苍松万古青"、"寿同松柏千里碧，品似芝兰一味清"、"松木有枝皆百岁，蟠桃无实不千年"等。

竹是"岁寒三友"之二，也是"花中四君子"的一位。它根生大地，渴饮甘泉，中空有节，质地坚硬，冬夏常青，所以它象征正直、坚贞、有气节、有骨气和虚心自恃。中国人很喜欢竹子，在许多古典文献中，都记载了上古先民对竹子的崇拜。历朝历代有许多爱竹的"痴迷者"，其中最有名的要数晋代（265–420）大书法家王羲之的儿子王徽之。用一句现代时髦的话来说，他可算"追竹族"中的发烧友。他爱竹爱到一听说某士大夫家有好竹，便跑去观看，甚至只顾看竹，连主人打招呼、让座也不加理会。有一次，他暂时寄居在一个地方，他马上叫人在宅旁种竹，并指着竹子说："何可一日无此君？"由此竹子得了一个"此君"的雅号。另一位爱竹的痴迷者是宋代大诗人苏东坡。他爱竹爱到不吃肉可以、没有竹子不行的程度。他说："宁可食无肉，不可居无竹。无肉令人瘦，无竹使人俗。"还有一位就是清代扬州八怪之一的郑板桥，他画竹、赞竹。他说："四十年来画竹枝，日间挥写夜间思"。他称赞竹子不畏强暴、敢于斗争的精神，"秋风昨夜渡潇湘，触石穿林惯作狂。惟有竹枝浑不怕，挺然相斗一千场。"由此可见，人们在赞美竹子的同时，更是在颂扬中华民族的高尚气节和美好的情操。

在“岁寒三友”和“花中四君子”中都有梅花。它在百花凋谢的严冬季节开放，因此人们喜爱它凌霜傲雪的品格。它又是“万花敢向雪中出，一树独先天下春”的“东风第一枝”，所以梅花象征高雅纯洁、坚贞不屈、清丽中而含铁骨之气、独领风骚而不争春的精神。古往今来，爱梅之人多不胜数，诗词歌赋画，以梅为题也是最多。其中以宋代林逋为代表。林逋隐居杭州西湖的孤山，一生不当官，也不娶妻，没有孩子，整日以种梅放鹤为乐，所以有“梅妻鹤子”之语。他的《山园小梅》被人们称做千古传颂的咏梅绝唱：“众芳摇落独喧妍，占尽风情向小园。疏影横斜水清浅，暗香浮动月黄昏。霜禽欲下先偷眼，粉蝶如知合断魂。幸有微吟可相狎，不须檀板共金樽。”南宋（1127–1279）爱国诗人陆游也以梅自喻，颂扬梅的洁身自好、淡泊功名的高贵品格。他在《卜算子·咏梅》中写道：“驿外断桥边，寂寞开无主。已是黄昏独自愁，更著风和雨。无意苦争春，一任群芳妒，零落成泥碾作尘，只有香如故。”元代（1206–1368）的王冕画梅成癖，他名扬古今的《墨梅》诗是：“我家洗砚池头树，朵朵花开淡墨痕。不要人夸颜色好，只留清气满乾坤。”这些都是赞颂梅花的标格秀雅和品德高尚的著名诗词。

梅文化对中国人产生了深远的影响。有的男人也以梅为名，如清代文人陈梦梅；有人以梅花为号，如南宋史达祖号梅溪；也有人以梅为书名，如《梅村集》；地名中有“梅岭”，动物中有“梅花鹿”，乐曲中有“梅花三弄”，曲艺中有“梅花大鼓”等。

兰花也深受中国人的喜爱。它被称为“空谷佳人”，又有“香祖”、“国香”、“王者香”、“天下第一香”等别号。它花开四季，早春开花的叫春兰；春末夏初开花的叫蕙兰；夏季开花的叫建兰；秋末和冬季开花的叫墨兰和寒兰。兰花清雅含蓄，幽香四溢，文人们把它比做君子。它象征纯洁、高雅和真诚，更以“兰熏桂馥”表示历久不衰。《孔子家语》中说：“孔子曰，与善人交，如入芝兰之室，久而不闻其香，而与之俱化。”就是说与正人君子在一起，如在养兰花的房间里，被香气所化。可见古人将兰花看做“正气之宗，君子之喻”。王羲之曾在会稽山勾践种兰处建一兰亭，邀请当时名士42人饮酒赋诗，写下了名扬千古的《兰亭集序》。爱国诗人屈原在《离骚》中也有这样的诗句：“扈江蓠与辟芷兮，纫秋兰以为佩。……时暖暖其将罢兮，结幽兰而延伫。……户服艾以盈要兮，谓幽兰其不佩。”唐宋八大家之一的唐朝大诗人韩愈赋诗：“兰之猗猗，扬扬其香。不采而佩，于兰何伤。”宋代文人苏辙有诗云：“幽花耿耿意羞香，纫佩何人香满身？一寸芳心须自保，长松百尺有为薪。”这些都是赞扬兰花的美丽和品德高尚的。至于宋末元初郑思肖画的《墨兰图》，画兰不画土，更是表现了画家寓意国土被异族践踏、不愿为奴的崇高民族气节。

菊花是在深秋时节傲霜而开的花卉。它被人们看做坚毅、清雅、淡泊功名的品格象征。诗人屈原就有“朝饮木兰之坠落，夕餐秋菊之落英”的诗句。东晋（317–420）诗人陶渊明更是以爱菊、咏菊而闻名。他的“采菊东篱下，悠然见南山”向世人描绘了一幅恬淡、宁静的田园生活景象，令人不胜向往。唐代诗人陈叔达的《咏菊》：“霜间开紫蒂，露下发金英。但令逢采摘，宁辞独晚荣。”宋代朱淑贞的《黄花》：“土花能白又能红，晚节由能爱此工。宁可抱香枝头老，不随黄叶舞秋风。”这些诗句都歌颂了菊花不随波逐流、保持高尚晚节的可贵情操。

牡丹也是中国人非常喜爱的一种植物，它被誉为“国色天香”。牡丹雍容华丽，象征富贵荣华，幸福吉祥。有人提议，应定它为中国国花。赞赏牡丹的诗文很多。宋代大文学家欧阳修的《洛阳牡丹记》，堪称一篇写牡丹的专著。他对牡丹的历史、栽培、品种、风俗等，都写得非常清楚。另外还有陆游的《天彭牡丹谱》，明代薛凤翔的《亳州牡丹史》都是描写牡丹的。诗人们也都写下了许多歌咏牡丹的诗词，像唐朝刘禹锡的《赏牡丹一首》：“庭前芍药妖无格，池上芙蕖净少情。唯有牡丹真国色，花开时节动京城。”五代（907-960）时皮日休的《牡丹》：“落尽残红始吐芳，佳名唤作百花王。意夸天下无双绝，独立人间第一香。”这些都是脍炙人口的咏牡丹佳作。

民间也流传着一则关于牡丹的故事。传说，武则天初春游上苑，见苑中花朵都含苞未放，于是她下令催开，写了一首催花诗：“明朝游上苑，火速报春知。花须连夜发，莫待晓风吹。”众花全都开放，唯有牡丹抗旨不开。武则天大怒，下令把牡丹贬到洛阳。可见牡丹不独容貌华美，她还有一股子蔑视权贵、刚毅倔强的性格。

水仙被称为“凌波仙子”。人们赞赏它“一盆水仙满堂春，冰肌玉骨送清香”。它象征素洁高雅、超凡脱俗的品格。宋代诗人刘邦直写道：“得水能仙天与奇，寒香寂寞动冰肌。仙风道骨今谁有？淡扫蛾眉簪一枝”。黄庭坚在《次韵中玉水仙花两首》中，也写道：“借水花开自一奇，水沉为骨玉为肌。暗香已压酴醾倒，只比寒梅无好枝。”这些都写出了水仙的风韵和品格。

在其他花卉中，中国人还以桃花比喻美人；以荷花比喻高洁，有“出淤泥而不染”之说；昙花表现好事物不久长，有“昙花一现”之语；红豆象征爱情和相思等。

另外，人们还用“家花”比喻妻子，用“野花”比喻男人外遇的女人，有一首歌叫“路边的野花不要采”，它告诫人们对爱情要忠贞。

中国人对野草也是很赞赏的，人们赞美小草不求名、不图利、内心平安、怡然自乐的精神。有首歌词写道：“没有花香，没有树高，我是一棵无人知道的小草。从不寂寞，从不烦恼，你看我的伙伴遍及天涯海角。”唐代大诗人白居易的一句“野火烧不尽，春风吹又生”更是流传千古。他赋予野草的这种顽强精神，也深深地扎根在中国人的精神世界里，这也正是了解中国植物文化的意义所在。

Attaching symbolic value to plants, flowers, and trees is a phenomenon common to all languages and cultures. In China, the cultivation and appreciation of plants is something that began thousands of years ago. From those times, Chinese people had endowed many plants with special significance. Writers, poets and painters have long depicted flowers and trees in their artistic pursuits. Over time, the symbolism of plants has become a complex part of Chinese culture. Historically, plants have also been thought to embody certain spiritual features that have shaped the customs and character of China as a nation.

China is famous as being home to many thousands of varieties of flowers, many of which are cultivated for the personal pleasure of Chinese people. The ten most widely appreciated and culturally significant are peony, Chinese herbaceous peony, camellia, azalea, narcissus, chrysanthemum, plum blossom, lotus, Chinese flowering crab apple and orchid. Pine and bamboo are also very popular. Many different aspects of plants, flowers and trees are admired, including their shapes, colors, and scents. Furthermore, they are often endowed with spiritual and human attributes. In Chinese, the expression Three Friends in Cold Winter refers to pine, bamboo and plum trees. Similarly, the expression Four Men of Honor refers to plum, orchid, bamboo and chrysanthemum, and Four Elegancies refers to the simple yet graceful orchid, chrysanthemum, narcissus and calamus.

Pine is held in high esteem as one of the Three Friends in Cold Winter because it is evergreen, grows straight and tall, and can endure cold weather with relative ease. People value it as a symbol of integrity, tenacity and uprightness. Confucius once said "Only after it turns winter are we aware of the survival of the pine and cypress." The famous Tang Dynasty (618-907) poet Li Bai wrote:

A giant pine grows on Mt Taihua,
Erect and upright over hoar frost and snow;
Reaching the sky tall and strong,
It never bends when wind blows.

Another equally gifted poet, Bai Juyi wrote:
I love pine tree for thy integrity in even old age,
I adore pine tree for thy uprightness.
Wishing to see thee every day,
I plant thee in front of my house.
I know thee will grow strong and high,
If thee does not die.

Pine represents a spirit of strength and perseverance, and of maintaining one's integrity regardless of circumstances.

Due to the fact pine trees grow to a great age, they are also a symbol of longevity. In Chinese art pine trees and cranes represent long life. When being sent as greetings to older people on their birthdays, these especially popular couplets are often used:

As auspicious as the unceasing water in the eastern sea. As timeless as the longevity pine of the southern mountain.

A thousand year old crane. An evergreen pine tree.

As long living as the pine and cypress. As graceful as an orchid.

Every branch on a pine tree is over one hundred years. Every fruit of a peach tree is over a thousand years.

Bamboo is depicted in both Three Friends in Cold Winter and Four Men of Honor, and has many rhetorical implications in Chinese culture. Somewhat similar to pine, the fact that it is evergreen, and its stems are strong and hard make it an apt symbol of integrity, strength and loyalty. In Chinese, the hollow aerial culms and the nodes of bamboo are homophones for modesty with self-esteem. The worship of bamboo as a form of divine being was recorded in several classical history books, including *The Annual of the Huayang Kingdom*, which was one of the earliest chronicles of southeast China. It was also mentioned in *The History of the Later Han Dynasty*.

Chinese history is replete with bamboo aficionados, but three of them are particularly worth discussing.

The first was Wang Huizhi, son of Wang Xizhi, the great master of calligraphy in the Jin Dynasty (265-420) . One day Wang Huizhi heard of a remarkable variety of bamboo growing at the house of a scholar-official. Going to view it, he became so entranced in its exquisiteness that he did not hear the greetings of the host of the house. Another time, he stayed away from home for some days. So much did he miss his beloved bamboo that he asked to have some planted beside his temporary home. "How could I live without gentleman bamboo?" he asked rhetorically. Ever since then, bamboo came to be commonly referred to as "gentleman bamboo".

The great Song Dynasty poet and food connoisseur Su Dongpo once noted that "To live without meat will only make one thinner. But to live without sight of bamboo, this will make one vulgar."

Finally, Zheng Banqiao, a prodigiously talented Qing Dynasty artist noted for his writing, painting, and calligraphy not only painted bamboo but also wrote poetry praising its qualities. He boasted that not only had he painted bamboo for over 40 years, he also spent a great deal of time reflecting on its virtues and aesthetic value. In one of his poems, he wrote:

Harsh autumn wind has come to the south,
Sweeping stone and wood furiously.
Among the plants, only bamboo fears not,
Standing erect against the wind for many rounds courageously.

The high degree of esteem in which bamboo is held in Chinese culture is accurately expressed in this poem.

Like bamboo, the plum blossom holds a place in both Three Friends in Cold Winter and Four Men of Honor. The graceful blossom can withstand freezing cold that kills other flowers, and also has a delightful scent. Because it is the earliest blossom to bloom after winter, it stands out among its peers. And like bamboo and pine, the plum blossom also had its legion of fans. Lin Bu, a Song Dynasty hermit who lived at Mt Gushan near the West Lake in Hangzhou was famous for his love of both plum trees and cranes. An idiom, 梅妻鹤子, literally meaning plum as wife and cranes as children, actually was generated from Lin Bu's way of life, as a metaphor for a lifestyle free of worldly worries. Lin Bu's poem on plum was regarded the most classic in praise of the plant, but there were others who also expressed it artistically, including Lu You in the Southern Song Dynasty (1127-1279) , and Wang Mian from the Yuan Dynasty (1206-1368), who both wrote and painted. In poetry, the plum blossom is often praised for its ability to preserve purity and charm, and help lead an honorable life.

The character 梅 (*mei*, plum) has over time been incorporated into the names of people, places, books, music and art forms. The name of a noted Qing Dynasty scholar, Chen Mengmei, means dreaming of plum. A scholar of the Southern Song, Shi Dazu, gave himself the additional name of "plum creek." A famous book is called *An Anthology of Plum Village*, and a piece of folk music is known as *Three Variations of Plum Blossom*. Finally, there is an art form known as Plum Drum.

Orchid is admired for its charming fragrance and grace, and is often referred to as a beauty in an echoing valley. Because there are so many varieties, at least one will be in bloom at any given time of the year. One of the more poignant quotes of Confucius was "To be a friend with a true gentleman is like staying in a house filled with the fragrance of orchids. After a time, one notes not the fragrance, because it is intrinsically present." That is to say, if one befriends a gentleman, one becomes a gentleman.

The great master of calligraphy, Wang Xizhi, built a pavilion named Orchid on Mt Kuaiji. He invited 42 respected scholars to the pavilion to drink wine and engage in a poetic jam session. He then collected these poems for a book, *The Collection of the Orchid Pavilion* and wrote a preface to it. This piece of writing is highly respected for both its prose and the high aesthetic value of its running script calligraphy. In successive dynasties, many more poets wrote about or artistically expressed the orchid's beauty and grace. A powerful image painted at the turn of the Song and Yuan dynasties showed an orchid surviving without soil. The artist, Zheng Sixiao, was using this metaphor to convey that although the Yuan Dynasty, a khanate of the Mongols, took over, he would remain loyal to the Song Dynasty.

In late autumn, when hoar frost has already formed and the temperatures in the early morning dip below freezing, the chrysanthemum flourishes. It is regarded by Chinese people as strong, graceful, and with no egotistical desire for fame or gain. To indicate high-minded loftiness, the poet Qu Yuan of the State of Chu once wrote:

In the morning I drink water off fallen magnolia petals,

In the evening I have fallen chrysanthemum petals as sustenance.

Tao Yuanming of the Eastern Jin Dynasty (317-420) expressed his deep love for this flower through his poem:

While picking chrysanthemum beneath the eastern fence,

My gaze upon the southern mountain rests.

A tranquil, peaceful scene to be sure! Over time many other poets have written about how the chrysanthemum flourishes in autumn, and maintains its delicate scent despite the cold wind attempting to sweep it away. For Chinese people, these are values to be held in high esteem.

Peony is another flower prized in Chinese culture. It is enjoyed for its stately color and heavenly fragrance. Due to its grace and poise, it is a fitting symbol of splendor, wealth, and happiness. Among others, it was proposed as the national flower of China.

The most highly regarded classical piece of writing about peony is *Notes on Peony in Luoyang City*. This was written by Ouyang Xiu, a Song Dynasty man of letters. He elaborated on the peony's history, methods of planting, varieties, and related customs. Literary figures of the Song and Ming dynasties also composed similar works. Liu Yuxi, of the Tang Dynasty, wrote a poem *Admiring Peony*:

Compared to other flowers,
Peony is the only to possess stately beauty.
It touches everyone in the capital city
Where it blooms.

There is a legend that describes how peony came to be associated with the city of Luoyang. The Empress Wu Zetian planned to visit her Upper Garden in early spring. At the time, the plants were budding but not yet in bloom. The fussy monarch issued an imperial decree in the form of a poem:

I will visit the Upper Garden tomorrow,
Spring shall be let known in time.
All flowers shall overnight bloom and grow
And wait not for vernal wind.

The Empress had her wish – almost. Although the other flowers did as commanded, peony declined, due to its pride. Wu Zetian was furious and ordered peony be demoted to Luoyang. Peony has been endowed with the quality of indifference to the powerful and the influential, and the strength to stay true to its own principles.

Narcissus, the water fairy, is considered special because it grows in clean water and exudes an elegant and pure fragrance. Due to these attributes it is regarded as possessing pure and refined qualities. Similar to the other flowers mentioned in this chapter, it has been subject matter for many poems.

There are still many other flowers that have symbolic value in Chinese culture. Peach blossoms are thought to represent pretty ladies. Due to the fact it grows in mud but manages to achieve to be visually pleasing, lotus stands for grace and purity. The broad-leaved epiphyllum represents a brief duration, according to the expression "lasting as briefly as the broad-leaved epiphyllum". The seed of the red bean shrub is a token of love. Interestingly, with regards to love, sometimes Chinese refer to one's wife as a flower at home. On the other hand, wild flower describes a woman one has an affair with. A popular Chinese song includes the line "Don't pick a wild flower by the roadside", meaning it is better to stay faithful to one's love.

Grasses also have their place in the Chinese cultural realm. They are admired because they do not seek fame or attention, but are content with their lot in life. The resilience of grasses is also admired by the Chinese people. The lyrics of one song note:

I am a nameless piece of grass,
I never feel lonely,
I am never disturbed,
I have friends
At the most remote corners of the earth.

The Tang Dynasty's Bai Juyi penned the most famous lines regarding grass:

Balefire never extinguishes grasses,
They continue to grow in the vernal wind.

生词 New Words

1.历代	lìdài	successive dynasties
2.寄托	jìtuō	to place on
3.牡丹	mǔdān	peony
4.芍药	sháoyao	Chinese herbaceous peony
5.山茶	shānchá	camellia
6.杜鹃	dùjuān	azalea
7.水仙	shuǐxiān	narcissus (the plant and its flower)
8.菊花	júhuā	chrysanthemum
9.梅花	méihuā	plum blossom

10.荷花	héhuā	lotus
11.海棠	hǎitáng	Chinese flowering crab apple
12.兰花	lánhuā	cymbidium, orchid
13.艳丽	yànlì	bright-colored and beautiful
14.醇美	chúnměi	pure and sweet
15.品格	pǐngé	one's moral character
16.情操	qíngcāo	sentiment
17.君子	jūnzǐ	a man of noble character; a man of virtue
18.高昂	gāo'áng	high; to hold high
19.挺拔	tǐngbá	tall and straight
20.正直	zhèngzhí	honest, upright, fair-minded
21.不屈不挠	bùqū-bùnáo	unyielding, indomitable
22.刚直不阿	gāngzhí-bù'ē	upright and above flattery
23.凌云	língyún	to reach the clouds; to soar to the skies
24. 蟠桃	pántáo	flat peach; peach of immortality in Chinese mythology
25.气节	qìjié	integrity; moral courage
26.骨气	gǔqì	strength of character
27.虚心	xūxīn	open-minded, modest
28.痴迷	chīmí	infatuated, obsessed, crazy
29.时髦	shímáo	fashionable
30.雅号	yǎhào	elegant name
31.强暴	qiángbào	ferocious adversary; brute force
32.铁骨	tiěgǔ	firm and unyielding
33.风骚	fēngsāo	literary excellence
34.隐居	yǐnjū	to live in seclusion; to withdraw from society and live in solitude

35.绝唱	juéchàng	the peak of poetic perfection
36. 洁身自好	jiéshēn-zìhào	to refuse to be contaminated by evil influence; to preserve one's purity
37.淡泊功名	dànbó gōngmíng	not to seek fame and wealth
38.佳人	jiārén	a beautiful woman; beauty
39.幽香四溢	yōuxiāng sìyì	to give out a delicate fragrance
40.名士	míngshì	a person with a literary reputation
41.恬淡	tiándàn	indifferent to fame or gain
42.宁静	níngjìng	quiet, peaceful
43.田园生活	tiányuán shēnghuó	idyllic life
44.不胜	búshèng	very, extremely
45.向往	xiàngwǎng	to yearn for; to look forward to
46.随波逐流	suíbō-zhúliú	to drift with the tide; to go with the stream
47.国色天香	guósè-tiānxiāng	ethereal color and celestial fragrance
48.雍容华丽	yōngróng-huálì	elegant and poised; stately
49.专著	zhuānzhù	monograph
50.脍炙人口	kuàizhì-rénkǒu	(of a piece of good writing, etc.) to win universal praise; to enjoy great popularity
51.贬	biǎn	to demote, to relegate
52.含苞	hánbāo	in bud
53.蔑视	mièshì	to despise; to show contempt; to scorn
54.权贵	quánguì	influential officials; bigwigs
55.刚毅	gāngyì	resolute and steadfast
56.倔强	juéjiàng	stubborn, unbending
57.超凡	chāofán	to transcend the worldly; out of the ordinary
58.脱俗	tuōsú	free from vulgarity; refined
59.风韵	fēngyùn	graceful bearing; charm

60.出淤泥而不染	chū yūní ér bù rǎn	to emerge unstained from the filth
61.昙花一现	tánhuā yí xiàn	to flower briefly as the broad-leaved epiphyllous; to be a flash in the pan
62.相思	xiāngsī	to pine with love; to yearn for sb.'s love
63.外遇	wàiyù	extramarital relations
64.告诫	gàojiè	to warn, to admonish
65.忠贞	zhōngzhēn	loyal and steadfast
66.怡然自乐	yírán zìlè	to be happy and pleased with oneself
67.烦恼	fánnǎo	vexed, worried
68.天涯海角	tiānyá-hǎijiǎo	the end of the earth; the remotest corners of the earth
69. 扎根	zhāgēn	to take root

语法聚焦 Notes and Examples

一、反之，这种植物文化……发挥了重要的作用

"反之"是连词，连接两个意思相反的分句，起转折作用，有"否则"、"不然"的意思。

Conjunction 反之, indicating a turn in tone, links two clauses with opposite meanings. For example:

1. 只有大家团结起来才能成功，反之，必定失败。
2. 物体的热膨胀与温度有关，一般是温度高，膨胀就大，反之，温度低，膨胀就小。

二、总之，人们把松视为一种坚贞顽强、处乱世而不改节的精神象征

"总之"是连词，是"总而言之"的意思。表示下文是总结性的话。

Conjunction 总之, abbreviation of 总而言之, means in summary. For example:

1. 金小姐能歌善舞，能文能武，总之，是个多才多艺的人。
2.《红楼梦》、《三国演义》、《战争与和平》，总之，世界名著，他差不多都读过。
3. 总之，我不知道他说了些什么。

三、其中最有名的要数晋代（265–420）大书法家王羲之的儿子王徽之

"其中"是名词，用在后一分句里。"其"复指前一分句中提到的人或事物，"中"是"中间"的意思。

Used in the second clause, noun 其中 refers to someone or something mentioned in the first clause, while 中 means amongst. For example:

1. 全校有教师五百多人，其中女教师占二分之一。
2. 这个城市有商店两千多家，其中有五百家是今年开的。
3. 北京有许多名胜古迹，颐和园就是其中的一个。

四、他可算"追竹族"中的发烧友

"算"是动词。这里表示"认做"、"认为"、"当做"，有时后面可以带"是"。

算 is a verb meaning to be regarded, 是 sometimes follows it. For example:

1. 郭强可算全班最好的学生。
2. 今年不算热。
3. 就算你有理，你也不能这么气势汹汹。
4. 他的英文水平算不错了。

五、甚至只顾看竹，连主人打招呼、让座也不加理会

"甚至"是连词，它提出突出事例，表示强调，有进一层的意思，有时和"连……也……"一起用。

Conjunction 甚至 emphasizes what follows it, meaning even. Sometimes it is used with 连… 也…. For example:

1. 他眼睛越来越不好了，甚至戴上眼镜也看不清楚。
2. 这篇文章他念得很熟，甚至都能背下来了。
3. 这里不但老年人能骑马，甚至连六七岁的孩子也会骑。

4. 约翰的中文水平提高得非常快，甚至一些中文小说原著，他都能读了。

六、东晋（317–420）诗人陶渊明更是以爱菊、咏菊而闻名

这里的“以”是“因为”、“由于”的意思，“以……”表示原因，“而……”表示结果。这个结构常用于书面语。

以… 而… is often seen in written Chinese, 以 introduces a reason and 而 introduces a result. For example:

1. 吐鲁番以盛产葡萄而闻名。
2. 妈妈以有这样的儿子而感到骄傲。
3. 李大夫以解除病人的痛苦而感到幸福。

七、堪称一篇写牡丹的专著

“堪”是文言文用词，用于书面语，是“可以”、“能”的意思。

堪 is a word of classical Chinese, meaning can, to be able to. For example:

1. 你如果这样干下去，后果不堪设想。
2. 我想白江先生堪当此重任。
3. 这些苏绣堪称刺绣中的上乘之作。

八、唯有牡丹抗旨不开

“唯”是文言虚词，用来限定事物或动作的范围，强调“独一无二”。它与“有”组成固定格式，意思是“只有”。

唯 is a word of classical Chinese, used to limit the scope of an action or affair, with an emphasis on uniqueness. In modern Chinese, it is used with 有 as a fixed pattern meaning there's only. For example:

1. 唯有改革创新，才是企业发展之路。
2. 代表团下午要去参观一个纺织厂，唯有梁太太不去。
3. 在孔教授诸多论文著作中，唯有这一篇论据有些不妥。

想一想 Questions

1. 中国的十大名花是哪些?
   What are the ten famous flowers in China?
2. “岁寒三友”是指什么?
   What are the Three Friends in Cold Winter?
3. “花草四雅”是指什么?
   What are the Four Elegant Plants?
4. 请说出几种花的象征意义。
   Can you name the symbolism of a few flowers?

超级链接 Super Links

王羲之（321–379）

中国古代著名的书法家。其书法作品，博采众长，精研体势，推陈出新，将前人质朴的书风，改成了妍美流畅的新字体。由于其书法字势雄壮多变化，而被历代学书者崇尚，影响极大。

苏东坡（1037–1101）

姓苏名轼，号东坡居士。中国古代著名的文学家、书画家、散文家和诗人。其诗清新豪健，善用夸张比喻，在艺术表现方面独具风格。词开豪放一派，对后代影响深远。他不仅诗词写得好，还擅长行书、楷书、绘画。可以称之为中国历史上不可多得的文学和艺术天才。

郑板桥（1693–1765）

姓郑名燮，号板桥。清代画家、文学家。其诗、书、画世称“三绝”，善画兰竹。其书法自成一派，将隶体融入行楷，非古非今，自称“六分半体”。

欧阳修（1007–1072）

北宋古文运动的领袖。散文说理畅达，抒情委婉，诗风与其散文近似，语言流畅自然，其词深婉清丽。

武则天（624–705）

中国历史上唯一一位女皇帝。她开创殿试制度，亲自考试贡生，令九品以上的官员可自行荐举；但她也任用酷吏，屡行大狱，许多朝臣被牵连冤杀。武则天执政初年颇能纳谏，晚年却豪奢专断，颇多弊政。

黄庭坚（1045–1106）

北宋时期诗人、书法家。其诗多写个人日常生活，讲究修辞造句，力摈轻俗之风气。其书法作品以侧险取势，纵横奇绝，自成风格。

唐诗欣赏

静夜思
李白
床前明月光，
疑是地上霜。
举头望明月，
低头思故乡。

NIGHT THOUGHTS
Li Bai
I wake, and moonbeams play around my bed,
Glittering like hoar frost to my wandering eyes.
Up towards the glorious moon I raise my head,
Then lay me down – and thoughts of home arise.

Translated by Herbert A. Giles

春晓
孟浩然
春眠不觉晓，
处处闻啼鸟。
夜来风雨声，
花落知多少。

DAWN IN SPRING
Meng Haoran
How suddenly the morning comes in spring!
On every side you hear the sweet birds sing.
Last night amidst the storm – Ah, who can tell,
With wind and rain, how many blossoms fell?

Translated by John Turner

登鹳雀楼
王之涣
白日依山尽，
黄河入海流。
欲穷千里目，
更上一层楼。

ON TOP OF STORK–BIRD TOWER
Wang Zhihuan
As daylight fades along the hill,
The Yellow River joins the sea.
To gaze unto infinity,
Go mount another storey still.

Translated by John Turner

渭城曲
王维
渭城朝雨浥轻尘，
客舍青青柳色新。
劝君更尽一杯酒，
西出阳关无故人。

FAREWELL TO AN ENVOY ON HIS MISSION TO KUCHA
Wang Wei
The morning rain has washed the Weicheng dust away,
The willows round the inn their fresh green robes display.
I urge thee, friend, another cup of wine to drain,
Since west of Yangkwan Pass you'll seek for friends in vain.
Translated by Tsai Tingkan

游子吟
孟郊
慈母手中线，
游子身上衣。
临行密密缝，
意恐迟迟归。
谁言寸草心，
报得三春晖。

THE SONG OF THE WANDERING SON
Meng Jiao
In tender mother's hands the thread
Made clothes to garb her parting son.
Before he left, how hard she spun,
How diligently wove; in dread
Ere he returned long years might run!
Such lifelong mother's love how may
One simple little heart repay?
Translated by W. J. B. Fletcher

中国的色彩文化

Colors

8

A Kaleidoscope of Chinese Culture

有一次，一个老师在汉语课堂上问学生一个问题："如果我去参加你的婚礼，打着一条洁白的领带，你见了以后，有何感想？"美国学生回答："我会感到很奇怪。"日本学生回答："我非常高兴。"香港学生回答："我气死了。"由此可以看出，同样的一种颜色，不同的国家或不同的民族，对它有不同的好恶情感。这是因为人们赋予了颜色不同的含义，形成了不同民族的色彩文化心理。

中国人自古对颜色就有丰富的认识，汉语中存在着大量的颜色词。而且人们又从传统的哲学思想、民俗文化、色彩联想等出发，赋予了各种颜色不同的象征意义，形成了独特的中华色彩文化。

颜色本身是一种客观存在的现象，它不存在高低、贵贱之分，可是一旦人们把它与社会政治、文化、礼仪等问题联系起来，它便有了三六九等的差别。古时候，中国人把颜色分为两大类：一类是"正色"，包括青、赤、黑、白、黄；另一类是"间色"，包括绀（红青色）、红（赤之浅者）、紫、缥（淡青色）、骝黄五种。这可能是很早的时候，古人在诸多的颜色中，发现了有些颜色是基本色，它们互相按照一定的比例搭配，就能产生新的颜色，所以称之为"正"，而有些颜色是在搭配中产生的，所以称之为"间"。久而久之人们对色彩逐步形成了不同的爱憎情感。据《论语》中记载："子曰，'恶紫之夺朱也，恶郑声之乱雅乐也，恶利口之覆邦家者'"这句话的意思是：我讨厌用紫色代替红色，讨厌用郑国的乐曲代替典雅的乐曲，讨厌用花言巧语颠覆国家的人。在这里，孔子把他的观点和爱恶感情注入了色彩之中。

另外，中国人赋予各种颜色的文化含义，还与中国阴阳五行学说有着密切关系。阴阳五行学说，最早创立人是子思及其门徒孟子，而实际上完成此说的人，是战国末齐国人邹衍。他的著作《邹子》和《邹子始终》都已经失传，我们只能在其他史书中见到他的理论。邹衍把水、火、木、金、土这五种元素称之为“五德”，也叫“五行”。他认为这“五行”之间是互相制胜的，木胜土，金胜木，火胜金、水胜火，世界按照这个规律，循环更替，改朝换代。他的理论当然受到了当时统治者的欢迎，因为未当上皇帝的地方军阀，希望自己有机会夺得王位；当上皇帝的，认为自己是顺乎天意掌握了政权。

这种阴阳五行学说，把东西南北中五方，春夏秋冬四季和青、赤、白、黑、黄五种颜色联系在一起。根据《吕氏春秋》、《礼记》、《周礼》、《淮南子》等书中记载，它们相配的情况是这样：东方天帝是太皞，属木，主春，木为青色，所以叫青帝；南方天帝是炎帝，属火，主夏，火为赤色，所以叫赤帝；西方天帝是少皞，属金，主秋，金是白色，所以叫白帝；北方天帝是颛顼，属水，主冬，水是黑色，所以叫黑帝；中央是属于“土德”的黄帝，为黄色。宋代理学家朱熹说：“黄，中央土之正色。”传说轩辕黄帝得“土德”，穿黄袍，戴黄冕，所以黄色便成了帝王之色，是皇权的象征，代表着尊贵、威严和至高无上。我们到北京故宫去看一看，整个故宫的大部分屋顶都是黄色琉璃瓦，皇帝的衣服是黄色龙袍，出巡时打的是黄色龙旗，坐的是黄色龙辇，后宫寝室是黄色的龙被、龙帐，皇帝的诏书更是写在黄绫子上。总之，黄色成了皇帝的专用色，其他人是绝对不能用的，如果用了，就会有生命危险，因为擅自使用黄色意味着有谋反篡位之心。唐朝时，黄巢写了一首《咏菊》诗，歌颂黄色的菊花，自然被定为“反诗”之列，他是借题抒发自己的造反之心。这首诗是：“待到秋来九月八，我花开后百花杀；冲天香阵透长安，满城尽带黄金甲。”这首诗正是用满城遍布黄色的菊花，暗喻起义军希望推翻统治者，夺取政权的愿望。

在近代，中国人的色彩文化融入了西方文化，赋予了“黄色”一些新的意义。人们把一些色情、淫秽的事物冠之以“黄”，如：黄色画报、黄色小说、黄色电影、黄色录像、黄色酒吧等，进而把取缔这些不良现象，叫做“扫黄”。有人传言这种观念来源于美国。19世纪时，美国报业巨子普利策创办的《世界报》与另一报业巨子威廉·赫斯特主持的《纽约新闻报》两种刊物竞争时，《纽约新闻报》将原《世界报》栏目《黄孩儿》挖走，由此掀起了两份报纸对《黄孩儿》的争夺，之后，两份报纸借人们对此事的关注大肆策划刺激性报道，争夺群众。由此被人们戏称为“黄色新闻”，这种说法很快被人们接受并沿用至今。无论这种观念源自何方，中国人对黄色的理解是中西合璧的。由此可见各种文化是互相交流、互相影响的。

红色是中国人最喜爱的喜庆之色。不管是逢年过节、贺寿嫁娶、买卖开张、竣工典礼等各种庆祝活动，人们总是用红色作为主色。结婚时，要贴大红双喜字，新娘子穿红色衣服，戴红花，坐大红花轿，新郎要十字披红，洞房要布置得红彤彤，点红蜡烛，铺红被褥。人们称“结婚”为“红喜”。春节时，家家贴红春联、红福字，挂大红灯笼，放红爆竹，给孩子的压岁钱用红纸包上。各公司、商店发的奖金，也是装在红袋内，叫做给“红包”。妇女生小孩，要送红鸡蛋等。所以红色在中国是幸福、欢乐的象征。

在近代，红色又与政治意义相结合，出现了红区、红军、红色根据地等词语。近年来，随着市场经济的发展，有些人富起来了，这引来了一些人的嫉妒，人们把这种嫉妒心理称为“红眼病”。

中国人对红色也有一些禁忌。在给别人写信的时候，禁用红色笔，因为这是一种断交的表示。也不用红笔写别人的名字，或在别人的名字上画红钩、打红叉，因为中国古时候，在处死罪犯时，才在他们名字上打红钩。

白色对于世界上很多国家的人们来说，是纯洁明亮、高雅和坦率的象征，所以在西方举行婚礼时，新娘子身着白色婚纱；在日本则穿白色日本服装，客人打白领带。可是在中国人的传统观念中，白色表示肃穆和哀悼，因此在举行传统葬礼时，才使用白色。灵堂的布置使用白花，用白布做“台裙”，供桌上点着白色蜡烛，四周墙壁上，挂着白色的挽联。死者的亲属穿白孝衫、白孝鞋和戴白孝帽。出殡时，打的是白纸幡，撒的是白纸钱。总之，白色给人带来静穆、哀伤的气氛。中国古书《礼记》中说：“素服（白衣），以送终也。”因此人们称葬礼是“白喜”。但是由于受西方的影响，现代中国的年轻人在婚礼上会先穿白婚纱、黑礼服举行典礼，之后再换上红色的旗袍参加酒宴，展现了中外文化交融的景象。

白色和红色一样，在近代也带上了政治色彩，出现了白区、白色恐怖、白色政权等词语。另外，在京剧表演艺术中，白色脸谱象征奸诈、阴险和歹毒。历史上的奸臣，如曹操、赵高、严嵩都施以白色脸谱。

黑色因为其颜色本身较暗，给人一种庄重、沉稳的感觉，所以它象征严肃和刚毅。中国古代夏朝（约前2070-前1600）和秦朝（前221-前206）是崇尚黑色的，当时的官服和旗帜是黑颜色，秦朝老百姓是用黑布包头，所以被叫做“黔首”。中国京剧脸谱中，黑色表示刚直、勇猛、淳朴和铁面无私。多少年来，一直为广大人民喜欢和爱戴的清官——包拯，就是画黑色脸谱，被人们称做“包黑子”。其他还有李逵、尉迟恭、张飞、呼延庆等人物，他们有的是草莽英雄，有的是勇猛的斗士，都有憨直、无私、可爱的一面。

在西方国家，黑色用在葬礼之中，人们穿黑色服装，带黑领带、黑围巾、黑面纱，以表示肃穆、庄严，寄托对逝者的哀思。这种文化习俗也传到中国，在一些大城市，追悼会上人们戴白花，臂上缠黑纱，已是很普遍的事情了。

另外，黑色又和黑暗相关联。中国古代有一种侮辱性的刑罚叫“墨刑”，就是在人的脸上刺上记号或文字，再涂上黑色的墨，使之永远不掉。虽然这种刑罚很久以前就被禁止了，但很多有刑罚意思的字还是以“黑”为偏旁。在汉语中，黑字也出现在许多贬义词中，凡是不光明正大的坏勾当，常常与“黑”联系在一起，如：黑社会、黑手、黑货、黑市、黑名单、黑帮、黑后台等。

“黑”字还有表示狠毒的含义，如：黑心肠。近年来，又在此义上进行了引申，将那些贩卖假货、抬高物价、坑害别人、牟取暴利的行为评价为“真黑”或“太黑了”。

绿色也是人们喜爱的颜色，它象征青春、希望、和平和充满活力。在国际上，它是穆斯林国家偏爱的颜色。现代中国在很多方面也与世界其他国家一样，采用绿颜色，比如：邮政局工作人员穿绿服装，邮筒、邮箱涂成绿色；外科医生手术时，穿绿色手术衣；交通信号的绿灯表示通行等。近年来，人们把那些没有受到化学污染的食品，称之为“绿色食品”。

绿色在中国古代是底层人民的标志。官在七品以下穿绿衫，屠夫、酒保戴绿色巾帽，唐代乐府妓院里的男人戴绿纱巾，所以汉语中有“戴绿帽子”一语，明朝郎瑛在《七修类稿》中说：“吴人称人妻为淫者为绿头巾。”此语在今天也含有同样的意思，是一句非常不好听的话，十分令人避讳。因此，千万不可错用，以免引起人们心理上的不愉快。

人们为色彩赋予了语言，更在艺术创作中用色彩表达人们丰富的情感。在中国传统书画作品中，画家们常用色彩体现不同的意境。有这样一个小故事：明朝时，有一次皇帝想考一下天下的画师，于是宣旨把全国的画家都召到北京，出题让他们作画，优胜者自然得到重赏。画题是：万绿丛中一点红，动人春色无须多。画家们根据这个题目，画了起来。过了几天，画家们纷纷把画作交了上来。评审官们对几千张画进行了评审，最后选出了三张作为前三甲。这三张画的第一张是一片苍绿色的松林，松林中站着一只丹顶鹤，只有鹤顶上有一点红，称做“丹顶红”；第二张是一片青绿色的丛山峻岭，只有山凹处夕阳落山留下的一点红，称做“夕阳红”；第三张是春天的河边，一片嫩绿色的柳林里，一个浣纱姑娘手提竹篮，前来浣纱，只有她的嘴唇上有一点红，称做“胭脂红”。这三张画画得都非常漂亮，评审官们经过反复讨论，最后大家一致认为，第三张应为最好，因为这三张画虽都描绘了“万绿丛中一点红”，但对于“动人春色无须多”这句的表现，第三张就略胜一筹了。

色彩对人的心理作用，来源于人的生活经验。人对色彩的反映是普遍的，色彩的象征性也是非常鲜明的，不同时代、不同文化、不同地域、不同国家与民族喜欢的色彩不同，色彩的忌讳也不同。因此，在国际交往日益频繁的今天，我们更需注重色彩在不同文化交流中的作用。

Colors represent different things in different cultures. Consider the question: "How would you feel if somebody went to your wedding wearing a white tie?" Depending on the nationality of the person you asked, you would get a variety of answers. An American would respond "I would think that person is weird." A Japanese person may respond "I would feel happy." One from Hong Kong would, however, say "I feel very angry." We can deduce from the different responses that colors symbolize different ideas and feelings, and have different psychological implications.

In ancient times, Chinese people had already developed a complex culture surrounding colors, and their language included many descriptive color-based words. Different colors were endowed with different philosophical or customary symbolism. The Chinese thus developed a unique culture of color.

Colors are, in themselves, objective and with no inherent qualities to suggest one is better than the other. However, in a socio-political, cultural, or ritual context, colors unavoidably become grouped into different categories. In ancient China, blue, red, black, white, and yellow were classified as "direct" colors, and reddish blue, light blue, light red, purple, and reddish yellow were classified as "indirect" colors. This may be due to the fact ancient Chinese regarded some colors as basic or primitive, which they labeled "direct". Combinations of these colors in different proportions created new colors, which they labeled "indirect". According to *The Analects of Confucius*, Confucius once said, "I hate the color purple for it contends red, I hate State Zheng's music for it mingles with elegant music, I hate those who overthrow their state by sweet words." Here Confucius already had a bias towards colors.

The cultural significance of color in China is closely tied to the Theory of Yin Yang and the Five Elements. This theory was first developed by Zi Si and his disciple Mencius, and was mostly completed by Zhou Yan from the State of Qi during the Warring States Period. Although Zhou Yan's two works were both lost, his philosophies have been referred to in other historical works. Zhou Yan regarded the five elements of water, fire, wood, gold and soil as "five virtues". According to him, wood can overcome soil, gold overcome wood, fire overcome gold, and water overcome fire. It made sense, therefore, that the world followed the rules of the five elements to recur and subrogate, and dynasty replaced dynasty. This belief was particularly favored by both upstart feudal rulers and established kings or emperors who sought to legitimize their claims to power. The former took it that they had the right to challenge the established power base, and the latter could claim they had followed philosophical conventions and held the mandate of heaven.

The philosophical beliefs of Zhou Yan also connected the five colors of green, red, white, black and yellow, with the five directions of east, west, south, north and center. It also linked them with the four seasons. According to several classics, including *The Book of Rites* and *Huai Nan Zi*, the King of Heaven in the east, Taihao (太皞), was connected with the nature of wood, and in charge of spring. He was also known as the Green King, because green is connected with spring. The King of Heaven in the south, Yandi (炎帝), was lord of summer and fire, and known as the Red King, because red is the color of fire. The King of Heaven in the west, Shaohao (少皞), was lord of gold and in charge of autumn. He was known as the White King, because the color of gold was thought to be white. The King of Heaven in the north was named Zhuanxu (颛顼). He held power over water and winter, and was known as the Black King, because black was the color of water.

The King of Heaven in the middle was named Huangdi (黄帝), the Yellow Emperor. His nature was of the virtue of the soil, represented by yellow. Zhu Xi, a Song Dynasty philosopher who perfected the doctrines of the Neo-Confucianism, remarked, "Yellow is the pure color of the soil in the middle." Legend had it that the Yellow Emperor who was born at Xuan Yuan Hill gained the virtue of the soil. His fate, therefore, was to be clothed in a yellow gown and a yellow crown. As a result yellow became the color that symbolized imperial power, nobility, stateliness and supremacy. Yellow is everywhere in the Imperial Palace in Beijing, known as the Palace Museum. Most of the roofs are laid with yellow-glazed tiles. The flags, the dragon carriage, clothing and bedding of the emperor were all yellow, and the emperor's scripts were written on yellow damask silk.

The use of yellow was reserved exclusively for the emperor. Anyone else who dared to use it was deemed a dangerous rebel, possibly trying to overthrow the emperor. As a result they would put lives at risk by this mere act. Huang Chao, who led a peasant revolt in the Tang Dynasty, wrote a poem called *Ode to Chrysanthemum*:

On the eighth of September when autumn comes,

All other flowers are dead but chrysanthemums are flourishing in the cold weather.

The vigorous fragrance of the yellow flowers penetrates the entire city of Chang'an,

And like yellow armor the flowers are seen everywhere.

This poem was actually using yellow chrysanthemum as a metaphor to express the wish of the uprising force to seize imperial power. Incidentally, Huang Chao's surname, Huang, also means yellow.

More recently, the Chinese culture of colors has incorporated some elements of western culture. One such color is yellow, which now carries the connotation of being pornographic or obscene, as in yellow books, yellow novels, yellow movies, or even yellow bars. Crackdowns on materials seen as pornographic or obscene are known as sweeping the yellow.

It is said that this meaning of yellow is originated in the US in the 19th century. The term refers to journalism that featured sex scandals, sensationalism, or other unethical practices. The competition between Joseph Pulitzer and William Randolph Hearst, each with his own brightly-colored comic strip, *The Yellow Kids*, sealed their fates together and provided future historians with the convenient title of "yellow journalism". The Chinese apprehension of yellow is both local and western, and is a good example of the intermingling of different cultures.

Red is the favorite color of the Chinese. It is widely used for celebratory occasions such as festivals, birthdays, weddings, business openings, and project completion ceremonies. Red is consistently the dominant color at these events. At traditional weddings, big red characters "double happiness" are prominently displayed. Dressed in red and wearing red flowers, the bride is carried on a red sedan. The groom wears a red silk cloth wrapped over his wedding suit. The bridal chamber is decorated with red candles, and all the bedding is also red. Traditional weddings are even referred to as red happiness.

During the Spring Festival, every household places Spring Festival scrolls and the character "fu" in red on doors and walls. Red lanterns are hung out for display and red firecrackers set off. Children are given gifts of money wrapped in red paper, and New Year bonuses are given to employees in red envelopes. Red eggs are also given to women who have just given birth. Red is a symbol of happiness and blessing.

Red has also become a political tag, with common terms such as the red base, the red army, and others coming into being. It has still other connotations, although not all of them are positive. If you hear the expression "red-eye syndrome", it is referring to somebody being in a state of jealousy. This humorous expression has come about due to the explosion of wealthy people in China following the adoption of a market economy. People jealous of wealth are said to have jealously red eyes.

Red also attracts some taboos. One should never write a letter in red ink, because this signifies that you in fact wish to break off your friendship with the recipient. Likewise one should never write another person's name in red ink, or tick or cross the name. It is because historically criminal's names were ticked in red ink when they were sentenced to be executed.

In many cultures, white is a symbol of purity, brightness, frankness and elegance. At western-style weddings the bride wears a white wedding dress. In Japan, the bride wears a traditional Japanese costume, and male guests wear white ties. Due to western influences, many modern Chinese young people now wear white wedding dresses and black suits to their weddings, but then change into mandarin gowns for the banquet that follows. The bride wears a red gown and the groom a black one. This is an interesting fusion of western and Chinese customs. However, traditionally in China white is a solemn color that symbolizes grief and mourning and was used in funerals. The hall in which guests mourned was decorated with white flowers. A white cloth and white candles were also placed on a credence table. The walls were decorated with white elegiac scrolls, and the relatives of the deceased all dressed in white. During the funeral procession, white paper flags were flown and white paper money was thrown. It was noted in *The Book of Rites* that "White attire is for funerals." Resilient and open-minded people who tried to look for the positives in death regarded funerals as "white happiness".

White also became associated with politics in China a few decades ago, with terms such as white area, white terror, and white regime being used. This was seen in contrast to red. White also symbolizes bad faith, cattiness and viciousness in Peking Opera. The characters Cao Cao, Zhao Gao, and Yan Song, are regarded as treacherous court officials in history. Their faces are all painted white. The expression "White-face Cao Cao" refers to a person of bad faith.

Black is considered to be a steady, sober, serious and masculine color. In the Xia Dynasty (about 2070 BC-1600 BC) and Qin Dynasty, officials' gowns and flags were all black. Qin Dynasty commoners wrapped their heads with black turbans and hence earned the nickname "black heads". In Peking Opera, black masks represent honesty, uprightness, bravery, impartiality and unsophistication. The role of Bao Zheng, or Black Bao, an esteemed Song Dynasty official, wears a painted black mask. Other characters, such as Li Kui, Yuchi Gong, Zhang Fei, and Huyan Qing also wear painted black masks. They are heroes and fighters, and are esteemed for their frankness, selflessness and purity.

In the west, black is used for funerals. People wear black suits, ties, and scarves or veils as a sign of mourning. This custom has also found traction in China, especially in cities, where people now sometimes also wear black at funerals.

Black is also reminiscent of darkness, and perhaps because of this it also suggests crime and unlawful activity. In ancient China, there was a black ink punishment. This meant that criminals would have certain characters tattooed on their face in black ink. This punishment has long been discarded, but many characters to do with punishment still include the radical for black. The character for black is also often used in many words or sayings with derogatory implications. Black heart, for example, is ascribed to a person who is considered to be malicious. Shady business people are criticized as being too black. Evil deeds and things associated with them are also referred to as being black, such as black society, black hand, black goods, black market, blacklist, black gang, and black background.

Green stands for somewhat contradictory meanings. On the one hand, it is a symbol of youthfulness, hope, peace and vigor. Along with many other countries, the postal service in China uses green. Surgeons wear soothing green gowns during surgery. Green traffic lights mean it is acceptable to go. In recent years, food uncontaminated by chemicals has been known as green food. Green represents health.

On the other hand, green has some more negative meanings. Historically, green was the color of the lower classes. Officials who were ranked outside the top seven grades wore green clothes, butchers and bartenders wore green cloth caps, and male staff in Tang Dynasty brothels and performance venues wore green scarves to show their identity. In the Ming Dynasty a renowned book collector and scholar named Lang Ying noted that people from the State of Wu called a man with a loose wife a green scarf. Later, this became "wearing a green hat". Saying to a man that he is wearing a green hat is regarded as highly insulting and should be avoided.

In Chinese paintings, colors are used to express feelings and artistic concepts. In the Ming Dynasty, an emperor ordered all the painters in the land to come to the capital for a contest. The emperor gave the painters the theme for the competition, which was "Some red in green, a simple but touching spring scene." Within a few days, thousands of paintings had been submitted. A shortlist of three was selected by a panel of experts. Third place went to a painting of a dark green pine forest, with a red-crowned crane among the trees. Second place went to a picture of a tall lush green mountain range, with a red sun setting in the distance. The winner, however, was a painting of a young lady washing silk yarn by a creek. She was in a green willow wood, and had a touch of red rouge on her lips. All three paintings were very skillful in depicting "some red in green", but the winner had a more intelligent portrayal of "simple but touching spring scene".

The psychological interpretations of colors come from people's living experience. Colors always have some symbolic meaning for people, depending on their culture, time and location. The taboos of color also vary. Colors thus have a role to play in interpersonal and intercultural exchanges.

生词 New Words

1.色彩	sècǎi	color, hue
2.情感	qínggǎn	emotion, feeling
3.赋予	fùyǔ	to give, to entrust
4.含义	hányì	meaning, implication
5.丰富	fēngfù	rich, abundant
6.客观	kèguān	objective
7.存在	cúnzài	to exist; reality
8.现象	xiànxiàng	appearance, phenomenon
9.一旦	yídàn	once; in case; now that
10.政治	zhèngzhì	politics
11.三六九等	sānliùjiǔděng	various grades and ranks
12.类	lèi	kind, category
13.比例	bǐlì	scale, proportion
14.搭配	dāpèi	collocation, match
15.花言巧语	huāyán-qiǎoyǔ	sweet words; fine words
16.颠覆	diānfù	to overturn, to subvert

17.学说	xuéshuō	theory, doctrine
18.创立人	chuànglìrén	founder, originator, initiator
19.门徒	méntú	disciple, follower, adherent
20.失传	shīchuán	to be lost
21.循环	xúnhuán	to circulate; cycle
22.更替	gēngtì	to replace
23.改朝换代	gǎicháo-huàndài	change of dynasty or regime
24.统治者	tǒngzhìzhě	ruler
25.军阀	jūnfá	warlord
26.王位	wángwèi	throne
27.顺乎	shùnhū	to comply with; to conform to
28.天意	tiānyì	God's will; the will of heaven
29.政权	zhèngquán	political (or state) power
30.理学	lǐxué	a rationalistic Confucian philosophical school that developed during the Song and Ming dynasties, known to the West as Neo-Confucianism
31.尊贵	zūnguì	honorable, respectable
32.威严	wēiyán	dignified; prestige
33.至高无上	zhìgāo-wúshàng	most lofty; paramount
34.琉璃瓦	liúliwǎ	glazed tile
35.出巡	chūxún	to go on an inspection tour
36.诏书	zhàoshū	imperial edict
37.绫子	língzi	twill-weave silk
38.谋反	móufǎn	to conspire against the state; to plot a rebellion
39.借题抒发	jiètí shūfā	to make use of the subject under discussion to put over one's own ideas
40.造反	zàofǎn	to rise in rebellion; revolt

41.融入	róngrù	to mix together; to fuse
42.色情	sèqíng	sex
43.淫秽	yínhuì	obscene, salacious, pornographic
44.取缔	qǔdì	to outlaw, to ban
45.竞争	jìngzhēng	to compete
46.中西合璧	zhōngxī hébì	a good combination of Chinese and Western elements
47.压岁钱	yāsuìqián	money given to children as a lunar New Year gift
48.罪犯	zuìfàn	criminal, offender
49.纯洁	chúnjié	pure; clean and honest
50.坦率	tǎnshuài	candid, frank
51.肃穆	sùmù	solemn and quiet
52.葬礼	zànglǐ	funeral
53.灵堂	língtáng	mourning hall
54.挽联	wǎnlián	elegiac couplet
55.出殡	chūbìn	to carry a coffin to the cemetery
56.脸谱	liǎnpǔ	types of facial makeup in operas
57.奸诈	jiānzhà	fraudulent, crafty
58.阴险	yīnxiǎn	sinister, insidious
59.歹毒	dǎidú	sinister and vicious
60.奸臣	jiānchén	treacherous court official
61.刚毅	gāngyì	resolute and steadfast
62.铁面无私	tiěmiàn-wúsī	impartial and incorruptible
63.坏勾当	huài gòudang	criminal activities; a dirty deal
64.浣	huàn	to wash
65.胭脂	yānzhi	rouge
66.略胜一筹	luèshèng-yìchóu	a notch above; slightly better

语法聚焦 Notes and Examples

一、我气死了

“死”在这里是形容词，放在动词或形容词后面作补语，表示程度极高，达到顶点，多用于口头语。

死 functions as an adjective and is a complement for the verb or adjective before it to indicate the highest degree, often seen in spoken language. For example:

1. 快打开窗户，我热死了。
2. 有什么吃的给我拿来，我简直要饿死了。
3. 老黄穿了这么一件不中不洋的衣服，大家见了，快笑死了。

二、可是一旦人们把它与社会政治、文化、礼仪等问题联系起来

“一旦”是副词，表示“如果”的意思。它用在假设句里，表示条件。

一旦 is an adverb meaning if in a suppositional clause to indicate a condition. For example:

1. 我们这个科研项目，一旦研究资金到位，我们马上开始。
2. 你这样做是不合法的，群众一旦了解了事实真相，大家会把你告上法庭。
3. 这种技术一旦被坏人掌握了，后果不堪设想。

三、结婚时，要贴大红双喜字，……新郎要十字披红

“要”在这里是助动词，表示做某事的意志、意愿，有时也表示“必须”、“应该”。

要 is used as an auxiliary verb to show the will or intention in doing something. It sometimes means must or should. For example:

1. 我们要争取提前完成今年计划。
2. 每到年终，郭先生要写总结，要做报表，要订明年规划，简直忙得不得了。
3. 我们要提倡勤俭持家。

四、多少年来，一直为广大人民喜欢和爱戴的清官——包拯

“一直”是副词，表示动作或行为在一定时间里，不间断进行或始终不变。

Adverb 一直 indicates an action continues or remains the same over certain period. For example:

1. 从早到晚雪一直在下。
2. 1990年以来，孙海波一直在科学院工作。
3. 这些年，我一直惦念着你们。

五、在西方国家，黑色用在葬礼之中

"之中"表示在某范围或过程里面，多用于书面语。

之中 is used more in written language to indicate among or in the process of. For example:

1. 在这几个孩子之中，彬彬年纪最小。
2. 你们如果在学习之中有什么困难，可以找韩老师帮助。
3. 纳斯达克指数一天之中就上涨了3个百分点。

六、人们把那些没有受到化学污染的食品，称之为"绿色食品"

这里的"受"是动词，表示"遭受"的意思。

受 as a verb means to suffer or bear. For example:

1. 小李因为违反了安全守则，受到了领导的批评。
2. 今年的台风使这里老百姓的财产受了很大的损失。
3. 有的旅客在机场受到了不公平的待遇。

七、只有鹤顶上有一点红，称做"丹顶红"

"只有"是副词，表示唯一可能做的事或情况。

Adverb 只有 means only, indicating only one thing that can be done or there is only one situation. For example:

1. 我们只有与东方集团公司兼并这一条路，别无办法。
2. 在这种情况下，只有你能帮助我。
3. 现在只有开闸放水，才能保住大坝。

想一想 Questions

1. 中国古时候，人们对颜色有哪些看法?
   In ancient China, what kind of views did people have towards colors?
2. 北京故宫为什么到处是黄色?
   Why yellow can be seen in many places in the Palace Museum?
3. 中国人最喜欢的喜庆颜色是什么?
   What is the color the Chinese mostly use for happy and celebratory occasions?
4. 请你谈一谈你最喜欢的颜色。
   Can you please talk about your favorite color(s)?

超级链接 Super Links

英语颜色词拾趣

像汉语中“白吃”、“白喝”、“白费劲儿”，“白”并不表示具体颜色一样，英语中一些颜色词同样被赋予了不同的文化内容和特殊意义。

green—绿色

1. green eyes 嫉妒
2. green hand 没经验的生手
3. green old age 老当益壮
4. green house 花房，温室
5. greenback 美钞

red—红色

1. red alert 紧急警报
2. see red 大怒，生气
3. red meat 牛、羊肉
4. in the red 亏损，负债
5. red gold 纯金

blue—蓝色

1. blue moon 很难遇见的事
2. blue flu 生病请假
3. in a blue mood 情绪低落
4. blue fear 极度恐惧
5. out of the blue 出乎意外

white—白色

1. white day 吉利日子
2. white hands 诚实
3. white alert 解除警报
4. white nights 不眠之夜
5. white sale 大减价

black—黑色

1. black sheep	害群之马，败家子
2. black deed	恶劣行为
3. black coffee	没有牛奶或糖的咖啡
4. black tea	红茶
5. a black letter day	倒霉的日子

yellow—黄色

1. yellow steak	胆怯
2. a yellow dog	卑鄙的人
3. yellow boy	金币
4. yellow belly	可鄙的胆小鬼
5. yellow looks	尖酸多疑的神情

brown—褐色

1. brown paper	牛皮纸
2. brown rice	糙米
3. brown sugar	红糖
4. to do sb. brown	使某人上当
5. brown bread	黑面包

中国的饮食文化

Food

9

A Kaleidoscope of Chinese Culture

中国有句古语："民以食为天"。此语出自《史记》："王者以民人为天，民人以食为天"。唐代司马贞注释说，此乃管仲之语，管子说："王者以民为天，民以食为天，能知天之天者，斯可矣。"当然，"食" 在古时是指粮食，但不管怎样，中国人自古便把吃饭看做生活中的头等大事。随着历史的发展和社会的进步，饮食已不只是为了满足人们的生存需要，它与社会多种文化活动紧密结合在一起，形成了丰富多彩的饮食文化。

中国人的饮食文化是中国文化的一个重要组成部分。今天中国饭店遍布世界各地，可以说凡有中国人的地方，就有中餐馆。中国饭"色香味形器"的饮食特色，得到了世界各国人民的赞赏，中国人的饮食文化，也受到其他民族的称誉。下面我们从生存享受、礼仪祭典、交际情感、美学情趣等几方面，对中国饮食文化加以介绍。

众所周知，饮食是人类维持生命必不可少的活动。中国人的饮食有如下几个特点：

一、以植物性食品为主，辅之以肉食。这是因为中华民族最早发源于中国黄河流域，长期以来一直以农业生产为主要经济方式，因此形成了农业文化的特点。反映在饮食上，中国的传统饮食习俗以粮食和蔬菜为主，以肉食为辅。在古代，人们吃的粮食是"五谷"，即：麦、黍、稷、豆、稻，后来又增至"九谷"。蔬菜有竹、瓜、芋、韭、葱等。汉唐元明以来，从中亚、南美、欧洲引进了黄瓜、大蒜、茄子、菠菜、胡萝卜、西红柿、马铃薯、花生等。古人食肉不多，只有上层统治者和富豪人家才多吃肉，所以他们被古代下层人民称为"肉食者"。

二、以熟食和热食为主。很早以前，中国人便知道了使用火，结束了自然饮食状态，而最初火的使用，主要是烧、烤两种方式。传说到轩辕黄帝时期，人们知道了蒸、煮的烹调方法。三国（220-280）谯周在《古史考》中说："黄帝始蒸谷为饭，烹谷为粥"，所以中国人把黄帝奉为中国饮食文明的创始者。《吕氏春秋》中也说：食物"九沸九变"，可以"灭腥、去臊、除膻"，所以食熟食、热食成为贯穿古今的中国烹饪指导思想。

三、聚餐制。从出土的一些中国古建筑的遗址中，人们可以看到，中国古代房屋中间有灶和烟囱。古人吃饭是大家围坐在一起，共同进餐的。在今天，中国人仍旧非常喜欢一家人围坐在桌旁，将饭菜摆放在桌上，一起用饭，显示出家庭的团聚和温馨。

随着社会生产的发展和物质财富的增加，饮食已不仅仅是为了填饱肚子，它逐渐变为一种生活享受。春秋时代的孔子曾说："食不厌精，脍不厌细"，这就是说，吃的东西越精美越好，做工越细致越好。中国菜是十分讲究用料、刀工和火候的。多年来，烹饪技术精益求精，不断发展变化，出现了花样繁多的各种烹调方法，如：煮、蒸、炸、炒、煎、烧、炖、溜、焖、熬、煨、熏、烩、扒、烤、涮、汆、烙、爆、炝、拌、腌、渍、烹、滑、煸、泡、糟、卤、酱等。中国的烹调可称得上选料讲究，做工细致，盛名天下。

另外，中国幅员辽阔，各地物产不同、饮食习惯不同，因此出现了风味独特的地方菜系。著名的有八大菜系，即江苏菜、浙江菜、山东菜、安徽菜、广东菜、福建菜、湖南菜、四川菜。有人将这八大菜系作了形象的比喻：苏、浙菜宛如清秀素丽的江南美女；鲁、皖菜好像古拙淳朴的北方健汉；粤、闽菜酷似风流典雅公子；川、湘菜犹如才艺满身的名士。每个菜系都有拿手传统菜，如：江苏菜的清蒸鲥鱼、清炖蟹肉狮子头；浙江菜的西湖醋鱼、龙井虾仁；山东菜的荷花大虾、鸡腿扒海参；安徽菜的葫芦鸭子、雪冬烧山鸡；广东菜的烤乳猪、蚝油牛肉；福建菜的佛跳墙、菊花鲈鱼；湖南菜的东安鸡、红煨鱼翅；四川菜的怪味鸡、麻婆豆腐。这些色、香、味、型俱全的美味佳肴，真是格调不同、异香纷呈。

中国自古崇尚礼仪，称为礼仪之邦，所以中国饮食文化也具有丰富的礼仪文化内涵。中国古代的重要典章制度书籍——《礼记》中就记载了许多中国古时候的用餐礼仪，像用餐时人们的座位应该如何坐，盘碗菜肴应该如何放，饮酒、食肉、吃饭的进餐顺序应该怎样，主宾应该如何敬酒，以及吃饭时不许“反鱼肉”，不许“扬饭”等。到了孔子时代，孔子更是倡导饮食礼仪，他说“食不言，寝不语”、“席不正，不坐”、“割不正不食”、“虽蔬食菜羹，必祭，必齐如也”、“有盛馔，必变色而作”、“乡人饮酒，杖者出，斯出矣”等。在后来封建社会的宴饮活动中，出现了左为上、面东为尊、长幼有序等饮食礼仪。今天，随着时代的发展，过去的一些繁缛的礼仪制度已经不再被人们所遵循了，但在现代的宴饮活动中，仍然体现出菜肴丰盛、尊长爱幼、敬宾侍客、心情放松、气氛热烈的形式美和人情美。

再有，中国人的宴饮活动，还与人际交往、增进友谊联系在一起。有句俗语说：“酒逢知己千杯少”。因此无论过去还是现在，人们在举办婚礼、丧礼、祝寿、生子等活动中，都要设置宴席，邀请亲朋好友相聚，增进彼此交往，维系感情。如今，有些企业、事业单位，在生意开张、大厦落成、合同签订、年终结业时，都要组织员工或客户相聚，在推杯换盏和欢声笑语中，增进员工的凝聚力和与客户的友好感情。在家庭宴请或公司聚会中，中国人有一些特别的饮食习俗：

一、食物要丰盛、菜要多，酒要足。虽然现在大家从节约的角度出发，对剩下的菜肴“打包”，但餐后如能多剩余一些，会使聚会者感到气氛热烈，场面圆满。

二、在传统的饮食习俗中，席间主人有布菜的习俗，就是主人常常用筷子把好吃的菜、肉夹送到客人的盘、碗之中，并且劝告客人多吃一点，吃好、吃饱，以表示主人的热情好客。现在出于健康的考虑，主人通常会把名贵的菜放到客人旁边，方便客人食用，或使用专用的筷子为客人夹菜。

三、有劝酒的习俗。在席宴间，人们互相敬酒、劝酒，希望都不要客气，吃得酒足饭饱。在改革开放初期，有些地方将劝酒发展为豪饮，出现了迫使人喝酒的现象，造成了客人有心理压力。因此，现在的宴请，主人通常会向客人敬酒，但不再过分劝酒。

四、主人有斟茶倒酒的习俗。在人们进餐中，主人常常给客人斟茶或倒酒，一般客人把杯子放在桌子上，将一只手放在杯旁，表示谢意。在中国南方的一些城市，人们还用弯曲的中指和食指叩击桌子来表示感谢。据说这是来源于这样一个故事：清朝乾隆皇帝下江南，微服私访，他扮仆人模样，他的侍从扮做主子。他们来到饭店吃饭，为了不暴露身份，乾隆皇帝只好给侍从斟茶，侍从心中十分惶恐，但又不能表露，只好用手指叩击桌子，以表示奴才下跪，叩拜谢恩。人们总是喜欢编出各种故事，来为自己的一些文化现象作解释。

五、请客吃饭时，中国人点菜喜欢双数，如四菜一汤、四冷四热、四碟八碗等。有人说这是出于中国人阴阳平衡的文化心理，因肉食属阳，金属器皿也属阳，如果食用菜数也是属阳的话，阴阳便失去平衡，所以菜品的数量采用属阴的偶数。今天人们已经很少关注这种饮食阴阳理论了，大家只是出于习惯罢了。

中国人不仅追求食物的味香色美，更追求食物的美学效应。有些菜肴用各种蔬菜雕制成花鸟鱼兽等精美造型，并命名为富贵牡丹、孔雀开屏、松鹤延年等，一个菜就是一件精美的艺术品，真是使人不忍下箸。

除此之外，中国人的饮食审美情趣还突出地表现在菜肴的名字上。有的菜名联系着历史典故，比如：有一道菜叫“霸王别姬”，这是用历史上项羽被刘邦打败，与他的爱姬死别的故事来命名的，实际上是把鳖肉和鸡肉合做在一起的一个菜；有一道用蟹黄和燕窝做的菜，叫“鸿门宴”，这也是取自于楚汉相争的故事。有的菜名俗中见雅，比如：有一道菜叫“樱桃肉”，是将一块块红似樱桃的肉做好后，四周配上绿色豆苗，使人想起“红了樱桃，绿了芭蕉”的诗句。还有些菜名直接引用诗词中的好词佳句，令人诗情、食情倍增，如：翠堤春晓、花报瑶台、珠圆玉润、红粉佳人、玉楼夜照、醉里乾坤、满天星斗、紫气东来、玉女晚妆、八仙过海、桂楫兰桡、鱼跃清溪等。

另外，在菜名中也能反映出中国人的祈求吉祥的心理，比如：用鸡和蛇肉做的菜叫“龙凤呈祥”或“龙凤烩”；四个丸子的菜叫“四喜丸子”；发菜豆腐汤叫“发财多福”；黄花炖豆腐叫“金镶玉”；各种菜杂烩在一起叫“全家福”；祝寿时的面条叫“长寿面”；结婚时用百合和莲子做的羹叫“百年好合”等。这些菜食名使人未食其物，就产生了喜庆吉祥的心情。

还有一些菜食的名字叫得很怪，故意以拙见巧，俗中见奇，用怪名加深人们的印象，以此扩大菜食的知名度，如：狗不理包子、耳朵眼儿炸糕、叫花子鸡、蚂蚁上树、猫耳朵、佛跳墙、油炸鬼、驴打滚儿、熊瞎子上炕（满族菜）、平地一声雷、臊子面、杠子头、姑嫂饼等。

另外，中国自古就有以人名来命菜食名的传统，如：“永加王烙羊”、“成美公藏蟹”、“虞公断醒酢”等。今天则有：宫保鸡丁、麻婆豆腐、东坡肉、老边饺子、老孙家羊肉泡馍、李连贵大饼等。

中国饮食文化是中华各族人民在几万年的生产和生活实践中创造、积累起来的，其中丰富地蕴含着中国人认识事物、理解世界的哲理。它不仅是中国的骄傲，而且是影响周边国家和世界的物质财富及精神财富。只有了解了菜肴所体现的中国文化的背景，才能更好地理解中国人的饮食习俗。

An age-old Chinese saying says "Food is of the utmost importance to everyone." *The Records of the Historian* noted, "His people are of the utmost importance to a king, food is of the utmost importance to people." Sima Zhen, a historian in the Tang Dynasty, explained that this remark was from Guan Zhong, a politician in the Spring and Autumn Period, and Guan Zhong also added, "He who knows what is of the utmost importance to Heaven is the most able one." The Chinese have long regarded food as their primary want. With social and economic progress, food has been related to many cultural events and a rich culture of food has evolved.

Food is an essential part of Chinese culture. Chinese restaurants can be found everywhere in the world, and Chinese cuisine is widely appreciated for its combination of color, aroma, taste, arrangement, and even utensils. Chinese food culture has many unique features.

1. **The Chinese generally eat more vegetables than meat.** The Chinese people have their cultural origins in the fertile Yellow River basin. Over centuries their economy and culture were closely linked to agricultural production. Grain and vegetables were historically the major part of the average person's diet, with meat being a supplement. Grain for the ancient Chinese meant wheat, broomcorn millet, foxtail millet, soybean, and rice. Later on, grains were classified into nine different types. Vegetables included bamboo, gourd, dasheen, leek and onion. In the Han, Tang, Yuan, and Ming dynasties, cucumber, garlic, spinach, carrot, tomato, potato and peanut were introduced to China. People who were rich or from the upper classes could afford to eat more meat, and were known as meat-eaters by the lower classes.

2. **The Chinese are very devoted to cooked and hot food.** The

discovery of how to use fire for cooking marked the end of Chinese people eating uncooked food. Fire was originally used to bake and roast food, but by the period of the Yellow Emperor, people had begun to learn how to cook by steaming and boiling.

A Three Kingdoms (220-280) scholar and historian named Qiao Zhou recorded that the Yellow Emperor began to steam grains and boil them to make congee. Chinese recognize the Yellow Emperor as the inaugurator of civilized cooking in China. *Lü's Spring and Autumn Annals* noted that well-cooked food is rid of raw and foul smells. Thus having cooked and hot food is an age-old principle of Chinese cuisine.

3. Chinese people have always been partial to dining together. Excavations have revealed that kitchens were an important part of ancient houses and that people sat and ate together. Even today, mealtimes are an occasion for the whole family to come together and share food. Dining together is considered an essential part of a happy family reunion.

As society continued to develop economically, dining became more than a desire to satisfy a basic need, but a way to enjoy life. Confucius said, "To have rice finely cleaned is not disliked by anyone; to have meat mince finely cut is not disliked by anyone." So even by the time of Confucius, it was thought that food should be finely prepared and cooked. Chinese cuisine is very concerned with choosing ingredients, cutting skills and the cooking method and duration. Culinary skills have been refined and improved over many centuries, and there are now numerous ways used to cook food, including boiling, long-boiling, quick-boiling, steaming, deep-frying, stir-frying, slippery-frying, quick-frying, grilling, braising, stewing, smoking, baking, roasting, mixing, pickling, and preserving, to name just a few.

Due to the size of the country, many different styles of cooking have developed in different areas. Today the eight most famous are Jiangsu cuisine, Zhejiang cuisine, Shandong cuisine, Anhui cuisine, Cantonese cuisine, Fujian cuisine, Hunan cuisine and Sichuan cuisine. Metaphors can be used to tell the differences between these styles. Jiangsu and Zhejiang styles can be likened to southern beauties, whereas Shandong and Anhui styles are like northern males. Canton and Fujian styles have parallels with elegant gentlemen, and Sichuan and Hunan styles are like talented scholars.

With regard to signature dishes, Jiangsu style is famous for Steamed Shad, and Lightly-braised Crab Meat Balls. Zhejiang style is famous for West Lake Fish, and Shrimp with Longjing Green Tea Leaves. Shandong style is known for Lotus-shape Prawns, and Sea Cucumbers with Chicken Drumsticks, Anhui style for its Duck with Gourd, and Pheasant with Bamboo Shoots. Cantonese style is renowned for Roast Suckling Pig, and Beef with Oyster Sauce. Fujian Style is famous for Assorted Seafood and Fowl Meat Casserole, and Chrysanthemum-shape Sea Bass, whereas Hunan style is for Dong'an Style Chicken, and Shark's Fin Stew. Last but not least, Sichuan style is known for Special-flavor Chicken and Hot-and-Spicy Bean Curd. Each one of these dishes is unique, yet they are all perfect combinations of color, aroma, taste and shape.

Courtesy and propriety are especially important in Chinese culture. The etiquette of dining is no exception. *The Book of Rites*, an ancient work recording the correct ways to behave, included many rules and regulations regarding table manners. Among these were the seating order of the participants, the arranging of the dishes, the order of drinking, and how to propose toasts. During meals it also included such precise guidelines as saying that a piece of fish or other meat taken out of the dish plate could not be taken back to it again, and the temperature of staple foods should remain constant.

Confucius was very particular about dining etiquette. He noted "One should not converse while eating," and "If the sitting mat is not placed in the correct manner, do not sit." And even more specific, "Do not eat food that has not been cut." True to the spirit of civility and politeness embodied in his philosophy, he also said "Always make a solemn offering, even for a simple meal of soup and vegetables," and "When attending a grand feast, be sure to offer thanks to the host." With regards to age, he made the comment "After a drinking session for the village, the elders will depart before others."

At feudal banquets, the seat to the left of the host was reserved for the guest of honor. Seats facing east traditionally symbolized respect, and the guests were seated according to age. Nowadays, many of the more complicated conventions are no longer followed, but dining remains an occasion in which elders are respected, the young taken care of, guests are fussed over, and plenty of dishes are supplied.

Dining is also closely related to friendship and interpersonal exchanges. A proverb says "When like minds meet, there can never be too many cups," or "For congenial friends a thousand toasts are too few." Weddings, funerals, birthdays, and other celebrations are and have for millennia been occasions in which feasts are held for friends and relatives. Businesses also have dinners for their staff or clients at a new office launch, for the signing of an agreement, or a year-end party. During these occasions, people propose toasts and chat heartily. Business and family feasts share some common features.

1. **There must be more than enough food and drink.** Nowadays people tend to order a little less and may take home the leftovers, however quantity remains important. Chinese people like to order more food than the guests are likely to eat. If there is food left over, the guests will feel their host is indeed very hospitable, and the host will feel comfortable that he has organized a perfect feast.

2. It used to be considered polite for the banquet host to use his own chopsticks to place food onto the plates of the guests, and urge the guests to take more food. Nowadays this is considered a little unhygienic, so a better way is to put the most expensive dishes near close to the guests, or for the host to use special serving chopsticks to choose food for the guests.

3. The host also urges the guests to drink more. Banquet guests are encouraged to behave as if they are at home, and a way to do this is for the host to encourage them to eat and drink. Occasionally, guests may even be forced to drink against their will and actually feel some pressure when invited to a banquet. These days better hosts still propose toasts, but try to steer clear of urging their guests to drink excessively.

4. The host normally refills the guest's drinks. And as he is doing so, the guest should put the cup on the table and rest their hand beside it, to show their gratitude. In some southern cities, the guest taps his or her index and middle finger on the table in order to express gratitude. This custom is said to have originated in the Qing Dynasty. Emperor Qianlong toured southern China, but wanted to hide his identity from his subjects. In order to achieve this, he wore plain clothes, and instructed his servants not to show public expressions of respect. One day, he went to a restaurant, and, perhaps wanting to experience life as a common person, poured tea for his servant. This placed the servant in an unusual and uncomfortable position – one he got around by ingeniously crooking his two fingers to represent kowtowing and tapped them on the table, which represented the floor.

5. Chinese people tend to order dishes in even numbers, for example, four dishes and a soup, four cold dishes and four hot dishes, or four plates and eight bowls. This practice comes from the desire to balance the Yin and Yang. In earlier times, meat and metal utensils were considered to represent Yang. Because even numbers are thought to represent Yin, even numbers of dishes were needed to balance out Yang. In recent times people have tended to pay less attention to the Yin and Yang of dining formalities, but the practices still remain.

The Chinese feel that food should not only be great to eat, but should also be pleasing to the eye. Different vegetables are often carved into delicate shapes such as flowers, birds, fish and other animals. Peony Abundance, Peacock Fanning Out Tail, and Longevity Crane by Pine Tree, are a few kinds of dishes that are designed to be visually appreciated before being eaten.

Dishes are also named for imaginative reasons. Some are related to historical anecdotes and others for the poetic nature of the name. A considerable number are named after generals, scholars, and historical events. Cherry Meat, for example, is not made of cherries but port cooked with special ingredients to the color of cherry, with green vegetables to make a visual contrast. Poetic names are appetizing in themselves, for example, Spring Morning at Green Bank, Flowers at Fairy Palace, Pearl Round and Jade Pure, Beauty in Pink, Moonlit Jade Tower, Fairy Stars, Lucky Purple Air, Eight Immortals Crossing Sea, Laurel and Orchid Oar, and Fish Jumping Over Clear Brook.

The names of some dishes address the Chinese appetite for auspiciousness as well as good food. One dish made of chicken and snake is known as Auspicious Dragon and Phoenix, and another is Four Meat Balls of Happiness. A bean curd soup with moss fungi is known as Fortunate and Lucky, because bean curd and this particular type of fungus are homophones of luck and becoming wealthy. A dish consisting of bean curd and daylily flowers is known as Gold Inlaid with Jade, because of its colors. One containing a hotchpotch variety of vegetables and meats is called A Whole Happy Family, and another food taken on birthdays is named Longevity Noodles. A soup made of lily bulbs and lotus seeds which is served at weddings is called Lifetime Devotion and Happiness. Once again, in this dish, homophone plays a role. In Chinese, lily sounds like long term devotion and harmony.

Some other dishes or food have rather strange names in order to help them stand out among so many other delicacies. However, they are often very tasty! Some examples are Steamed Filled Bun that Dogs Never Pay Attention to, Beggar's Chicken, Ants Climbing Trees, Monk Jumping Over the Wall, and Thick Stick, to name just a few. It is also interesting that both in the past and at present family names or given names of people related to some dishes have been incorporated into the names of those dishes.

The culture surrounding food and dining in China has evolved over many centuries, and reflects the world view and philosophy of Chinese people. Chinese cuisine is not only the pride of Chinese nation, but also part of the world's heritage and legacy. A better understanding of the cultural elements of Chinese food will help one comprehend the formalities and customs related to food and dining.

生词 New Words

1.饮食	yǐnshí	food and drink; diet
2.遍布	biànbù	to be found everywhere
3.特色	tèsè	characteristic; distinguishing feature
4.赞赏	zànshǎng	to admire, to appreciate
5.生存	shēngcún	to subsist, to live
6.享受	xiǎngshòu	to enjoy, to treat
7.发源	fāyuán	to rise, to originate
8.引进	yǐnjìn	to introduce from elsewhere
9.上层	shàngcéng	upper levels
10.富豪	fùháo	rich and powerful people
11.传说	chuánshuō	it is said; they say
12.贯穿	guànchuān	to run through; to permeate
13.烹饪	pēngrèn	cooking; culinary art
14.遗址	yízhǐ	site (where sth. was)
15.灶	zào	kitchen range; cooking stove
16.温馨	wēnxīn	warm; soft and sweet
17.讲究	jiǎngjiu	to be particular about; to pay attention to; to stress
18.刀工	dāogōng	(in preparing food) cutting and slicing skill
19.火候	huǒhou	duration and degree of heating, cooking, smelting, etc.
20.精益求精	jīngyìqiújīng	to constantly improve sth.; to keep improving
21.花样繁多	huāyàng fánduō	a great variety
22.盛名	shèngmíng	great reputation
23.风味	fēngwèi	special flavor; local color

24.清秀	qīngxiù	delicate and pretty
25.古拙	gǔzhuō	primitive and crude
26.公子	gōngzǐ	a pampered son of a wealthy or influential family
27.名士	míngshì	a person with a literary reputation
28.美味佳肴	měiwèi-jiāyáo	delicious food; delicious dainty
29.遵循	zūnxún	to follow; to abide by
30.酒逢知己千杯少		jiǔ féng zhījǐ qiān bēi shǎo for congenial friends a thousand toasts are too few
31.彼此	bǐcǐ	each other
32.生意	shēngyi	business, trade
33.开张	kāizhāng	to open a business
34.落成	luòchéng	to be completed
35.欢声笑语	huānshēng-xiàoyǔ	happy laughers and cheerful voices
36.凝聚力	níngjùlì	cohesive force; cohesion
37.好客	hàokè	to be hospitable; hospitality
38.劝酒	quànjiǔ	to urge sb. to drink (at a banquet)
39.酒足饭饱	jiǔzú-fànbǎo	to have drunk and eaten to one's heart's content
40.豪饮	háoyǐn	to drink with abandon; to drink heavily
41.微服私访	wēifú sīfǎng	to travel incognito
42.侍从	shìcóng	attendants, retinue
43.惶恐	huángkǒng	terrified
44.谢恩	xiè'ēn	(usually of a minister to an emperor) to express gratitude for a favor
45.孔雀开屏	kǒngquè kāipíng	a peacock spreading its tail
46.延年	yánnián	to prolong life
47.典故	diǎngù	allusion; literary quotation
48.樱桃	yīngtao	cherry

49.龙凤呈祥	lóngfèng-chéngxiáng	the dragon and the phoenix bring prosperity
50.全家福	quánjiāfú	hotchpotch
51.百年好合	bǎinián-hǎohé	life-long happiness and perfect harmony
52.周边	zhōubiān	periphery

语法聚焦 Notes and Examples

一、随着历史的发展和社会的进步

“随着”是介词，表示“跟”。它所组成的介词词组表示，在此条件下，产生某种结果。

Preposition 随着 means following and the prepositional phrase with 随着 indicates a result from the condition introduced by 随着. For example:

1. 随着年龄的增长，他变得更加成熟和老练了。
2. 随着经济的发展，人们的生活水平也在提高。
3. 随着时间的推移，这件事逐渐被人们忘记了。

二、可以说凡有中国人的地方，就有中餐馆

“凡”是副词，表示在某个范围之内毫无例外，有“只要是”的意思，后面常与“就”、“便”、“都”等词相搭配。

Adverb 凡, sometimes used together with 就, 便, 都 etc., indicates that there is no exception within certain range. For example:

1. 凡在我厂工作十年以上的职工，都可拿到一笔奖金。
2. 凡是见到过他的人，没有不称赞他的。
3. 凡能找的地方，我们都找过了，可就是没找到。

三、长期以来一直以农业生产为主要经济方式

“以来”是助词，用在某些时间词或含有时间意义的词语后边，表示从那个时间开始直到现在这一段时间。

Auxiliary word 以来 is used with words or phrases of time to indicate from that time on. For example:

1. 这个学生到美国以来，每天十点以前没有睡过觉，都在学习。
2. 周老师参加工作以来，没请过一天假。
3. 近十年以来，这个地方灾害不断。
4. 交易会开幕以来，每天交易额都大幅攀升。

四、中国人仍旧非常喜欢一家人围坐在桌旁，将饭菜摆放在桌上，一起用饭

"将"是介词，表示对人或事物的处置，用法与"把"相同，多用于书面语。
Preposition 将, similar to 把, means disposal of a person or thing. For example:

1. 妹妹将哥哥的病情写信告诉了妈妈。
2. 法庭将案情重审一遍。
3. 必须将这些过时的数据清理出去。

五、像用餐时人们的座位应该如何坐，盘碗菜肴应该如何放

"如何"是疑问代词，多用于书面语，有"怎么"、"怎么样"的意思。
Interrogative 如何 means how or how things are going. For example:

1. 这叫我如何向大家交代。
2. 不知你近况如何，请来信告我。
3. 我买时，厂家说如何之好，回来才发现问题很多。

六、但在现代的宴饮活动中，仍然体现出菜肴丰盛……气氛热烈的形式美和人情美

"仍然"是副词，表示某种情况没有改变，在句中作状语。
Adverb 仍然 as an adverbial in a clause means things remain the same. For example:

1. 上班时，我看见这个老头坐在这里，下班看见他仍然坐在这里。
2. 关于工作时间，每周仍然休息两天。
3. 多年不见，常先生仍然是热情、健谈，一副老样子。

七、因此无论过去还是现在，……

"无论"是连词，表示条件不同而结果或结论不变。它后面常有"谁"、"什么"、"怎么"、"还是"等词相搭配。
Conjunction 无论, often followed by 谁, 什么, 怎么, 还是, shows that the conclu-

sion or outcome remains the same whatever the condition may be. For example:

1. 这个方案无论谁反对，我们都要坚持。
2. 无论遇到什么情况，你都要保持克制。
3. 别人的意见，无论是对还是错，你都要听。

八、大家只是出于习惯罢了

“只是”是副词，它限定动作范围，是“仅仅是”、“只不过”的意思。
Adverb 只是 means merely, only, or no more than. For example:

1. 我只是说说而已，没有别的意思。
2. 这个学生非常聪明，只是做事有些马虎。
3. 学习外语，不能只是写，还应该多说多听。

想一想 Questions

1. 中国人的饮食有什么特点?
   What are the features of Chinese food and Chinese cuisine?
2. 中国有几大菜系?
   How many major schools of cooking are there in China?
3. 中国人在饮宴中有哪些习俗?
   What kinds of customs and etiquettes do the Chinese have at banquets?
4. 中国菜的名字有哪些文化内涵?
   What kinds of cultural elements are included in the names of Chinese dishes?
5. 谈一谈你对中国饮食的一些看法。
   Please share your views on Chinese food and Chinese cuisine.

超级链接 Super Links

《史记》

中国历史上第一部纪传体通史，作者是西汉时期（前206–公元25）的司马迁。该书成书于公元前104年至公元前91年。全书共一百三十篇，分为本纪、书、表、世家、列传五种形式。“本纪”是按年代顺序记叙帝王的言行和政迹；“表”是按年代谱列出各个时期的重大事件；“书”记录了各种典章制度的沿革；“世家”载述诸侯国的兴衰和杰出人物的业绩；“列传”记载各种代表人物的活动。《史记》一书本是没有书名的，司马迁完成这部巨著后曾给当时的大学者东方朔看过，东方朔非常钦佩，就在书上加了“太史公”三字。“太史”是司马迁的官职，“公”是美称，“太史公”主要表明了作者。但后人因尊敬司马迁，故将此书称为“太史公书”。

管仲（？–前645）

春秋时期齐国人，中国古代著名政治家，官至宰相。管仲注重经济，反对空谈，主张通过改革以富国强兵。从政期间，他确立了通过三级审核选拔人才的制度；主张按照土地好坏分等征税，禁止官兵掠夺家畜；并且用官府力量发展盐铁业，铸造和管理货币，调节物价。诸多改革措施推行后，取得了显著的成效，使得国力大振。后人尊称他为“春秋第一相”。

“王者以民为天，民以食为天，能知天之天者，斯可矣。”

这句话可理解为：执政者首先要以民为本，而老百姓安居乐业、社会稳定的关键在于基本生活资料供应的保障与持续稳定。

谯周（201–270）

中国古代著名的儒学大师和史学家。

《古史考》

书名。谯周撰写。该书搜罗众多古籍补充了《史记》记载的先秦史实的缺漏，是研究中国古代史重要的参考书之一。原书25卷，现已无存世。

《吕氏春秋》

战国末期秦国宰相吕不韦（？–前235）集合门客共同编写。全书共26卷，汇合了先秦各派学说，为当时秦国统一天下、治理国家提供的思想理论。

《礼记》

该书是中国古代一部重要的典章制度书籍，也是儒家经典著作之一，记录了秦汉以前的各种礼仪制度，是研究中国古代社会情况、儒家学说和文物制度的参考书。

反鱼肉

反鱼肉是指：吃中餐时，将自己没有吃完的鱼、肉再放回盘中。

扬饭

用食具扬起饭粒以散去热气。

布菜

吃中餐时，主人为了表示热情，把菜肴分给座上的客人，即夹菜给客人。

端午节民俗趣谈

Folk Customs of the Dragon Boat Festival

10

A Kaleidoscope of Chinese Culture

端午节指农历五月初五，它是中国一个古老的传统节日，从春秋战国算起，已有两千多年历史了。端午节又叫端阳节、重午节、天中节、天长节等，老百姓俗称“五月节”。“端”就是“初”的意思。在唐朝以前，人们把这个节日叫“五月五日”，而不是叫“端午节”，到了唐朝时，才出现了“端午”这个名字。

端午节是中国民间的传统节日，它的起源众说纷纭，古时有人在此日纪念战国时楚人伍子胥，有人纪念东汉时孝女曹娥，更有闻一多先生认为它是古代吴越族的一个图腾祭。但流传最广、影响最深远的说法是为了纪念爱国诗人——屈原。屈原是战国时楚国人，他学识渊博，善于外交，得到了楚国国王楚怀王的信任，任过左徒、三闾大夫等官职。当时正是七国争霸的时代。屈原主张联合齐国抵抗秦国，可是国内的一些亲秦派在楚怀王面前讲了许多屈原的坏话，使楚怀王不再重用他。后来楚怀王被骗到秦国并死在那里，他的儿子顷襄王接位以后，把屈原放逐到湖南一带。屈原满腔悲愤，忧国忧民，写下了许多爱国诗篇。公元前278年，在他62岁那年，他听到了秦国大军攻陷楚国国都的消息，悲痛万分，在五月五日这一天，怀抱一石，投汨罗江自尽了。老百姓非常热爱这位为国为民的诗人，大家纷纷划船来寻找他，并且把包好的粽子抛到江中喂鱼，以免鱼虾伤害他的身体。端午节赛龙舟、吃粽子习俗正是由此而来。宋朝时，屈原被封为“忠烈公”，这就使端午节更富有纪念屈原的意义了。抗日战争时，人们又把农历五月五日定为“诗人节”，直到今天，各地诗社、诗词协会等，都在端午节这天举办各种赛诗、赏诗活动，借以弘扬源远流长的中华端午文化。

过端午是中华民族两千多年来的传统习俗。虽然中国幅员辽阔、民族众多，但各地过端午的习俗大致相同。主要有：挂艾叶、菖蒲，赛龙舟，吃粽子，饮雄黄酒，游百病，佩香囊，备牲醴等。其中有些活动，如赛龙舟等，已得到新的发展，突破了时间、地域界线，成为了国际性的体育赛事。

插艾叶、菖蒲的风俗大致起源于南北朝（420–589）时期。艾叶是一种含有挥发性芳香油的植物，可以驱蚊虫、净化空气；菖蒲是一种水生植物，也含有挥发性芳香油，可以提神通窍、杀虫灭菌。按照传统习俗，人们在农历五月五日这天会打扫庭院，并将艾叶、菖蒲插在门楣上。这种民俗是有一定的科学道理的。因为夏至是在农历的五月，这一天太阳几乎直射北回归线，从此以后，阳光直射的位置逐渐南移，白昼逐渐变短，黑夜逐渐变长，气候也开始由热转凉，中医认为，在寒气暑气交换之时，人们要特别注意在饮食、穿衣、行动上防止疾病入侵。而艾叶和菖蒲与大蒜一样都有杀菌的作用。因此，从农历五月五日这天开始挂艾叶、菖蒲可以起到预防疾病的作用。从明朝开始，人们在端午节这天，还要饮用少量的菖蒲雄黄酒。雄黄是一种中药材，中医认为雄黄可以治百种虫毒、虫伤，所以在中国古代也有用雄黄酒治疗蚊虫咬伤的案例。

在端午节诸多的习俗中，南方水乡的“龙舟竞渡”被人们极为称道。这一天，人们穿着节日盛装来到江边，一声炮响，各条参赛龙舟有如箭发，各个争先恐后，奋力拼搏，欢呼声、鞭炮声响成一片，情景欢快动人。关于举办龙舟竞渡的起因，人们认为是为了纪念爱国诗人屈原。相传屈原投汨罗江后，楚国百姓因舍不得贤臣屈原投江而死，纷纷划船营救。他们争先恐后，追至洞庭湖时却不见了屈原的踪迹。之后每年五月五日人们划龙舟以纪念他，逐渐形成了端午节龙舟竞渡的习俗。

端午节的另一重要习俗是吃粽子。其实粽子在很早的时候就有了，它最早的名字叫角黍，本来是农民用来祭祀祖先的供物。它的做法从古至今变化不大，古人是用黍米来做，明朝以后改为糯米。先将泡好的糯米用竹叶或苇叶包成三角形或四角形，再用线绳扎紧，放在锅中煮熟，便可食用。后来人们在粽内又添加了各种果料。之后，粽子逐渐发展成端午节的“节日食品”，人们可以用粽子馈赠亲友。一直到今天，每年五月初，中国许多家庭仍要浸糯米、洗粽叶、包粽子，其馅料也更为丰富，北方多以大枣、豆沙、枣泥为馅，南方多以蛋黄、奶油、腊肉、火腿为馅。总之，千百年来，吃粽子的习俗在中国长盛不衰，而且也影响了亚洲许多国家。

端午节除了赛龙舟、吃粽子外，还有一项活动颇受小朋友喜爱，那就是系五色丝线、挂荷包。古代中国人崇拜青、白、红、黑、黄五种颜色，人们认为它们分别对应着东、南、西、北、中五个方位，蕴含着神奇的力量，因此，人们以五色为吉祥色。端午节这天的清晨，各家大人起床后第一件大事便是在孩子手腕、脚腕、脖子上拴五色线。系线时，小孩子不能说话。五色丝线不可任意折断或丢弃，只能在夏季第一场大雨或第一次洗澡时抛到河里。传说，系五色丝线的儿童可以避开蛇蝎类毒虫的伤害；扔到河里后，可以让河水将瘟疫、疾病冲走，儿童能保安康。除戴五色丝线外，古代中国人在过端午节的时候，必戴的物件还有荷包，有的用五色丝线缠成，有的用碎布缝制，里面多装有香料，佩戴在身上香气扑鼻。

时至今日，端午节作为中华民族的传统节日深受人们喜爱。中国政府从保护传统节日文化和中华民族文化遗产的角度出发，现已将端午节列为了国家法定节假日。

The Duanwu Festival, known as the Dragon Boat Festival in the west, is a Chinese tradition that began more than 2,000 years ago in the Spring Autumn and Warring States Period. In actual fact, the festival has several different names, including the Duanyang Festival, Chongwu Festival, Tianzhong Festival, Tianchang Festival, and the Festival in May. Before the Tang Dynasty, it was known as “the Fifth Day of the Fifth Lunar Month”, but then it was changed to Duanwu. Duan (端) means the first.

The origins of the festival are obscure, and vary according to different folk traditions. One tradition holds that it was to commemorate Wu Zixu, a loyal official of the State of Wu during the Warring States Period. Another tradition believes it was started in memory of Cao E, a filial daughter of the Eastern Han Dynasty. A famous scholar named Wen Yiduo in modern times believed it was originally a totemic sacrifice in the ancient southern Yue and Wu tribes. However, the most widespread belief is that it was originally to commemorate the great patriotic poet Qu Yuan.

Born in the State of Chu during the Warring States Period, Qu Yuan grew up to be an able diplomat and extremely knowledgeable man of letters. As a trusted confidant of King Huai, he held many important positions. At the time, there were seven states fiercely struggling for supremacy. Qu Yuan proposed that the State of Chu should ally with the State of Qi in order to be able to better contest the supremacy of the powerful State of Qin. However, the court was full of intrigue and bitter rivalries. Pro-Qin court officials said many evil things about Qu Yuan, and sowed distrust toward Qu Yuan in the King's mind.

Later, King Huai was duped into visiting the Kingdom of Qin, and subsequently died there. His son, Xiang, became the next king and sent Qu Yuan into exile in a remote part of Hunan Province. During his exile, Qu Yuan was highly concerned with the fate of the State of Chu and penned many patriotic poems.

In 278 BC, when Qu Yuan was 62, tragedy struck the State of Chu when Qin troops overran the capital. On the fifth day of the fifth month, Qu Yuan was so devastated that he held a big stone in his arms and threw himself into the Miluo River. Because he was such a respected figure, local people rowed boats out on the river to search for him, but it was too late. When they realized that he was indeed dead, they threw dumplings of rice wrapped in reed leaves into the water, in the hope that the fish would eat these instead of Qu Yuan's body.

Holding dragon boat races and celebrating with this kind of food, known as zongzi, evolved into a custom that continues to this day. During the 1940s, the celebration was named Poet's Day, and since then many people have used the day to compose and appreciate poems, and to celebrate its other customs.

The tradition of the Dragon Boat Festival has now been continued for over 2,000 years, but its customs have remained largely the same. Dried Chinese mugwort or calamus is usually hung on doors, zongzi is symbolically prepared and eaten, and rice wine with realgar powder is served. People carry small pouches stuffed with fragrant spices, sacrifices are prepared for ceremonies, and, of course, dragon boat races are held. Dragon boat racing has also become an international sport with its own set of rules.

Hanging Chinese mugwort or calamus is a custom that originated in the period of the Southern and Northern dynasties (420-589). The fragrance of mugwort is not only pleasant, but also has the power to deter worms and mosquitoes. Calamus is a kind of aquatic plant that has similar effects. On the fifth day of the fifth lunar month, houses and courtyards are traditionally cleaned and scrubbed and dried Chinese mugwort or calamus is hung on door lintels to help kill germs and hence prevent disease.

This custom has some basis in scientific reasoning. Summer arrives in the fifth lunar month and the days are therefore longer and hotter. According to the theories of traditional Chinese medicine, people should pay particular attention to what they eat, how they dress, and their daily activities at the intersection of the seasons because of the health risks associated with cool air meeting hot air.

For the same reason, a small amount of realgar powder is consumed on the day. This practice was started in the Ming Dynasty. In Chinese medicine, realgar has been used to cure worm bites since ancient times.

By far the favorite event of the day is the dragon boat races that take place in river towns across southern China. As mentioned above, the original intention behind the boat races was to save the life of Qu Yuan. Nowadays, however, the racing is an exciting and happy event and the participants dress in festive costumes. Races are kicked off with starting guns, and the colorfully decorated boats are cheered on by riverside spectators. The festive atmosphere is also enhanced by the sounds of firecrackers being set off.

In its earliest form, zongzi was named angled broomcorn millet, and was used as a part of the sacrifices made to the ancestors. By the Ming Dynasty, the broomcorn millet was changed to glutinous rice, but the method of preparation remained the same. The rice is first soaked in water for a couple of days, after which it is wrapped in triangle or rectangle-shaped bamboo or reed leaves, which is then bound with cotton thread. To improve the flavor, dates or beans are often added in northern China, and egg yolk, preserved meat, ham or even cream is often added in southern China. Zongzi is often given as a festival gift to relatives and friends. This delicacy is not only a Chinese favorite but has also become popular in many Asian countries.

Another Dragon Boat Festival custom is concerned with the well-being of the family's children. On the morning of the festival a five-colored thread, representing the five directions of north, south, east, west and center, will be tied about the wrist, ankle and neck of children in the family. The children must stay silent while this is being done, and after that, the threads should not be torn, cut or thrown away at will. Only when the first summer rain comes, or when the children take their first summer bath, the threads are untied and thrown into a river. People believed that the magical properties of the auspicious thread would protect the children from being bitten by scorpions or snakes, and after it is thrown in the river, any possible disease would be washed away by the water, leaving the children healthy and well. Apart from this practice, sometimes one would wear a pouch at the festival that may be wrapped in five-colored threads, or sewn with small pieces of cloth that would be filled with fragrant essence.

The Dragon Boat Festival remains to this day one of the favorite festivals of Chinese people. For preservation purposes, it has even been listed as a national holiday.

生词 New Words

1. 端午节	Duānwǔ Jié	the Dragon Boat Festival (the 5th day of the 5th lunar month)
2. 众说纷纭	zhòngshuōfēnyún	varying opinions
3. 流传	liúchuán	to spread, to circulate
4. 学识渊博	xuéshí yuānbó	to have great learning
5. 善于	shànyú	to be good at; to be adept in

6. 争霸	zhēngbà	to contend (or struggle) for hegemony
7. 坏话	huàihuà	malicious remark; vicious talk
8. 重用	zhòngyòng	to put sb. in an important position
9. 放逐	fàngzhú	to send into exile; to banish
10. 满腔	mǎnqiāng	to have one's bosom filled with
11. 忧国忧民	yōuguó-yōumín	to be concerned about one's country and one's people
12. 悲痛	bēitòng	grieved, sorrowful
13. 自尽	zìjìn	to commit suicide
14.龙舟	lóngzhōu	dragon boat
15.粽子	zòngzi	zongzi, a pyramid-shaped dumpling made of glutinous rice wrapped in bamboo or reed leaves
16.艾叶	àiyè	Chinese mugwort
17.菖蒲	chāngpú	calamus
18.雄黄酒	xiónghuángjiǔ	realgar wine
19.夏至	xiàzhì	the Summer Solstice – the 10th of the 24 solar terms
20.几乎	jīhū	almost
21.回归线	huíguīxiàn	tropic
22.白昼	báizhòu	daytime
23.争先恐后	zhēngxiān-kǒnghòu	to strive to be the first and fear to lag behind
24.馈赠	kuìzèng	to present (a gift); to make a present of sth.
25.亲友	qīnyǒu	relatives and friends
26.香料	xiāngliào	perfume, spice
27.时至今日	shízhìjīnrì	at this late hour; even to this day

语法聚焦 Notes and Examples

一、人们把这个节日叫“五月五日”，而不是叫“端午节”

“而”是连词，连接意义相反或意义转折的两个分句。有时也连接语义相承、递进的分句或句子，表示递进关系。多用于书面语。

Conjunction 而 connects two clauses with opposite or contrasting meanings, and sometimes connects a clause with progressive meaning. It is more used in written language. For example:

1. 这里是一片冰天雪地，而南方早已春暖花开了。
2. 他想买汽车，而妻子想买房子，他们一时拿不定主意。
3. 这些水果不是温室里长的，而是秋天储存起来的。
4. 我们必须掌握一种外语，而学外语不是一天能学好的，要持之以恒。

二、到了唐朝时，才出现了“端午”这个名字

“才”是副词，用在动词前作状语，表示时间晚或长、事物数量少。

Adverb 才, used before a verb, indicates the action done by the verb comes late, slowly or in small quantity. For example:

1. 你怎么才来?
2. 他们学了半年，才学了两课。
3. 这本大辞典才三块钱。

三、使楚怀王不再重用他

“使”是动词，表示派遣、指使，也表示使动或致使，与“让”、“叫”相似。

Verb 使 means dispatch, ask, or let someone do something. For example:

1. 明天我使人给你送去。
2. 你别着急，院长已使人打电话去了。
3. 你这么说，使我非常不好意思。
4. 听完报告，使我们更加了解了这里的情况。

四、这一天太阳几乎直射北回归线

“几乎”是副词，表示接近某数量或接近某种情况。“几乎”也有“差一点就……”的意思。

Adverb 几乎 means almost, nearly, etc.. For example:

1. 你不提起这件事，我几乎忘了。
2. 那座厂房几乎有两个篮球场大。
3. 要不是他用车送我，我几乎误了大事。

五、关于举办龙舟竞渡的起因，人们认为是为了纪念爱国诗人屈原

“关于”是介词，它组成的介词词组，可以作定语和状语，表示涉及的人或事物。

The prepositional phrase with the word 关于 functions as an attribute or adverbial, meaning on the subject of or concerning. For example:

1. 这是一本关于中医理论的书。
2. 关于签订合同的事，我们明天再谈。
3. 关于学习方法问题，我已经说了很多了。

六、本来是农民用来祭祀祖先的供物

这里的“本来”是副词，表示“原先”、“先前”，作状语。

Adverb 本来 means originally, previously and functions as an adverbial. For example:

1. 我朋友本来是学化学的，现在改学物理了。
2. 陈太太本来不想买，可大家都劝她买，她就买了。
3. 这个旅行团本来只有十个人，现在四十多人了。

七、它的作法从古至今变化不大

“从”是介词，它表示起点，用在表示时间或地点的词语前，后面常跟“到”、“至”等词语。

Preposition 从 leads a word or phrase indicating time and location, meaning from. 到 or 至, meaning usually, follows. For example:

1. 他从早到晚都埋头在实验室里。
2. 从一九八五年到一九八九年，王平先生任我校校长。
3. 从今天开始，我每天锻炼一小时。
4. 从古至今，不知有多少文人雅士来这里诵诗作画。
5. 火车提速后，从上海到南京，只用1小时55分钟。

想一想 Questions

1. 中国的端午节是哪一天？它有几个名字？
   Which day is the Dragon Boat Festival? What are the different names of it?

2. 端午节有哪些风俗？
   What kinds of customs are there in this festival?

3. 什么是龙舟竞渡？它的来源是什么？
   What is dragon boat racing? What is its origin?

4. 粽子是一种什么样的食品？
   What kind of food is zongzi?

超级链接 Super Links

《史记》中对屈原的记载

屈原者，名平，楚之同姓也。为楚怀王左徒。博闻强志，明于治乱，娴于辞令。入则与王图议国事，以出号令；出则接遇宾客，应对诸侯。

译文：

屈原名平，与楚国的王族同姓。他曾担任楚怀王的左徒。见闻广博，记忆力很强，通晓治理国家的方法，擅长外交辞令。在朝内与楚怀王商议国事，发号施令；对外接待宾客，应酬诸侯。

其文约，其辞微，其志洁，其行廉。其称文小而其指极大，举类迩而见义远。其志洁，故其称物芳；其行廉，故死而不容。自疏濯淖污泥之中，蝉蜕于浊秽，以浮游尘埃之外，不获世之滋垢，皭然泥而不滓者也。推此志也，虽与日月争光可也。

译文：

他的文笔简约，词意精微，他的志趣高洁，行为廉正。他的文章写到的都是小事，但表达的意义却非常重大，列举的事例虽然浅近，但含义却十分深远。由于他志趣高洁，所以文章中多用香花芳草作比喻，由于他行为廉正，所以到死也不为恶势力所容。他独自远离污泥浊水，像蝉脱壳一样摆脱浊秽，浮游在尘世之外，不受浊世的玷辱，保持高洁的品质，出污泥而不染。由此推断屈原的志向，可以和日月争辉。

腊八节民俗趣谈

The Eighth Day of the Twelfth Lunar Month and the Porridge Eaten on the Day

11

A Kaleidoscope of Chinese Culture

腊八，是指中国农历十二月初八，它是中国一个传统节日，由来已久，是古代中国人年终祭祀的一个节日，叫做“腊祭”。在古代农业社会，人们的许多风俗习惯都与农业生产有着密切的联系。每当农业生产获得丰收，人们便认为这是天地诸神及祖先护佑的结果，于是便要举行盛大的祭典，来祭祀掌管风、雨、田、农的天地诸神和自己的祖先，以示感谢，并乞求来年风调雨顺。又因为在农民的生活中，人们春耕、夏耘、秋收、冬藏，前三季都是比较忙的，只有冬藏之季比较空闲，所以，腊祭常于年底举行。久而久之，人们就把举行腊祭的岁终之月称为“腊月”了。元明之后，腊祭日益不被人们所重视。至清乾隆时，皇帝终于下令废除腊祭，但是，腊月的一些习俗仍然保留在民间，这就是吃腊八粥的风俗。

关于腊八粥的起源，众说纷纭。一种为大家普遍接受的说法是，它来源于佛教。唐代道世和尚在《诸经要集》中说，腊月初八是佛祖释迦牟尼的生日和降伏六师外道之日，为了纪念这个日子，佛教各寺院在这一天作浴佛会，煮七宝五味粥以供佛斋众。所以扬州人有去金山寺喝用一百零八种食物做成的粥的习俗。另外一种解释是，相传佛祖释迦牟尼原为古印度北部迦毗罗卫国净饭王的儿子，因他痛感人生充满了生、老、病、死各种苦痛，于是寻求解脱之道，他于二十九岁时，毅然舍弃王位，出家修行。经过六年艰苦奔波，他走遍印度名山大川，求师访贤，于十二月初八这一天，来到了比哈尔的尼连河畔。因为又饥又累，他昏倒在地上。这时有一个叫释迦罗越的牧羊姑娘看见了，她用自己身带的杂粮和野菜，煮熟了乳糜粥来喂他，佛祖因而得救。他在尼连河内洗了一个澡，然后向着东方，盘腿坐在菩提树下，深思悟道。到了十二月八日的夜里，他忽然大彻大悟，觉悟成佛。所以佛教称这一天为“成道节”。各寺院在这一天，用香谷和干菜熬成粥，以此供佛，也布施给众人。据南宋孟元老的《东京梦华录》中记载：“十二月八日，诸大寺作浴佛会，并送八宝五味粥与门徒，谓腊八粥。”南宋周密在《武林旧事》中也记载："八日，则寺院及人家用胡桃、松子、乳蕈、柿、栗之类做了粥，谓之腊八粥。"后来，这种喝腊八粥的习俗由佛寺扩展到了民间。北京一些主要街道出现了许多粥棚，而且做粥的用料也越来越讲究，越来越丰富。清代富察敦崇在《燕京岁时记》中记载："腊八粥者，用黄米、白米、江米、小米、菱角米、栗子、红豇豆、去皮枣泥等，合水煮熟，外用染红桃仁、杏仁、瓜子、花生、榛瓤、松子及白糖、红糖、琐琐葡萄，以作点染。"由此可见，腊八粥是一种多样谷物粮食和果类熬成的杂米粥。

喝腊八粥是符合中医养生理论的。制作腊八粥主要是选用豆类和谷物类作原料，这些原料除含有人体正常饮食需要的碳水化合物外，还含有B族维生素和多种人体必需微量元素、蛋白质、脂肪及膳食纤维等营养成分。更为重要的是，腊八粥所含的营养成分比一般单一原料制成的粥更能满足人体的多种营养需要。其中莲子可补气健脾，绿豆对高血压有辅助治疗的功效，赤豆能消水肿、治脚气，松子仁能滋润心肺、调理肠道，栗子能补益肾气、治腰酸腿软。这些对于提高人体免疫力、延缓衰老不无裨益。按中国传统养生观点，腊八粥具有健脾、开胃、补气、安神、清心、养血之功效，并有御寒作用，是冬令的滋补佳品，故能传承百代而不衰。随着国民生活水平的提高和对饮食养生保健需求的日益增加，人们不再满足只在腊八这天喝腊八粥，而是会根据自身的体质选择不同的原料调配腊八粥，经常食用。

中国喝腊八粥的的历史已有一千多年。每逢腊八这一天，不论是朝廷、官府、寺院还是黎民百姓家都要做腊八粥。到了清朝，喝腊八粥的风俗更是盛行。在皇宫内廷，每到腊八，就在宫内支起能装一百多斤米的大锅，于初七晚上，通宵熬粥，一共有六口大锅。第一锅粥供佛，第二锅献皇上及朝政元老，第三、四、五锅赏王公大臣、封疆大吏。这五锅用剩下的粥连同第六锅，拿到宫外，施舍百姓，并向各个寺院发放米、果等供僧侣食用，以表示"皇恩浩荡"。

腊八粥也叫“七宝五味粥”，传说吃了以后可以得到佛祖的保佑，所以穷人把它叫做“佛粥”。据说杭州名刹天宁寺内有储藏剩饭的“栈饭楼”，平时寺僧每日把剩饭晒干，积一年的余粮，到腊月初八煮成腊八粥分赠信徒，称为“福寿粥”、“福德粥”，意思是说吃了以后可以增福增寿。

普通的平民百姓在这一天家家也要做腊八粥。粥中用料根据各自家庭的经济状况而定。人们除了用粥供佛祀祖外，还馈赠给亲朋好友、街坊邻里。但送礼时，一定要趁早送去，最迟也不能超过中午。人们还给猫、狗、鸡、猪等动物也吃一点。北京有句童谣：“腊八粥、腊八饭，小鸡吃了就下蛋。”就是院内的果树花卉，也涂抹一点，据说来年会枝叶繁茂，果实累累。如果家中有亲丧“守制”的，不能熬粥。由此可见，腊八粥被人们视为吉祥之物。每年此时，粮米店老板会将各种米类、豆类掺和在一起出售，称之为“腊八米”，借此小赚一笔。

腊八这一天，除了喝腊八粥，各地还要制作不同的美食。例如，在安徽的农村，人们在腊八前后都要晒制豆腐，民间将这种自然晒制的豆腐称做“腊八豆腐”。在北京，腊月初八这天要泡制“腊八蒜”。其实材料非常简单，就是醋和大蒜。做法也不复杂，将剥了皮的蒜瓣放到一个可以密封的罐子里面，然后倒满醋，密封后放到一个冷的地方。慢慢地，泡在醋中的蒜就会变绿，最后会变得通体皆绿，如同翡翠碧玉。

腊八食粥，实际上是揭开了春节的序幕。从这一天起，许多人家就开始忙于杀猪、打豆腐、腌制腊肉、采购年货，为春节的庆祝活动作各种准备。所以有一童谣说：“老太太，你别馋，过了腊八就是年。腊八粥，喝几天，哩哩啦啦二十三。”虽然，现在的腊八节已经没有了最初的那些敬神、供佛、祭祖的事项，但过了腊八，过新年的味道便越来越重了。

On the eighth day of the twelfth lunar month, the traditional Laba Festival is held. *La* (腊) is another name for the twelfth month, and *ba* (八) is eight in Chinese. The festival originated from the ritual sacrifice held at the end of the year.

In the traditional agricultural economy many customs were linked to the cycles of agricultural production. During spring, summer and autumn, farmers were busy plowing, attending to their crops, and harvesting. They were less busy in the winter. They took one day in the last month of the lunar year to hold a grand ritual sacrifice, in order to extend their gratitude to and ask for the blessings of the gods and their ancestors. However, this ritual diminished in importance during the Yuan and Ming dynasties, and was finally abandoned in the Qing Dynasty. The one custom that has managed to survive through the centuries is to prepare and eat a special food, known as laba porridge.

There are several different explanations of the origins of laba porridge. The most popular ones are linked to Buddhism. One explanation is that the day was the birthday of Sakyamuni, the historical Buddha. Porridge is made at Buddhist temples to celebrate it. Another story begins with Sakyamuni's early life in northeast India. He was the son of the king of the Sakya, Suddhodana, who ruled at Kapilavastu on the border of Nepal. When he turned 29, he became aware of pain, sickness and death, and decided to abandon his privileged life and embrace asceticism. He traveled, fasted, and meditated for six years in search of enlightenment. Making his way to the Nairanjana River in Bihar, he was so hungry and weak that he fainted. A shepherd girl saved him by feeding him with a porridge made of various grains and edible weed.

When he recovered a little, he sat beneath a bodhi tree, facing the east, and meditated on death and rebirth. On the eighth day of the twelfth month, he became a Buddha. This day became known as the day of the enlightening. Traditionally, Buddhist temples would prepare a porridge made of a variety of grains and dried vegetables on this day as an offering to Buddha and alms for Buddhist believers. A Southern Song scholar, Zhou Mi, noted that families as well as temples prepared laba porridge. This practice was also recorded by Meng Yuanlao in the same dynasty. Since the Song Dynasty, families have traditionally prepared this porridge. The streets of old Beijing also had their own porridge eateries.

Over time, the quality and variety of porridge grew and changed. A Qing Dynasty scholar noted "The ingredients of laba porridge include millet, rice, glutinous rice, glutinous millet, water caltrop kernels, chestnuts, red cowpeas, and jujubes without skin. Add water to these ingredients and boil until ready to serve. Before serving, add nut pieces dyed red such as walnut, almond, sunflower seed, peanut, hazelnut, pine nut, as well as white and brown sugar, and Xinjiang raisins. Lotus seeds, lentils, barley, or longan should not be added as they spoil the taste." It is clear from these records that laba porridge was a food made from a wide variety of grains, dried nuts and fruit.

According to theories of traditional Chinese medicine, laba porridge is a healthy food. The wide variety of grains and nuts not only provide carbohydrates, but are also rich in vitamins and minerals, protein, fat and fiber. It is, therefore, very nutritious. Chinese people believe that nutritious food is preferable to a medicinal remedy. Laba porridge, with its many nutrients, is thought to be a particularly good food for wintertime. Nowadays it is not just taken on this special occasion, but whenever people feel like it. Other ingredients can also be added.

On the evening of the Laba Festival in the Qing Dyansty, chefs of the imperial palaces prepared six gigantic woks of porridge. Each wok contained over 50 kilograms of grains and nuts, and was cooked throughout the night. Porridge from the first wok was offered to the Buddha. The second wok was for the imperial family and the most important officials of the court. The third, fourth, and fifth woks were given to other officials. The leftovers, along with the sixth wok, were taken out of the Forbidden City and given to the common people. Temples were given special grants of grains and nuts in order to prepare the porridge for the festival. It was an occasion to showcase imperial generosity.

Due to the belief that its origin was intertwined with his enlightenment, people believed that laba porridge also brought on the blessing of the Buddha. Buddhist devotees at Hangzhou's famous Tianning Temple gave the dish a suitable auspicious name – the porridge of fortune and longevity, or the porridge of fortune and virtue.

Ordinary people did not always use the same ingredients as the imperial family when they prepared laba porridge for themselves, and besides offering to Buddha and the ancestors, it was also shared with friends and neighbors. One rule associated with this practice was that it must be dished out before noon. Cats, dogs, chickens and even pigs were given a portion. A Beijing nursery rhyme goes "Laba grains, laba porridge, chickens lay eggs after taking porridge." Possibly the most unusual tradition was to paste a small portion of porridge on trees and plants in order for them to grow strong and bear fruit in the coming year. Also, if a family had experienced the death of a close relative in the past three years, they would not prepare the porridge. Perhaps the most fortunate people of the Laba Festival were the grain-store owners, who used to make a small fortune from charging higher rates for mixed grains.

Porridge is not the only specialty food enjoyed during the Laba Festival. In rural Anhui Province, in the south of China, beans are ground and bean curd is made. This is known as laba bean curd. In northern China, especially in Beijing, laba garlic is preserved to use as a side dish to dumplings. Cloves of garlic are sealed into a jar of vinegar and stored in a cool place on the eighth day of the twelfth lunar month. By the Spring Festival, which is still more than three weeks away, the garlic turns a jade green color. It is then ready to be served.

The Laba Festival is actually the prelude to the Spring Festival celebrations. According to custom, on the Laba Festival people begin to prepare food to be consumed during the Spring Festival, the most important holiday in the Chinese lunar calendar. Preparation in rural areas might include butchering a pig, preserving meat with spices, making bean curd, and steaming buns as staples. Another nursery rhyme goes: "Old lady, enjoy your laba porridge for now, and don't crave goodies; soon after Laba is New Year, and you will get more treats." Although the Laba Festival is no longer linked to Buddhism, it still leads into Chinese New Year celebrations.

生词 New Words

1.年终	niánzhōng	the end of the year
2.祭祀	jìsì	to offer sacrifices to gods or ancestors
3.风调雨顺	fēngtiáo-yǔshùn	good weather for crops; favorable weather
4.久而久之	jiǔ'érjiǔzhī	in the course of time; with the lapse of time
5.日益	rìyì	day by day; increasingly
6.废除	fèichú	to abolish, to abrogate
7.解脱	jiětuō	to free (or extricate) oneself
8.毅然	yìrán	resolutely, firmly
9.出家	chūjiā	to renounce the family (to become a monk or nun)
10.修行	xiūxíng	to practice Buddhism or Taoism
11.奔波	bēnbō	to rush about; to be busy running about
12.名山大川	míngshān-dàchuān	famous mountains and great rivers
13.盘腿	pán tuǐ	to cross one's legs
14.菩提树	pútíshù	papal; bodhi tree
15.大彻大悟	dàchè-dàwù	to fully recognize the truth; to come to understand thoroughly
16.黄米	huángmǐ	glutinous millet
17.江米	jiāngmǐ	polished glutinous rice
18.小米	xiǎomǐ	millet
19.枣泥	zǎoní	jujube paste
20.桃仁	táorén	walnut
21.杏仁	xìngrén	almond
22.瓜子	guāzǐ	sunflower seed; melon seed
23.松子	sōngzǐ	pine nut

24.碳水化合物	tànshuǐ huàhéwù	carbohydrate
25.蛋白质	dànbáizhì	protein
26.脂肪	zhīfáng	fat
27.莲子	liánzǐ	lotus seed
28.高血压	gāoxuèyā	high blood pressure
29.免疫	miǎnyì	immunity
30.元老	yuánlǎo	senior statesman
31.王公大臣	wánggōng dàchén	princes, dukes and ministers
32.封疆大吏	fēngjiāng dàlì	general name for high provincial officials
33.保佑	bǎoyòu	to bless and protect
34.街坊邻里	jiēfang línlǐ	neighbors
35.童谣	tóngyáo	children's folk rhymes
36.守制	shǒuzhì	to observe the prescribed period of mourning for one's deceased parent
37.吉祥	jíxiáng	luck; auspicious
38.翡翠	fěicuì	jadeite (a mineral)
39.碧玉	bìyù	jasper
40.序幕	xùmù	prologue

语法聚焦

一、元明之后，腊祭日益不被人们所重视

“日益”是副词，意思是“一天比一天更……”，一般用于书面语。

Often used in written Chinese, adverb 日益 means day by day. For example:

1. 这些年来，他的艺术日益趋向成熟。
2. 随着国民经济的发展，人民生活日益改善。
3. 由于他们沟通得不够，彼此间的矛盾日益加深。

二、佛祖因而得救

“因而”是连词，它表示因上文的原因或理由，引出了下文的结果或推论。它用于因果复句的后分句的句首。

Conjunction 因而 links the reason in the first clause and the outcome or conclusion in the second one. It is put at the beginning of the second clause of a cause and effect sentence. For example:

1. 孟江虚心好学，努力钻研，因而技术水平提高得很快。
2. 老宋寄出的信多，因而收到的信也多。
3. 大家觉得有个组织更能增进友谊，加强交流，因而成立了教师协会。

三、做粥的用料也越来越讲究

“越来越”是从“越……越……”发展来的固定格式。它表示某种情况在程度上，随着时间的推移而逐步加深，在句中作状语。

越来越 as a fixed pattern indicates something increases or develops over time. For example:

1. 天气越来越暖和了。
2. 这个学生的中文说得越来越好。
3. 这些科研成果发挥越来越大的作用。

四、人们除了用粥供佛祀祖外，还馈赠给亲朋好友、街坊邻里

“除了……（以）外”可以表示在已知的以外还有别的，也可以表示不计算在内。

除了…(以)外 means in addition to or except for. For example:

1. 这个地区除了一些大学以外，还有很多科研单位。
2. 吴太太除了会英语外，还会法语和德语。
3. 除了小赵以外，别人都去过桂林。
4. 除了妇女和孩子以外，别人都去抗险救灾了。

五、就是院内的果树花卉，也涂抹一点

这里的“就是”是连词，表示一种极端的情况，有“甚至”的意思。它后面常有“也”相呼应。

Conjunction 就是 introduces an extreme situation, meaning even. 也 usually follows it. For example:

1. 就是小学生，也能回答这个问题。
2. 这件复制品足以乱真，就是专家也难以鉴别。
3. 就是一些年老体弱的人，也来给他送行。

想一想 Questions

1. 中国的腊八粥是一种什么样的食品?
   What kind of food is the porridge eaten on the eighth day of the twelfth lunar month?
2. 你知道腊八粥的起源吗?
   Do you know the origin of this particular porridge?
3. 请说一个你的国家与民间习俗有关的童谣。
   Do you know a Chinese or foreign rhyme about folk custom?

超级链接 Super Links

在民间流传着一个与腊八粥有关故事：

从前，有一户人家。老两口只有一个儿子，自然爱如掌上明珠。两位老人整日辛勤劳作，早起晚睡地耕田种地。可是他们的儿子长大以后，非常懒惰，娶了个媳妇更是好吃懒做。两个人整日待在家中，过着饭来张口、衣来伸手的日子。老两口心中很是忧虑，他们感到自己一年比一年老了，将不久于人世。有一天，他们把儿子和媳妇叫到面前说：“我们已经年纪大了，不知道哪一天就要离开你们，有一句话你们一定要记住，‘谁家烟囱先冒烟，谁家高粱先红尖’”这话的意思是，谁家能起得早，谁家的庄稼就会长得好。不久，两位老人相继去世。可他们的儿子和媳妇根本没有把老人的话放在心上，依然故我，整天吃着爸爸妈妈为他们积攒下来的粮食。这样过了半年，不觉来到了冬季。一天傍晚，媳妇又去仓中拿米，发现粮食所剩无几，米缸也已见底。这一天正是腊月初八，天气异常寒冷。他们将缸中的剩米小心地拢起，将地上残留的豆子一点点捡起，就这样东捡捡，西凑凑，终于找到了一些杂粮。二人只好熬了一点粥。当他们捧着热乎乎、香喷喷的粥时，想起了爸妈的话“谁家烟囱先冒烟，谁家高粱先红尖”，这时，他们才真正明白了这句话的含义，心中很是悔恨。二人从此痛定思痛，每天早起晚睡，辛勤耕种，第二年秋天果然获得了丰收。

中华姓名杂谈

Surnames and Given Names

12

A Kaleidoscope of Chinese Culture

在中国，姓是表示有共同血缘关系的家族符号。为什么叫“姓”？班固说：“姓者，生也。人禀天气所以生者也。”许慎在《说文解字》中说：“姓，人所生也。”可见古代中国人是把姓与生育连在一起的。

中国有多少个姓呢？2007年8月16日，中国教育部和国家语委发布了《2006年中国语言生活状况报告》。通过2006年调查，全国姓氏有2.3万个，其中129个姓氏占总人口的87%。另外，根据抽样调查，在汉族姓氏中，占汉族人口二分之一以上的大姓有19个，它们是：王、李、张、刘、陈、杨、赵、黄、周、吴、徐、孙、胡、朱、高、林、何、郭、马。这与民间所说的“张王李赵遍地刘”很接近。

中国人的姓氏可分为单姓、复姓和极少的三字姓、四字姓。单姓占绝大多数，复姓在历史文献中出现过的有300多个，但沿用至今的大概只有几十个了，如：欧阳、司徒、端木、上官、诸葛等。至于三字姓和四字姓则少之又少，曾收录的有：朱可浑、步六孤、侯莫陈、井疆六氏等。另外，还有一些十分罕见的姓氏，如：死、难、黑、老、毒、妈、子、镜、蚋等。英美人也有一些罕见的姓，如：Broomstick (扫帚把)、Coffin (棺材)、Poison (毒药) 等。

有这样一个笑话：在美国，有一个青年人到一所大学图书馆申请工作。图书馆长在面试他的时候，问他：“贵姓？” 他答道：“你猜。” 馆长听了，火冒三丈，生气地说：“对不起，我工作很忙，没有时间来猜你的姓。” 说完拂袖而去。实际上，这个青年人的名字叫威廉·你猜(Wiliam Yo-gess) 。这份工作当然也就丢掉了。

在中国记录姓氏的典籍中，最为人熟知的是《百家姓》。此书是北宋初年编写的，共收姓494个，其中单姓434个，复姓60个。因为是宋朝人编的，所以宋朝皇帝的姓自然放在第一位，全书开头是：“赵钱孙李”。明朝人又编了一本《皇明千家姓》，自然把当朝皇帝的朱姓放在了第一名，开头是：“朱奉天运”。清朝皇帝亲自审定了一本《御制百家姓》，为了表示尊重儒家思想，故将孔子的姓放在了第一位，开篇第一句是：“孔师阙党”。可见编书谈姓，不那么简单，这里有文化政治问题。

关于中国人的姓氏的起源大致有十几大类，以图腾为姓：龙、云、熊、马；以封爵为姓：王、侯、伯；以国为姓：齐、鲁、韩、秦；以官职为姓：司马、太史、帅、尉；以职业为姓：卜、陶、巫、乐，等等，不一而足。英美人的姓氏来源也是多方面的，像以职业为姓：Tailor (裁缝)、Carpenter (木匠)、Smith (铁匠)等；以居住地为姓:York、Kent等；以地形地貌为姓: Hill (小丘)、Moor (荒野)、Lake (湖泊)等。

在中国，一个人除了姓之外还有名，姓是用来区别宗族血统，而名字是用来区别个人的。中国人对名字非常重视。许多老年人甚至认为，“赐子千金，不如教子一艺；教子一艺，不如赐子好名。”这种重视名字的现象与中国文化的关系极为密切，它反映了中国人的文化心理、道德传统、价值取向、爱好志趣等，而且带有明显的时代印迹，反映了不同时代的文化特征。上古时，人们用自己生日的干支作为名字，如：祖更、外丙等；魏晋南北朝时，因为受佛教影响，人名中出现了僧、昙、佛、法等；明清以后，按字排辈、以族谱名更为盛行，乾隆皇帝还为孔氏宗族赐过30个辈分用字，就很具有代表性，它们是：

希、言、公、彦、承，宏、闻、贞、尚、衍、兴、毓、传、继、广，昭、宪、庆、繁、祥、令、德、维、垂、佑，钦、绍、念、显、扬。

到了近代，人们的名字也随着时代的变迁而变化。如，男人名字有的取“建功立业”之意，如：邦、国、雄、良、栋等；有的取“发财致富”之意，如：财、贵、富、禄等；有的取“健康长寿”之意，如：龄、康、寿、鹤等，还有的取“美好道德情操”之意，如：忠、孝、仁、义等字眼。中国女人的名字往往要体现出“阴柔而美”的审美取向，所以有的以花草命名，如：芝、兰、莲、梅等；有的以鸟命名，如：凤、燕、鹃、鸾等；有的以闺中饰物命名，如：钗、钏、珠、环等；还有的以女人美德命名，如：贤、淑、静、贞等。英美国家女人的名字与中国一样，也采用一些典雅优美的词语，如：Lily (百合花)、Rose (玫瑰花)、Diana (源于希腊语，月亮女神)、Susan (源于希伯来语，优雅亲切)、Helen (源于希腊语，迷人的) 等。可见，人们对女性的审美要求和价值取向是比较相似的。

在现代中国人的姓名中，以单字为名特别多，很多人叫王静、刘伟、王涛，北京市叫“刘冰”的就有3000多个。另外，叠字名也大量存在，如：圆圆、毛毛、明明、菲菲等。近年来，人们开始追求名字的个性化。2007年8月16日，中国教育部和国家语委在发布《2006年中国语言生活状况报告》时，负责人就谈到，中国人的姓名结构逐渐发生变化，四个字以上的名字越来越多，还出现了“赵一A”、“奥斯锐娜王”等极端个性化名字。更有意思的是，有个孩子的名字叫@，家长解释说，全世界写电子邮件都用它，和汉语的发音“爱他”很相似。当然，起什么名字是个人的喜好和权利，好的个性化名字，会使人耳目一新、过目不忘，但极端个性化的名字，恐怕就会得不偿失。

中国人的名字有丰富的文化内涵，有时与人们的联想相结合，可以产生荣辱效应。清乾隆时，进士秦涧泉与友人同游杭州岳飞坟时，看见秦桧等四个佞臣的铁像跪在坟前，友人问他有何感想，他久久不语，后来说出一副对联：“人从宋后羞名桧，我到坟前愧姓秦”。此话不谬，在中国很少有人以“桧”为名，好端端的一个“桧”字，因为负载了“秦桧”这个人的信息，使人避之如虎。名字不仅能产生荣辱效应，而且在机缘巧合下，还能跟个人的前途命运联系在一起，搞好了能升官发财，搞不好就要倒霉了。清朝同治年间，有一个叫王国钧的人，会试考中了，殿试进了前十名，可当时垂帘听政的慈禧太后一听他的名字叫王国钧，马上联想到“亡国”、“亡君”，一下子把他从前十名降为三甲。他本来可以进翰林院的，结果成了榜下知县。这位王知县懊悔不已，将名字改为王颂平，想拍拍太后的马屁，但为时已晚。还有一个例子是中国末代状元刘春霖，他凭借一个好名字得以飞黄腾达，据说他参加科考那年适逢大旱，慈禧曾在宫中率人祈雨。太后一见“春霖”这个名字，甚是欢喜，于是他被点中状元。仅仅因姓名，王国钧与刘春霖的人生境遇，便有了天壤之别。此虽为历史趣事，但由此可见，中国人喜欢把名字同一定的含义、形象联系在一起。

In China, a surname is symbolic of blood relations. A clan or family has the same surname. The character for surname in Chinese is 姓 (*xing*). According to Ban Gu, historian and literary writer in the Eastern Han Dynasty, and Xu Shen, the author of *Explanations of Scripts and Elucidation of Characters*, 姓 means being born. Thus the understanding of ancient Chinese people was that the surname was intrinsically linked to reproduction and birthright.

How many surnames are there in China? According to *Language Situation in China 2006*, the latest official report by the Ministry of Education and the National Languages Committee, in total there are 23,000 in use. However a mere 129 names account for 87% of the population. The survey also revealed that the 19 most popular are Wang (王), Li (李), Zhang (张), Liu (刘), Chen (陈), Yang (杨), Zhao (赵), Huang (黄), Zhou (周), Wu (吴), Xu (徐), Sun (孙), Hu (胡), Zhu (朱), Gao (高), Lin (林), He (何), Guo (郭), and Ma (马). The results are consistent with what is widely believed to be the most popular names. The five most common are Zhang (张), Wang (王), Li (李), Zhao (赵), and Liu (刘).

The vast majority of Chinese surnames consist of only one character, however there are also surnames comprised of two, three, or even four. Throughout history more than three hundred surnames with two or more characters have appeared. Those with three or four characters, such as Zhu-ke-hun (朱可浑), Bu-liu-gu (步六孤), Hou-mo-chen (侯莫陈), or Jing-jiang-liu-shi (井疆六氏) sound very strange and are not in use anymore. There are also a few dozen surnames with two characters still used today, including Ou-yang (欧阳), Si-tu (司徒), Duan-mu (端木), Shang-guang (上官), Zhu-ge (诸葛). Interestingly, in both the Chinese mainland and Taiwan there also exist a few extremely odd surnames, such as 死 (*si*, dying), 难 (*nan*, difficult), 老 (*lao*, old), 黑 (*hei*, black), 毒 (*du*, poisonous), 妈 (*ma*, mom), 子 (*zi*, son), 镜 (*jing*, mirror), 蚋 (*rui*, mosquito). Of course, English also has its share of interesting surnames, such as Broomstick, Coffin and Poison.

There is a joke about one particular English name. In the US, a young man went to apply for a job at a university library. At the interview the chief librarian asked, "What's you name, please?" "You guess," said the man. The librarian was irritated and said, "I am very busy and have no time to guess your name!" He then stopped the interview and went away, and the poor young man was unable to get the job. The fact is that the young man was named William Yo-gess.

The most famous historical text regarding surnames is *The Collection of a Hundred Surnames*. Compiled in the Song Dynasty, this book records 494 names, of which 434 consist of one character and 60 consist of two characters. Understandably, the surname of the emperor of this dynasty is mentioned first – Zhao Qian Sun Li (赵钱孙李). In *The Collection of a Thousand Surnames* from the Ming Dynasty, the emperor's surname, Zhu (朱), is used in the first sentence of the book. This sentence translates as "The Zhu family inherits the blessing of heaven." However, in *The Collection of Surnames Approved by the Emperor of Qing*, the first name mentioned is that of Confucius, or Kong (孔), to show the emperor's respect for Confucius. The collections of names in different dynasties all were subject to the socio-political and cultural background of the times.

The origins of surnames fall into more than a dozen categories. 1. Some are inspired by certain historical tattoos, including Long (龙, dragon), Yun (云, cloud), Xiong (熊, bear), and Ma (马, horse). 2. There are those inspired by noble titles, including Wang (王, king), Hou (侯, marquis), and Bo (伯, earl). 3. Others are taken from the names of ancient states, including Qi (齐), Lu (鲁), Han (韩), and Qin (秦). 4. Some are from feudal titles, such as Si-ma (司马, a high military official), Tai-shi (太史, a high civil official), Shuai (帅, general), and Wei (尉, military officer). 5. Still others come from job titles, such as Bu (卜, fortune-telling), Tao (陶, pottery), Wu (巫, sorcery teacher), or Yue (乐, music).

These origins of names are not unique to China – English names also often come from job titles, such as Taylor, Carpenter or Smith, or place names such as York or Kent, or even natural formations such as Hill, Moor or Lake.

Surname is symbolic of blood relations and given name is more individual and personal. Chinese people have traditionally attached a great deal of significance to how they name a child. There is a proverb that says "To help children learn a skill is better than to pass wealth on to them, but to give a good name to children is better than to help them learn a skill." Given names reflect the cultural psychology, ethical traditions, values, aspirations and interests of Chinese people. As a result, popular names have varied with changing events in history.

For example, far back in pre-Buddhist times, people often used two characters that stood for the Heavenly Stem and the Earthly Branch at the time of one's birth, such as 祖更, 外丙. However, by the period of the Wei, Jin and Southern and Northern dynasties, due to the fact Buddhism had become widespread, people began to choose names with this philosophy's overtones.

It has only become common since the Ming and Qing dynasties that each generation share a common character as the first one of two-character names, and for the common characters for different generations to be recorded in the clan's genealogy. The first character of given names of 30 generations of Confucius' descendants was actually granted by Emperor Qianlong in the Qing Dynasty. They include: 希, 言, 公, 彦, 承, 宏, 闻, 贞, 尚, 衍, 兴, 毓, 传, 继, 广, 昭, 宪, 庆, 繁, 祥, 令, 德, 维, 垂, 佑, 钦, 绍, 念, 显, 扬.

Preference towards given names has changed over time, but generally speaking, male names are slanted toward the pursuit of fame and fortune, a healthy and long life, and virtues such as loyalty and responsibility. Female names show more of a tendency toward beauty, as reflected in names of flowers such as lotus and plum, birds such as phoenix or swallow, and jewelry such as pearl. Female names in both western and eastern culture have similar connotations of beauty and what were considered suitable aspirations of the female gender. There are many such names in English, including Lily, Rose, Diana, Susan and Helen.

Due to the fact the most popular surnames and given names in China today are taken by millions of people, and most names are normally only two characters long, many people share names. Some of these names include Wang Jing (王静), Liu Wei (刘伟), and Wang Tao (王涛). In Beijing alone there are over 3,000 people named Liu Bin (刘冰). There are also many given names with repeated characters, such as Yuanyuan (圆圆), Maomao (毛毛), Mingming (明明), or Feifei (菲菲).

Recently, people have developed more of a preference for unique individual names. At the launch of *The Language Situation in China 2006,* the spokesman noted that the structure of Chinese names has gradually changed. Names of four or more characters have appeared, along with other unusual attributes such as including letters of the English alphabet, as in the case of Zhao Yi A (赵一A). Another unusual one is Ao Si Rui Na Wang (奥斯锐娜王), which is not only five characters long but also sounds like the transliteration of a foreign name. One other child, a product of the dotcom generation no doubt, was given the name @. Although this sounds quite crazy to a westerner, his parents like the fact it is part of email addresses and also, it sounds like 爱他 (*ai ta*), meaning love him in Chinese. Given names reflect personal individual tastes. A nice one will stand out and be remembered, but an awkward one will leave people with a bad impression.

Names have rich cultural implications. Some names possess a sense of honor or glory, some a sense of disgrace, and others a sense of luck, good or bad. As such, stories attached to names are numerous, varied, and can be extremely fascinating.

During the reign of the Qing Dynasty's Emperor Qianlong, a highly regarded scholar named Qin Jianquan went sightseeing with a friend in Hangzhou. By the West Lake, they came across the tomb of Yue Fei, an honorable military leader from the Southern Song Dynasty. However although Yue Fei had been a brave soldier, his life had ended in tragedy and he was killed by a gang of treacherous officials led by Qin Hui (秦桧). At his tomb, where Qin Jianquan and his friend now stood, were kneeling statues of those treacherous officials. Upon seeing this, Qin Jianquan appeared lost in thought. When his friend asked him what he was thinking about, Qin Jianquan spoke two lines:

The given name Hui has not been used since the Song Dynasty,

I feel guilty to have the surname Qin while standing at the tomb of Yue Fei.

Indeed, there are very few people who use this particular given name 桧, because of its association with the treacherous Qin Hui.

Another story tells the contrasting fates of two scholars. During the reign of Qing Dynasty's Emperor Tongzhi, Wang Guojun passed both the metropolitan examination and the palace examination, and could be admitted to the Imperial Academy. However, the Empress Dowager did not like his name, because it sounds like the demise of the country and the emperor. As a result, he was immediately demoted to a lowly official rank, county magistrate. Wang changed his name with the aim to flatter the Empress Dowager, but it was already too late. Another participant, with the name Liu Chunlin, was awarded first place in the last metropolitan examination of the Qing Dynasty, and given a high-ranking position by the Empress Dowager Cixi because his name sounds like spring rain. At that particular time, the Empress Dowager was praying for some rain to relieve drought, and Liu Chunlin became a lucky man because of his name.

生词 New Words

1.杂谈	zátán	fragmentary writing
2.血缘	xuèyuán	ties of blood; blood relation
3.调查	diàochá	survey; to investigate
4.抽样	chōuyàng	sampling
5.历史文献	lìshǐ wénxiàn	historical documents
6.罕见	hǎnjiàn	seldomly seen; rare
7.典籍	diǎnjí	ancient codes and records; ancient books and records
8.皇帝	huángdì	emperor
9.开头	kāitóu	beginning, start
10.起源	qǐyuán	to originate; to stem from
11.图腾	túténg	totem
12.官职	guānzhí	government post; official position
13.职业	zhíyè	occupation, profession, vocation
14.不一而足	bùyī'érzú	no isolated case
15.宗族	zōngzú	patriarchal clan; clansman
16.道德	dàodé	morals, ethics
17.价值	jiàzhí	value, worth
18.志趣	zhìqù	aspiration and interest
19.印迹	yìnjì	trace, mark
20.发财致富	fācái zhìfù	to get rich; to make a fortune
21.闺中	guīzhōng	lady's chamber; boudoir
22.饰物	shìwù	jewelry; articles for personal adornment
23.个性	gèxìng	individual character; individuality
24.耳目一新	ěrmù-yìxī	to find everything fresh and new

25.得不偿失	débùchángshī	the loss outweighing the gain
26.荣辱	róngrǔ	honor or disgrace
27.效应	xiàoyìng	effect
28.佞臣	nìngchén	a sycophantic official or courtier
29.巧合	qiǎohé	coincidence
30.升官发财	shēngguān-fācái	to win promotion and get rich
31.倒霉	dǎoméi	to have bad luck; to be out of luck
32.会试	huìshì	the metropolitan examination held triennially in Beijing under the Ming Qing civil service examination system
33.殿试	diànshì	the palace examination (the final imperial examination, presided over by the emperor)
34.垂帘听政	chuílián tīngzhèng	(of an empress regent) to sit behind a screen to receive ministerial reports; to hold court from behind a screen
35.太后	tàihòu	mother of an emperor; empress dowager
36.一下子	yíxiàzi	in a short while; all at once; all of a sudden
37.翰林院	hànlínyuàn	the Imperial Academy (in feudal China)
38.知县	zhīxiàn	(in former time) county magistrate
39.懊悔	àohuǐ	to feel remorse; to regret
40.拍马屁	pāi mǎpì	to lick sb.'s boots; to flatter; to soft-soap
41.末代	mòdài	the last reign of a dynasty
42.飞黄腾达	fēihuáng-téngdá	to make rapid advances in one's career; to have a meteoric rise
43.适逢	shìféng	to happen to be present at the right moment (or on the occasion)
44.大旱	dàhàn	drought
45.祈雨	qí yǔ	to pray for rain
46. 天壤之别	tiānrǎngzhībié	as far apart as heaven and earth

语法聚焦 Notes and Examples

一、中国人的姓氏可分为单姓、复姓和极少的三字姓、四字姓

这里的“可”是能愿动词，相当于“可以”。它表示主、客观条件允许做某事。

可 in this context is a modal verb, same as 可以, meaning can or to be able to. For example:

1. 这本小说，我一天便可看完。
2. 可开可不开的会，就不要开。
3. 这个城市可参观的景点非常多。

二、至于三字姓和四字姓则少之又少

这里的“至于”是连词，它连接前后有类属联系的并列两部分，表示引起另一话题，把意思推进一步。

Conjunction 至于, connects the first clause with the second, introducing another topic and furthering the meaning. For example:

1. 我只知道他是一位科学家，至于他研究什么我就不清楚了。
2. 这件事应该办，至于什么时候办，大家可以商量。
3. 高长河决定去国外深造，至于去哪个国家，他还没定下来。

三、三字姓和四字姓则少之又少

“则”是连词，表示对比关系，有转折的意思，相当于“却”。

则 is a conjunction indicating contrast. For example:

1. 现在南方水涝成灾，北方则久旱不雨。
2. 这篇文章虽长，内容则很丰富。
3. 文教授是一位夫子型学者，不喜欢唱歌跳舞，他的太太则不同，是文娱活跃分子。

四、关于中国人的姓氏的起源大致有十几大类

“大致”是副词，表示一种约略的情况，意思与“大体上”差不多。

Adverb 大致, same as 大体上, means largely, more or less, and approximately. For example:

1. 这份计划我大致看了一下，我觉得还可以。
2. 我们对会议议程大致作了安排。
3. 公司的情况大致就这些，以后您可以慢慢了解。

五、赐子千金，不如教子一艺

“不如”是动词，表示比较，指前面谈到的事比不上后面所说的。

不如 means no better than, indicating a comparison that the former is no better than the latter. For example:

1. 借别人字典用，不如自己买一本。
2. 论技术，你不如牛师傅。
3. 爷爷的身体不如从前了。
4. 真是百闻不如一见。

六、中国女人的名字往往要体现出“阴柔而美”的审美取向

“往往”是副词，表示某种情况时常存在或经常发生。

Adverb 往往 means often, always, and frequently. For example:

1. 这里的春天往往刮很大的风。
2. 问题往往出在你不注意的时候。
3. 他的设计稿往往要修改几十遍。

七、搞好了能升官发财

“搞”原来是一个方言词，现在已经变成普通话常用词，代替许多动词，有“干”、“做”、“弄”等意思。

搞 is a word from certain dialects, but now frequently used in Mandarin Chinese in the place of many verbs, meaning to do. For example:

1. 我爸爸搞文艺工作几十年了。
2. 这件事搞不好要出大问题的。
3. 你们一定要搞清楚，这到底是谁的责任。

八、一下子把他从前十名降为三甲

“一下子”是副词，表示某种动作发生、完成得迅速，或某种现象出现得突然。

一下子 is an adverb meaning in a short while, all at once or all of a sudden. For example:

1. 我恨不得一下子就能学好中文。
2. 他的脸一下子吓白了。
3. 王大爷一下子就明白了这个年轻人的意思。

九、太后一见“春霖”这个名字，甚是欢喜

“甚”是文言虚词，用于书面语，表示程度很高。

甚, originally a function word in classical Chinese, is an adverb, meaning very. It is more used in written language. For example:

1. 用老办法去做，收效甚微。
2. 老兄建议甚好，定当照办。
3. 令郎几年来进步甚快，令人刮目。

想一想 Questions

1. 中国有多少个姓?
   How many surnames are there in China?
2. 中国人的姓氏起源有哪些?
   What are the origins of Chinese surnames?
3. 中国人的名字有什么特点?
   What kinds of features do Chinese names have?
4. 你能说出几个中国人名字的意思吗?
   Can you tell a few Chinese names and explain their meanings?

超级链接 Super Links

辈分用字

同一血缘姓氏中，同一辈分人的名字中都有一个相同的字，以此区分家族、亲友之间的世袭次第。辈分用字一般由本家族长辈或有一定社会地位的文臣儒士精心编排，确定后很少更改。例如，孔氏宗族中，人们就按这种方式起名，不仅为了区分个人在家族中的辈分，而且还有训导子孙发奋向上、光耀门庭之意。

中国百家姓最新排名次序

2007年4月24日，中国公安部公布了中国百家姓的最新排名。根据公安部治安管理局对全国户籍人口的统计分析，王姓是中国第一姓，有9288.1万人，占全国人口总数的7.25%；中国第二姓是李姓，有9207.4万人，占全国人口总数的7.19%；第三位是张姓，有8750.2万人，占全国人口总数的6.83%。这新百家姓的次序是：

王 李 张 刘 陈 杨 黄 赵 吴 周

徐 孙 马 朱 胡 郭 何 高 林 罗

郑 梁 谢 宋 唐 许 韩 冯 邓 曹

彭 曾 萧 田 董 袁 潘 于 蒋 蔡

余 杜 叶 程 苏 魏 吕 丁 任 沈

姚 卢 姜 崔 钟 谭 陆 汪 范 金

石 廖 贾 夏 韦 付 方 白 邹 孟

熊 秦 邱 江 尹 薛 阎 段 雷 侯

龙 史 陶 黎 贺 顾 毛 郝 龚 邵

万 钱 严 覃 武 戴 莫 孔 向 汤

汉语外来词与文化交流

Loanwords in Chinese and Cultural Exchanges

13

A Kaleidoscope of Chinese Culture

在中国有一个家喻户晓的外来词叫“可口可乐”，它是美国饮料Coca-Cola的中文名字。有意思的是，这个中文名字的发音与英文Coca-Cola极为相近，而中文意思却是“可口美味，饮而生乐”。正是这种音与意完美地结合，成功地帮助可口可乐在中国打开了市场。汉语吸收外来词并非改革开放以来的事情，而是自古就有，人们对外来语进行改造，使其逐步成为中华民族语言不可或缺的一部分。

世界上各个民族绝不是孤立地存在于世界之上的，各民族间总是处于彼此接触和相互交流之中。两种文化或多种文化的互相影响，互相渗透，突出地反映在语言上，就是外来词现象。也就是说，一种语言不管口语也好，书面语也好，它总是在各种交流中，吸收其他语言的词汇，并加以改造，使其适应本民族的语言特点。就拿英语来说，它既吸收了拉丁语的一些词汇，同时也吸收了法语的一些词汇，逐渐丰富和发展起来。

中国是一个多民族的国家，也是一个历史悠久的古国。在中华民族与其他民族长期相处之中，伴随着文化交流，汉语也吸收了大量的外来词。历史上对中国文化产生过重大影响的外来文化有中亚文化、印度佛教文化和近代欧美、日本文化。不同文化的交流，都给汉语带来了为数众多的外来词。不过汉语外来词大多数是经过改造后融入中国语言中的，这符合中国人的语言习惯。

公元前2世纪，汉武帝派张骞两次出使西域。据有关史料记载，张骞曾到达西域地区的大宛、大月氏、大夏、康居等国。张骞通西域在历史上产生了极为深远的影响，他开辟了中国汉朝与西域各国的经济、文化交流。他不仅把中国的丝绸、布帛等物品带到了这些地方，而且从西域各国带回了一些蔬菜和水果，从此以后，西域各国的使节和商人也纷纷来到中国，彼此建立了友好交往。当这些新的物品从西域传进中国时，人们便面临着一个汉语翻译问题，也就是如何给这些新事物定名。最初，汉语也像其他语言一样，采用了直接翻译的方法，即用一些与此物原音相同或相近的汉字进行对译，于是出现了目宿、蒲陶、流离、虎魄、师子、橐驼、批把等词语。这种直接音译法，固然反映了这些事物本来的名称，但不符合汉语的表述习惯。因为汉字本身既表音又表意，如果单取其音，弃其意不顾，不容易被大众接受。于是人们在汉字上动了脑筋，利用汉字偏旁部首表示事物种类的特点，把它们写成了苜蓿、葡萄、琉璃、琥珀、狮子、骆驼、琵琶等。这样，从这些字的偏旁中，便可清楚地判断它们的属性。这种方法也被后来汉语吸收外来词时所采用，其中比较突出的例子，就是对门捷列夫元素周期表的翻译。这些元素对当时的人们来说是完全陌生的，于是用这种音意结合的造字方法，轻松地解决了对元素类别和属性的认识。属于金属类的，就写成金字旁；属于气体类的，就写成气字头；属于矿石类的，就写成石字旁。于是，这些外来词便很顺利地转化成了汉语词汇。

在张骞出使西域的时代，人们在吸收外来词时，还采用了在中国某种原有事物的前边加一“胡”字的方法，以表示此物非中国所产，如：胡桃、胡葱、胡麻、胡豆、胡琴、胡瓜、胡荽、胡床等，后三种又逐渐演变成黄瓜、芫荽和交椅，已看不出是外来物了。这种方法也同样被后来人使用，如把“胡”字改为“西”、“番”、“洋”字，或干脆用来源地的名字，如：西红柿、西瓜、番薯、洋火、洋油、洋烟卷、荷兰豆、吕宋烟等。这些事物虽然都是来自他国，但是它们的名字不管是发音还是意义都与原语言没有关系了，可见，对外来事物的名字进行改造和再创造，使之成为新造词，是中国人吸收外来文化的一种方式。

佛教的传入是中国文化史上一件大事。它自汉朝传入中国以后，对中国历史文化、社会生活产生了极其重大的影响。佛经的传入和翻译，更是给汉语输入了大量外来词，而且汉语自身也由此创造出了不少新词语。一些本是佛教中的用语，今天已经成为中国人日常生活中的词汇，比如：世界、平等、绝对、实际、知识、现实、悲观、结果、刹那、觉悟、超脱、方便、信心、境界、智慧、圆满等；汉语中也有相当多的成语来源于佛教，例如：清规戒律、四大皆空、光明正大、生老病死、大慈大悲、心领神会、一尘不染、五体投地、功德无量、水中捞月、大千世界、超凡脱俗、慈悲为怀、弃暗投明、六根清净、皆大欢喜等；另外还有一些来自佛教的俗语、谚语和歇后语，如：跑了和尚跑不了庙，不看僧面看佛面，放下屠刀、立地成佛，平日不烧香、临时抱佛脚，善有善报、恶有恶报，泥菩萨过河——自身难保等。汉语从佛教吸收外来词还有些是直接音译，如：佛、劫波、浮屠、菩萨、袈裟、夜叉、罗汉、涅槃等，也有的采用音、意结合，如：辟支佛道、须陀恒道、阿鼻地狱等。

19世纪以来，欧美、日本文化进入中国，汉语随之出现了大量外来词，其中以来自英语和日语为主。开始时，人们往往采用音译法，如：德律风（电话）、士担（邮票）、开麦拉（照相机）、盘尼西林（青霉素）、梵婀玲（小提琴）、伯理玺天地（总统）、哀的美敦书（最后通牒）、巴力门（国会）等。这种音译外来词有的十分冗长拗口，使人费解难记，于是被意译或从被日语借用的一些汉字所代替。除此之外，还有“民主”代替了“德谟克拉西”，“科学”代替了“赛因斯”，“保险”代替了“燕梳”，“维生素”代替了“维他命”，“激光”代替了“莱塞”等。当然也有一些音译词一直被保留下来，如：沙发、咖啡、扑克、幽默、三明治、麦克风、逻辑等。

另外，人们还对一些音译词加以改造，在原音译词的后面加一个指示事物类别的名词，也就是指明了事物的属性，形成了音译加意译的造字方法，如：啤（beer）酒、坦克（tank）车、巧克力（chocolate）糖、沙丁（sardine）鱼、卡（card）片、高尔夫（golf）球、桑拿（sauna）浴、芭蕾（ballet）舞、吉普（jeep）车、香槟（champagne）酒、雪茄（cigar）烟等。

现代汉语不仅从西方语言中吸收了大量外来词，也从日语中吸收了很多词语。其中，有一些古汉语中的词，被现代日语用来翻译欧美语言中的词汇，之后又被现代汉语借用回来，如：文化、博士、法律、经济、环境等；另外，日本人用汉字造了一些新词，用来翻译西方书籍，这些词也被汉语借用回来，如：马铃薯、消防、美术、入场券、法人、瓦斯、混凝土、方针、政策等。

近年来中国实行了改革开放政策，人们在学习西方科学技术和进行各种交流中，更是吸收了大量的外来词，像bye-bye，goodbye，OK，cool等词，在汉语中大量出现。这些词不仅在城市知识阶层，就是在农村也不感到陌生。另外，近年来人们在吸收外来词时，也努力追求像“可口可乐”那样把音与意巧妙结合的方式，因此出现了百事可乐（Pepsi-Cola）、雪碧（Sprite）、香波（shampoo）、麦当劳（McDonald's）等词语。还有一些外文词加汉字或外文缩略词也直接进入了汉语之中，如：B超、T恤、AA制家庭、IP卡、MP3、卡拉OK、WTO、DVD、NBA等。

在汉语音译的外来词中，有些用方言音译的外来词也逐渐被其他地方所接受，例如："的士"是taxi的粤语音译，现在北京人也在使用。"的士"不仅成为汉语中的一词，而且由此又产生了一些新词语，如：坐出租车叫"打的"，出租车司机叫"的哥"，为出租车司机提供的快餐叫"的士快餐"，优秀出租车司机叫"的士明星"。另外还有一个字："吧"，它是由bar翻译而来，多被译做"酒吧"，可近年来又出现了各种各样的"吧"，像"玻璃吧"、"玩具吧"、"氧吧"、"布吧"、"陶吧"、"书吧"、"网吧"等。总之，人们愿意把一些休闲娱乐的场所叫做"吧"。

外来词是词汇中非常活跃的分子，它们伴着一个国家社会文化生活的发展而变化。中国人在赋予了外来词以新的面貌、新的内涵的同时，丰富了自身的语言，也为中国文化融合新事物、新概念、新思维等方面起到了积极作用。

The loanword 可口可乐 (*Kekou kele*), or Coca-Cola, is known to everyone in China. Not only does this word sound very similar to its English equivalent, it also has the very relevant and appropriate meaning of good taste and happy drinking. This intelligent combination of sound and meaning greatly assisted Coca-Cola's successful entry into the Chinese market.

The absorption of loanwords is not something new to China since the implementation of the opening up and reform policy, but a practice that began in ancient times. Words and expressions have long been imported and adapted, and become an integral part of the Chinese language.

The nations of the world do not live in isolation from one another. Through constant contact and exchange, different cultures have influenced each other throughout human history. A significant aspect of these influences is seen in the cross-pollination of languages, through the appearance of loanwords. It does not matter if the language is spoken or written, it will absorb words from other languages in the course of cross-cultural exchange and adapt them to original features. For example, English has absorbed numerous words from Latin and French, a process that has both altered the language and made it richer.

Over thousands of years Chinese has absorbed words from numerous languages and many disparate ethnic groups. Cultures that have made a linguistic impression on Chinese have been from Central Asia, India, and more recently Europe, America and Japan. These words have become an intrinsic part of the Chinese language, both linguistically and psychologically.

In the second century BC, the Wu Emperor of the Han Dynasty twice sent his envoy Zhang Qian on diplomatic missions to the west. Historical data shows that Zhang Qian went as far as Central Asia and Eastern Europe. His missions had far-reaching consequences, including opening up trade and cultural exchange between China and western lands. He took silk and cloth with him and returned with unfamiliar fruits and vegetables. As a result of his mission, diplomats and business people from western lands visited China with increasing frequency, and friendly cross-cultural exchange developed.

People thus had to find names for all the novel and unfamiliar goods pouring into the country. In the beginning, they used many awkward Chinese characters that imitated the pronunciations that the western people used for these strange goods. However, due to the way Chinese is structured, this method of incorporating new words was quite problematic.

Chinese is both phonographic and ideographic, and as such both the phonetic sound and the meaning of a word need to be taken into consideration to improve understanding. One clever method employed by Chinese people over time when forming new words was to add or change radicals that indicate sounds and thus create new words. In accordance with this method, when first introduced to Chinese clover was known as 目宿 (*muxu*). However, later it was altered to 苜蓿, because the radical 艹 indicates clover is a type of plant.

Lion was initially translated as 师子 (*shizi*), but later the radical 犭 for animals was added and it became 狮子. The same rule was followed when *The Periodic Table of the Chemical Elements* was translated into Chinese. The radical 钅 was added to the metal elements, the radical 气 was added to gases, and 石 was added to minerals. This method has been very effective in integrating these strange elements into Chinese.

During the time of Zhang Qian, many of the novel exotic goods that found their way to China had the character 胡 included in their names, to help indicate their foreign origins. Some examples of these are 胡桃 (a walnut foreign to the indigenous Chinese one), 胡葱 (shallot), 胡麻 (sesame), 胡豆 (legume), 胡琴 (western violin), 胡瓜 (cucumber), 胡荽 (coriander), and 胡床 (folding chair). Gradually, however, the Chinese words for cucumber, coriander, and folding chair were changed to 黄瓜, 芫荽 and 交椅, respectively, words that show no trace of their geographical origin.

Other characters besides 胡 that indicate an item is foreign are 西, 番, and 洋. Words such as 西红柿 (tomato), 西瓜 (watermelon), 番薯 (sweet potato), 洋火 (match), 洋油 (kerosene), 洋烟卷 (cigarette), 荷兰豆 (vegetable pea), and 吕宋烟 (Luzon cigar) are therefore not indigenous to China. Creating new words for goods imported into China has long been a way for the Chinese to assimilate aspects of foreign cultures.

The introduction of Buddhism in the Han Dynasty was a major cultural event in the history of China. A large number of loanwords as a result of the introduction and translation of the sutra appeared, and based on these loanwords new words were coined as well. Some expressions that evolved due to the introduction of Buddhism became expressions in daily life, such as 世界 (the world), 平等 (equality), 绝对 (absoluteness), 实际 (practicality), 知识 (knowledge), 现实 (reality), 悲观 (pessimism), 结果 (result), 刹那 (a brief moment), 觉悟 (consciousness), 超脱 (transcendence), 方便 (convenience), 信心 (confidence), 境界 (ambit), 智慧 (wisdom), and 圆满 (fulfillment).

There are also many idioms that have a Buddhist origin, including 清规戒律 (strict rules and commandments), 大慈大悲 (infinitely merciful), 心领神会 (to tacitly understand), 一尘不染 (stainless with no dust), 水中捞月 (to make vain efforts), 大千世界 (the boundless universe), 超凡脱俗 (to transcend secular affairs), 慈悲为怀 (leniency), 弃暗投明 (to forsake darkness for light), 苦海无边 (abyss of misery), 功德无量 (boundless beneficence), and many more.

From the 19th century onwards more and more loanwords have appeared, especially from English and Japanese. Initially transliteration was the most common method of absorbing these words into the language, such as with 德律风 (telephone), 士担 (stamp), 开麦拉 (camera), 盘尼西林 (penicillin), 梵婀玲 (violin), 伯理玺天地 (president), 哀的美敦书 (ultimatum), and 巴力门 (parliament). However these words were hard to understand, pronounce and remember. A new approach was needed. The meanings were translated, and some Japanese characters were incorporated to create the new Chinese words. Telephone then became known as 电话, stamp as 邮票, camera as 照相机, penicillin as 青霉素, violin as 小提琴, president as 总统, ultimatum as 最后通牒, and parliament as 国会. Similarly, the transliteration of democracy, 德谟克拉西 was replaced by 民主, science, 赛因斯 was replaced by 科学, insurance, 燕梳 by 保险, vitamin, 维他命 by 维生素 and laser, 莱塞 by 激光. However some transliterations remain in use today, including 沙发 (sofa), 咖啡 (coffee), 扑克 (poker), 幽默 (humor), 三明治 (sandwich), 麦克风 (microphone), 逻辑 (logic), etc..

In order to improve the inherent meaning of the transliteration, a noun is sometimes added. There are many examples of this type of word, including 啤 + 酒 = beer, 坦克 + 车 = tank, 巧克力 + 糖 = chocolate, 沙丁 + 鱼 = sardine, 卡 + 片 = card, 高尔夫 + 球 = golf, 桑拿 + 浴 = sauna, 芭蕾 + 舞 = ballet, 吉普 + 车 = jeep, 香槟 + 酒 = champagne, 雪茄 + 烟 = cigar.

Chinese has not only assimilated loanwords from western languages, but also from Japanese. A number of characters that were originally adopted by Japanese from Chinese came to be used in Japanese for adopted western words. Then, in a beautiful twist of cross-cultural exchange, some of these characters were imported back into Chinese. Some of these words are 文化 (culture), 博士 (doctor), 法律 (law), 经济 (economy), and 环境 (environment). New words were also formed in Japanese by using Chinese characters and subsequently came back into use in Chinese, including 马铃薯 (potato), 消防 (fire protection), 美术 (fine arts), 入场券 (admission ticket), 法人 (legal person), 瓦斯 (gas), 混凝土 (cement), 方针 (guideline), and 政策 (policy).

Following the opening up and reform policy, new loanwords such as bye-bye, goodbye, OK, and cool have begun to appear and become very popular. There are also many attempts at making transliterations suitable to Chinese in terms of the word's meaning. Some of the better combinations of sound and meaning, along with 可口可乐, are 百事可乐 (Pepsi-Cola), 雪碧 (Sprite), 香波 (shampoo), 麦当劳 (McDonald's).

On occasion, letters and acronyms are used by themselves or in conjunction with Chinese characters. Some examples of this are B超 (Ultrasonic B-scan), T恤 (T-shirt), AA制家庭 (AA family), IP卡 (IP card), MP3, 卡拉OK (Karaoke), WTO, DVD, and NBA.

Sometimes the characters used for loanwords are catalysts for the development of completely new words. One such loanword, 的士, is the transliteration of taxi in Cantonese, but became accepted as far away as Beijing. New offshoots of this word include 打的 meaning to take a taxi, 的哥 meaning male taxi driver, 的士明星, which means good taxi driver and 的士快餐, which is, intriguingly, taxi driver's fast food. Another commonly used transliteration that has followed this pattern is 吧, for a bar where alcoholic beverages are served. This word's offshoots include 玻璃吧 (glassware bar), 玩具吧 (toy bar), 氧吧 (oxygen bar), 布吧 (cloth bar), 陶吧 (pottery bar), 书吧 (book bar), and even 网吧 (the Internet bar). Some places for leisure activities are also named 吧.

Loanwords are among the most active elements of a given language. They usually evolve in tandem with a country's social and cultural development. In Chinese, loanwords have not only been given new appearances and connotations, but have also enriched the culture by drawing in new concepts, ideas and even ways of thinking.

生词 New Words

1.外来词	wàiláicí	word of foreign origin; loanword
2.饮料	yǐnliào	beverage
3.渗透	shèntòu	osmosis; to infiltrate
4.口语	kǒuyǔ	spoken language
5.书面语	shūmiànyǔ	written language
6.吸收	xīshōu	to absorb; to suck up; to assimilate
7.词汇	cíhuì	vocabulary; words and phrases
8.适应	shìyìng	to suit; to adapt to
9.拉丁语	lādīngyǔ	Latin (language)
10.符合	fúhé	to accord with; to tally with; to be in keeping with
11.公元	gōngyuán	the Christian era
12.世纪	shìjì	century
13.出使	chūshǐ	to serve as an envoy abroad; to be sent on a diplomatic mission
14.西域	xīyù	the Western Regions
15.深远	shēnyuǎn	profound and lasting; far-reaching
16.开辟	kāipì	to open up; to start
17.丝绸	sīchóu	silk
18.布帛	bùbó	cloth and silk; cotton and silk textiles
19.面临	miànlín	to be faced with
20.反映	fǎnyìng	to reflect, to mirror
21.琉璃	liúli	colored glaze
22.琥珀	hǔpò	amber
23.骆驼	luòtuo	camel
24.琵琶	pípa	pipa, a plucked stringed instrument

25.属性	shǔxìng	attribute, property
26.元素周期表	yuánsù zhōuqībiǎo	periodic table of elements
27.类别	lèibié	category, classification
28.胡桃	hútáo	walnut
29.洋火	yánghuǒ	match
30.吕宋烟	lǚsòngyān	Luzon cigar
31.音译	yīnyì	translieration
32.博士	bóshì	doctor (Ph.D)
33.经济	jīngjì	economy
34.环境	huánjìng	environment
35.马铃薯	mǎlíngshǔ	potato
36.消防	xiāofáng	fire fighting
37.入场券	rùchǎngquàn	(admission) ticket
38.法人	fǎrén	artificial person; legal person; corporation
39.瓦斯	wǎsī	gas
40.混凝土	hùnníngtǔ	concrete
41.方针	fāngzhēn	policy; guiding principle
42.政策	zhèngcè	policy
43.阶层	jiēcéng	(social) stratum
44.陌生	mòshēng	strange, unfamiliar
45.活跃	huóyuè	brisk, active

语法聚焦 Notes and Examples

一、不管口语也好，书面语也好，它总是在各种交流中，吸收其他语言的词汇

这里“……也好……也好”表示所列举的情形其结果都一样。前边可带有“不管”、“无论”等词语。

…也好…也好 indicates that what are cited makes no difference. Words such as 不管, 无论 can be used before this pattern. For example:

1. 不管他同意也好，不同意也好，事情就这样定了。
2. 无论话剧也好，京剧也好，我都爱看。
3. 是你的意见也好，还是领导的意见也好，我都不采纳。

二、就拿英语来说

“拿……来说”这个格式是在我们要用例子来说明问题时，把例子放在这个格式中，后面句子说明具体情况。

The pattern 拿…来说 cites an example, and the example is put between 拿 and 来说. The sentence follows it gives some details of the example. For example:

1. 这里的雨水非常多，就拿上个月来说，一个月就下了二十天雨。
2. 门球这种游戏多大年龄都能玩，就拿郝大爷来说吧，快八十岁了，每天还在打门球。
3. 这班学生的学习成绩非常好，就拿数学课来说，全班平均成绩是九十六分。

三、同时也吸收了法语的一些词汇

这里“同时”是连词，表示进一层，是“并且”的意思。

Conjunction 同时 means at the same time, meanwhile and furthers the meaning. For example:

1. 张先生是我们的老师，同时也是我们的朋友。
2. 这项任务是艰巨的，同时也是光荣的。
3. 对我们每个人来说，这是工作，同时也是学习。

四、西域各国的使节和商人也纷纷来到中国

“纷纷”是形容词，表示很多人接二连三地发出某种动作，进行某种活动。

Adjective 纷纷 indicates there are many people involved in certain action and the action is repeated for several times. For example:

1. 大家纷纷报名，要求献血。
2. 记者们纷纷向发言人提问。
3. 孩子们纷纷写信慰问他。

五、当这些新的物品从西域传进中国时

“当……时”也可以说成“当……的时候”。“当”是介词，介绍发生的时间。“当……的时候”表明事情发生在另一事情或另一种状态出现的时候。

当…时 is the same with 当…的时候. 当 is a preposition introducing the time of an action or when something happens. For example:

1. 当水温到达摄氏零度时，水会变成冰。
2. 当我一想起爸爸叮嘱我的话时，我全身就充满了力量。
3. 当老王赶到机场时，飞机已经起飞了。

六、固然反映了这些事物本来的名称

“固然”是连词，它与表示转折的连词“但是”、“然而”一起用，表示先肯定承认某种情况，然后又对该事物提出一种新情况，以转入正意。

Conjunction 固然 is used with 但是 or 然而 to indicate a transition, confirming one thing and introducing another thing that is meant. For example:

1. 你固然讲得很有道理，但是在现实生活中未必行得通。
2. 蛇液固然有毒，但可以入药。
3. 刘明固然是一个聪明能干的人，但是让他去做这件事，我还是不放心。

七、对中国历史文化、社会生活产生了极其重大的影响

“极其”是副词，一般用来修饰双音节形容词和某些动词，是“非常”、“很”的意思。

Adverb 及其 modifies a disyllabic adjective or some verbs, meaning very much or extremely. For example:

1. 这是一个极其深刻的教训。

2. 卫生部门对这种疾病极其重视。
3. 大家对孙家康先生的刻苦钻研精神，极其佩服。
4. 这种不良嗜好，对身体极其有害。

想一想 Questions

1. 你能举例谈一谈语言中外来词的现象吗？
   Can you give some examples of loanwords?
2. 中国汉朝时，有哪些文化交流？汉语吸收了哪些外来词？
   What kinds of cultural exchanges were there in the Han Dynasty of China? What loanwords were absorbed into Chinese?
3. 佛教对汉语有哪些影响？
   How did Buddhism influence Chinese language?
4. 近代和现代，汉语吸收了哪些外来词？
   What loanwords have appeared in Chinese over the past century?
5. 你国家的语言中有外来词现象吗？
   Are there any loanwords in your mother tongue?

超级链接 Super Links

看一看这些词，汉语怎么说：

1. AIDS	艾滋病	àizībìng
2. Benz	奔驰	Bēnchí
3. BMW	宝马	Bǎomǎ
4. bunge jumping	蹦极跳	bèngjítiào
5. carnival	嘉年华	jiāniánhuá

6. Carrefour	家乐福	Jiālèfú
7. clone	克隆	kèlóng
8. E-mail	电子邮件	diànzǐ yóujiàn
9. fans	粉丝	fěnsī
10. gene	基因	jīyīn
11. hacker	黑客	hēikè
12. hamburger	汉堡包	hànbǎobāo
13. Hollywood	好莱坞	Hǎoláiwū
14. hotdog	热狗	règǒu
15. ice cream	冰淇淋	bīngqílín
16. Kentucky Fried Chicken	肯德基	Kěndéjī
17. Oscar Award	奥斯卡奖	Àosīkǎjiǎng
18. party	派对	pàiduì
19. Pizza Hut	必胜客	Bìshèngkè
20. pudding	布丁	bùdīng
21. rally	拉力赛	lālìsài
22. salad	沙拉	shālā
23. Starbucks	星巴克	Xīngbākè
24. sundae	圣代冰淇淋	shèngdài bīngqílín
25. talk show	脱口秀	tuōkǒuxiù
26. tap dance	踢踏舞	tītàwǔ
27. The Beatles	披头士乐队	Pītóushì Yuèduì
28. the Internet	因特网	yīntèwǎng
29. TOEFL (Test of English as a Foreign Language)	托福	Tuōfú
30. Wal-mart	沃尔玛	Wò'ěrmǎ

跨文化交际与文化习俗琐谈

Cross-cultural Communication

14

A Kaleidoscope of Chinese Culture

语言作为一种交际工具是非常重要的，语言不通，交际无法进行。但语言又是一种载体，它负载着一定的文化内涵，在许多情况下，不同民族的跨文化交际受阻，出现了误解、不愉快或交际失败，并不是因为话语没说清楚，而是由于文化背景不同造成的。

有一对中国夫妇邀请一位美国朋友共进晚餐，因为彼此语言不通，所以请了一位青年学生给他们作翻译。这位美国客人很有礼貌地称赞主人的妻子说："You are very pretty."翻译将这句话译成了汉语："你很漂亮。"这位妻子回答："哪里，哪里。"这位翻译将汉语"哪里"直译为："Where? Where?"美国客人听了，真是丈二和尚摸不着头，心想：为什么问我哪里漂亮呢?于是回答："Everywhere."翻译又译成了汉语："每个地方都很漂亮。"

这种尴尬首先出自翻译对"哪里"的误译，而这种误译正是由于中美两国不同的文化心理造成的。在日常生活中，人们赞赏别人，或受到别人的赞赏，这是很普通的事，可是就此事而进行交流时就不一样了。在美国文化中，当一个人听到别人对自己的得体称赞时，他感到对方是真心实意地在表扬自己，所以在喜悦的同时，要对这种友善表示感谢，回答："谢谢。"当一个中国人听到别人称赞自己时，心中同样非常高兴，但表现出来的一定要谦恭有礼，绝不能默认对方的赞誉之词而沾沾自喜，要体现出"我离你的赞美还差得远呢"，所以回答是否定的："不好，不好"、"哪里，哪里"或"不敢当"。由此可以看出跨文化交际背后的文化差异。

再比如，一位美国人对一位中国人说：“我想请您用中文给中国公司写一封信，可以吗？”中国人说：“好吧，我试试吧。”美国人听了这句话后，又会糊涂起来：他到底能做还是不能做呢？这样一点小事，他做起来应该没问题，为什么要试试呢？其实，中国人这样说并不是他对做此事真的没有把握，而是他有信心能做好，但一定要表现得留有余地，不能把话说绝，所以用了一句“试试吧”，既表示接受这件工作，又显示了自己的谦逊。假如这件事发生在两个中国人之间，当一位中国人听到“我试试吧”这句话时，他会想，这是他的客气，他一定能做好这件事，所以常常说：“您别客气了，这件事对您来说是小菜一碟。”于是交流通畅进行。我们讲了上面的例子，似乎使人感到，中国人说话太不直爽，喜欢绕弯子。其实不然，美国人讲话很多时候也是非常婉转的。美国是一个高度重视“个体”的社会，个人的权利要受到高度的尊重，所以每当让别人做某件事情时，十分注意不要有打扰、强迫或不尊重别人的现象发生，因此表现在语言上，常用征询、反问、假设等语气，如：“Do you mind if ...?”、“Don't you think...?”、“Would you...?”遇到这种情况，作为交流一方的中国人应该明白，这是美国人想让你做这件事。

从上面事例中我们可以看到，文化背景在跨文化交际中的重要地位。而文化背景又是一个含义十分广泛的概念，它包括人们的世界观、价值观、思维方式、文化传统、风俗礼仪、生活习惯等许多方面，特别是一些风俗礼仪，更在人们交际中起着十分重要的作用。我们仅就中、美两国的一些生活礼仪习俗作简单的比较。

一、问候习俗。人们相见彼此打一声招呼，问候一声，这是再普通不过的一种习俗了。可是不同文化的民族，在打招呼的方式和用语上也存在着差异。美国人相见多用祝贺式或问候式打招呼，如："Hi"、"Hello."、"Good morning."、"Good evening."、"How are you?"、"How are you doing?"等。这种打招呼意在交流彼此的友好感情，绝不要你道出事情的真相，比如：问者说："How are you? "回答总是：" Fine."、" Very well, thank you."、"Wonderful, thank you. "等，虽然你此时也许内心烦事重重，或正遇到一些不愉快的事，但还是要闭口不谈，因为没有人喜欢听你诉苦。中国人打招呼的方式要比美国人复杂一些。除了祝愿、问候式的，像"你好！"、"早安。"、"晚安。"、"你好吗？"等，还有叙谈式，像"你去哪儿？"、"干什么去了？"、"忙什么呢？"也有晚辈或下级对长辈叫一声称谓，以表示尊敬，如："大妈"、"三叔"、"李大爷"、"王师傅"、"高院长"等。另外，中国人在关系非常亲密的朋友之间，往往在姓氏前加"老"、"小"、"大"等，而不叫名，如："老张"、"小刘"、"大杨"。这些打招呼只是人们相见时感情交流的一种手段，也不要求对方有准确的回答，比如："你去哪儿？"你可以如实回答："去商店。"也可以含糊其辞："出去一下儿。"中国人的问候方式和语言，反映了中国人的问候理念和文化心理，要在这短短的打招呼中，根据不同的人际关系，体现出尊敬、亲密、友善与和谐。有时非常好的朋友间还用幽默玩笑式，如："嘿，胖子！"、"呦，买这么多！"等。人们尽量将亲密友好的感情，浓缩在这短短几句问候语中。反倒是一些无关紧要、大家都不感兴趣的话，使人感到太生疏、太客套了，如："今天天气真不错呀"。但是在进行跨文化交际时，采用祝愿问候的形式更加稳妥，像"您好。"、"您好吗？"这样的问候语，显得很是得体，分寸也恰到好处。如果采用谈话式，往往会造成文化心理上的碰撞。假如一个中国人和一个美国人见面时问："你去哪儿？"美国人心里会很不舒服。

二、告辞和送别习俗。做客、聚会活动结束后的告辞和送别，各国的文化习俗也不完全一样。在美国，如果参加晚宴，一般在离开的时候，客人要向主人表示感谢，主人也对客人的光临致以谢意；在中国，当客人提出告辞时，主人要表示挽留，如："再坐一会吧，时间还早呢。"或"别着急，再玩一会儿。"等，藉此表示主人热情好客。在送别方式上，中、美也不一样。在美国，送别时，主人一般站在门内，向客人握手告别，双方常用的告别语是："Thank you for coming."、"Thank you for a wonderful afternoon."、"Thank you. I've enjoyed this beautiful evening."等。大家在热情友好的气氛中道别；而在中国，主人送客要送出门外，如果关系密切，甚至送至小区门口。送别时，主人常常说"再见"、"走好"、"慢走"、"欢迎你下次再来"等，客人也回敬说"再见"、"请回吧"、"请留步"、"别送了"等告别语，大家挥手告别，总之，整个告辞和送别要体现出感情深厚、依依惜别、热情友好的气氛。

三、见面礼习俗。中国自古便非常重视礼仪，被誉为"礼仪之邦"。过去致礼的方式很多，在不同场合和不同人际关系之间，所用的礼节也是不一样的，像请安、拱手、跪拜、长揖、顿首、肃拜、叉手、折腰等。随着时代的发展，历史上的一些致礼的形式已经不再为人们所使用了，今天中国使用的是世界各国通用的握手礼。这种礼节来源于西方，传入中国大约有一百年左右。在握手时，中、美两国无太大的差异，一般的原则是主客之间，主人先伸手；男女之间，女士先伸手；上下级之间，上级先伸手。但在美国，如果是老朋友久别重逢，还有拥抱和贴面礼，这一点在中国人之间是没有的，只有在美国生活了一段时间的人，才会"入乡随俗"，接受这种礼节并用在跨文化交际中。中国人除了握手礼以外，还保留有鞠躬礼和拱手礼。这两种礼节用得不多，只是在特殊场合才用，例如:中国人结婚时，新郎和新娘要向双方家长、客人、对方行鞠躬礼；人们在参加葬礼时，也要向遗体或遗像三鞠躬；另外，在歌舞文艺节目表演完毕，演员返回台上向观众谢幕时，也总是以鞠躬致意。至于拱手礼，用得更少了，多是在节日团拜和喜庆祝贺之时，人们行此礼以表示欢乐的心情，也有人急切求人帮忙时，用拱手表示。

四、送礼的习俗。 互赠礼品是人们交流感情、增进友谊的一种很好的方式。人们通过馈赠礼物，表达祝贺、感谢、慰问或哀悼的心情。中国自古便有“礼尚往来”的习俗。《诗经》中说：“投我以木桃，报之以琼瑶”。中国民间也有“千里送鹅毛，礼轻情义重”的俗语。所以中国人认为，送礼的主要目的，不是为了得到物质东西，更是看重物质背后的深情厚谊。中国人的送礼习俗大致有以下几方面：

1. 春节时送的礼，叫做“年礼”。 春节是中国的传统新年，是中国极为隆重的一个节日。从正月初一开始，亲戚朋友间要互相走动拜年，特别是子女、晚辈要到父母或长辈家拜年，这时人们要带一些礼物，像糕点、糖果、烟酒、茶叶或土特产等。另外，中国人有一种传统习俗，就是春节时长辈要给小孩子一些钱，称做“压岁钱”。过去给“压岁钱” 是很讲究的，钱要用新币，还常常用红纸包上。此风至今仍在中国保留着，而且近年来，因家中多是独生子女，长辈给钱的数目越来越大，一个春节，有的孩子会得到一笔不小的收入。

2. 中国人有给老人做寿和给小孩过生日的习俗。 给老人做寿送的礼叫“寿礼”，过生日送的礼，叫“生日礼物”。做寿因年龄和身份不同，规模也不同。一般是四十岁以上，逢十寿，叫做“大寿”，人们送的礼品有寿幛、寿桃、寿面等；如给孩子过生日时，礼物多是儿童衣物、玩具或金钱。

3. 结婚时送的礼叫“贺礼”。 结婚是人生中极其重要的一件大事，所以不论过去和现在，人们总是通过送礼的方式表示祝贺。送的礼物多是喜幛、艺术制品或生活中实用物品等。近年来，更多的人赠送花篮、发电子贺卡或馈赠现金。

4. 慰问病伤者时也要送礼。 有时人们要到医院或家中去看望有病的亲属，大家常常带去一些礼物以表示慰问之情。礼物多是鲜花、水果、罐头、营养品等。

5. **丧礼**。如果有亲朋好友去世，人们参加丧礼时，送的礼品多是花圈、挽联或鲜花，近年来，越来越多赠送金钱。

美国人送礼与中国人有相同之处，也有不同之处。美国人多是在圣诞节、生日、结婚、生小孩时送礼和致贺卡。遇到“父亲节”、“母亲节”，子女除了送礼外，写一张贺卡更是不可少的。美国人送礼时，可以事先问受礼者有何需要，以免送的礼不合适或过多，造成不实用。在接受礼物时，中、美也有不同。美国人很重视礼品的包装，接到后常常当面拆开，开前还要问赠送者一声：“我可以打开吗？”以表示尊重。中国人接到礼物时，在表示感谢以后，便把礼物放在一边，以免当场打开给人一种“重礼不重人”的感觉。

总之，习俗是不同民族在不同环境下形成的一种文化现象，人们在学习语言的同时，更应了解和认知交际者的文化背景和礼仪习俗，从而使自己在交际时能适应对方的文化心理。

People who learn Chinese do so to use the language as a means of communication. However although cross-cultural communication is closely linked with language, it is also more. Often, misunderstandings or communication breakdowns are not due to the language itself, but to differences in cultural background.

There is a popular Chinese joke that is also an excellent example of how language by itself is not always able to overcome the cultural divide. A Chinese couple invites an American friend to dinner, and a young student accompanies them to translate. The guest politely compliments the hostess, “You are very pretty.” “哪里, 哪里,” she replies, meaning, “I’m flattered.” The translator, who is not very experienced, translates this directly into English as “Where? Where?” Confused, the American says, “Everywhere!” He doesn’t realize that saying “哪里, 哪里” is a politely modest way of accepting praise.

The student interpreter is unaware of the differences in the cultural psychology of the Chinese couple and the American. An American will accept a compliment gladly and with a big thank you. However even if a Chinese person is happy to receive a compliment, he or she will feel the need of modesty in accepting it. For this reason he or she will normally accept a compliment by saying "No, no." or "I'm flattered." These kind of cultural differences are very important to understand when it comes to cross-cultural communication.

Another example involving modesty begins when an American asks a Chinese person "Can you write a letter in Chinese for me to send to a Chinese company?" The Chinese replies "Alright, I will try." This confuses the American, who is not sure whether his friend will or will not write the letter. However the meaning in "Alright, I will try" is that of course the Chinese person will do it. It's just that by saying he will try means he is not big noting himself. If, on the other hand, the conversation was between two Chinese people, the conversation would flow differently. When the person asking hears the reply "I will try", he or she will recognize it as modesty, and will respond "Come on, you are being too polite. This is really easy for you."

While this may lead some to believe that Chinese people do not speak to the point, it must be remembered that every culture has its own ways of expressing politeness. Americans place a lot of emphasis on individual rights, and regard this as a basis for a lot of social behaviors. When an American asks another person to do something, he takes care not to show disrespect to that person's individual rights by beginning the sentence with "Do you mind if…?" "Don't you think…?" or "Would you…?" If the addressee of this question is Chinese, he or she may not automatically realize that this is not a question, but a polite way of asking him or her to do something.

In cross-cultural communication, cultural background spans many potential problem zones, including world view, values, mentality, traditions, customs, and habits. In particular, traditions and customs play an essential role in interpersonal exchanges. For brevity's sake, we will keep our discussion to a brief comparison of some customs between China and the United States.

1. **Greetings.** Greetings are common feature of all languages and cultures, but are used in different ways. Common American greetings include "Hi." "Hello." "Good morning." "Good evening." "How are you?" or "How are you doing?" The last two are often not real questions, so responses to them are often the same, such as "Fine." "Very well, thank you." or "Wonderful, thank you." You may be upset or not fine at that moment, but that does not prevent you from answering "Fine." or "Very well."

The Chinese have a slightly more complex way of greeting. In addition to saying hello, they may ask "Where are you going?" "What are you doing?" A younger person may address an older person with their title, such as "Aunty", "Third Uncle", "Elder Uncle Li", "Master Wang", or "President Gao". Between close friends, Lao, Xiao, or Da, meaning old, young, or big may be added before somebody's surname, such as in Lao Zhang, Xiao Liu, or Da Yang. When you are asked the question "Where are you going?" in a greeting, it is considered acceptable to answer "Going to a shop" if that is what you plan to do, or something vague, such as "Going away for a while."

Greetings between Chinese vary depending on whether they are given between close friends or strangers. Close friends may even greet each other in humorous ways that sound rude or too casual to others, such as "Hi, you fat guy." or "Haven't you bought many things!" when seeing a friend at supermarket. Between friends, Chinese would consider a greeting such as "Isn't it a fine day" to be too distant. However, to be on the safe side and avoid any possible cultural transgressions, when meeting somebody the best thing is simply to say "*Ni hao ma*?" meaning "How are you?" A foreigner may feel uncomfortable being asked "Where are you going?"

2. Goodbyes. There are many different ways of saying goodbye in different cultures. In the US, the host often stands at the door and shakes the guest's hand, saying "Thanks for coming." The guest might respond, "Thanks for a wonderful afternoon." or "Thank you. I've enjoyed this beautiful evening."

In China, however, when the guest says that they must be off, the host will say "Please stay a little longer, it's still early", or "Don't hurry, stay longer", as a way of showing politeness and hospitality. While seeing the guest off, the host or hostess will accompany the guest out of the door, or maybe even downstairs to the entrance of the building. This show of reluctance to see the guest depart is considered to be quite courteous.

3. Gestures used in greetings. In the past, there have been many polite gestures used to accompany greetings in China. Depending on the relationship between the two people, they included drooping the right arm in front of oneself and bending the left knee, cupping one hand in the other before the chest, kneeling down, making a bow with hands clasped, kowtowing, raising one's folded hands to one's chin to salute, and even bending one's back to bow.

But most of these gestures are no longer used in daily life. Instead, similar to most western cultures, Chinese people usually shake hands when they meet. This was introduced to China more than a century ago. Usually the host takes initiative to extend his hand to the guest, the female extends her hand to the male, and the superior in position extends his hand to the subordinate. The Chinese do not usually hug or kiss each other's face. Apart from the handshake, two traditional greeting gestures are still used in formal situations. The first is bowing, and the other is cupping one hand in the other before the chest. These can be seen at weddings and funerals. At a wedding, the bride and bridegroom bow to each other, their parents, parents-in-law and wedding guests. At funerals, people bow to a photo of the deceased or the body of the deceased three times. Bowing is also a way for performers to thank their audience. Cupping one hand in the other before the chest is used much less. It is seen when people greet one another at Chinese New Year or on other happy occasions. When a person is in dire need of assistance, he may also use this gesture.

4. Gift giving. Giving gifts is a common way of expressing courtesy and friendship. In *The Book of Songs*, there are several mentions of gift-giving, including "You gave me a peach, and a ruby I offered you." There is also a Chinese saying: "The gift itself may be light as a goose feather, but when sent from afar, it conveys deep feelings." This reflects the belief that the value of a gift is not its material worth, but in the feeling that it represents. The Chinese give gifts on several occasions.

1. The Spring Festival gifts. Traditionally, relatives and friends visit each other at this time. In particular, married children come back to their parent's home, and younger generations visit older generations. Those visiting usually involve small gifts such as sweets, tea, cigarettes, spirits, wine, or something a little more special. Traditionally, elders also give some money to young children as a gift. The coins (as used in historical times) or notes given need to be new ones, and are wrapped in red paper or put in small red envelopes. Currently most Chinese families have only one child due to the government's one-child policy, and so the lucky child may get a considerable sum from his or her relatives.

2. Birthday gifts. Birthdays of older relatives and young children are particularly celebrated in Chinese families. Presents given to older family members are referred to as "longevity gifts". The change in a person's decade after the age of forty is always a big celebration. Traditional gifts to elders include silk birthday scrolls or cloth, peach-shaped birthday cakes, or birthday noodles. The quality of the present will vary according to the person's age and their position of seniority in the family. Common birthday presents for children include clothes, toys, or money for them to spend on things they like.

3. Wedding gifts. What is a wedding without gifts? Relatives and friends shower the bride and groom with presents. In the past, these might be a silk wedding scroll or cloth, or a piece of artwork. Nowadays it is more common to give the newlyweds something practical, like household goods, flower bouquets, wedding cards or money.

4. Gifts for the injured or patients. Flowers, fruit or nutriments may be given to people who are ill or injured.

5. Gifts at funerals. To express condolence over the death of a family member or friend, when attending a funeral people often have wreaths, elegiac couplets, or fresh flowers sent. It is also becoming more popular to bring some money for the bereaved.

There are both similarities and differences in the manner that Americans and Chinese give gifts. Americans give gifts at Christmas, birthdays, weddings, and when a baby is born. Americans also often celebrate Father's Day and Mother's Day by giving gifts and cards. Before an American chooses a gift, he or she may ask what the person wants in order to make sure they choose something suitable. The gift is almost always wrapped. When receiving a gift, an American will often politely ask "May I open it?" They will then open it in the presence of the person who gave them the gift.

Chinese people do not usually open gifts in the presence of those who gave it to them. In China it is considered more polite to thank the person giving the gift, and then politely put it aside. By doing this the person accepting the gift is considered to be paying less attention to the gift than the person who gave it to them.

As said, customs are cultural phenomena. When learning a language, one should also make an effort to understand something of the cultural background that has informed its development. This is a great help in overcoming cultural misunderstandings.

生词 New Words

1.载体	zǎitǐ	carrier
2.受阻	shòuzǔ	to be obstructed; to meet with obstruction
3.误解	wùjiě	to misread; misunderstanding
4.丈二和尚，摸不着头		zhàng èr héshàng, mōbuzháo tóu You can't touch the head of the ten-foot monk – you can't make head or tail of it; to be very in the dark
5.日常	rìcháng	everyday, daily
6.真心实意	zhēnxīn-shíyì	genuinely and sincerely; truly and whole-heartedly
7.表扬	biǎoyáng	to praise, to commend
8.谦恭	qiāngōng	modest and courteous
9.沾沾自喜	zhānzhān-zìxǐ	to feel complacent; to be pleased with oneself
10.差异	chāyì	difference, divergence
11.糊涂	hútu	muddled, confused
12.把握	bǎwò	assurance, certainty
13.信心	xìnxīn	confidence
14.留有余地	liúyǒu yúdì	to allow for unforeseen circumstances; to leave some leeway
15.小菜	xiǎocài	something extremely easy to do
16.通畅	tōngchàng	unobstructed, clear
17.直爽	zhíshuǎng	frank, candid, forthright
18.绕弯子	rào wānzi	to talk in a roundabout way; to beat about the bush
19.其实	qíshí	actually; in fact
20.婉转	wǎnzhuǎn	mild and indirect; tactful
21.重视	zhòngshì	to attach importance to; to pay attention to
22.个体	gètǐ	individualism

23.反问	fǎnwèn	rhetorical question
24.假设	jiǎshè	supposing; in case
25.世界观	shìjièguān	world view
26.价值观	jiàzhíguān	values
27.思维方式	sīwéi fāngshì	mode of thinking
28.问候	wènhòu	greetings
29.真相	zhēnxiàng	the real situation; the real facts
30.晚辈	wǎnbèi	the younger generation; one's juniors
31.长辈	zhǎngbèi	elder, senior
32.准确	zhǔnquè	accurate, exact
33.含糊其辞	hánhuqící	to talk ambiguously; to equivocate
34.亲密	qīnmì	close, intimate
35.友善	yǒushàn	friendly, amicable
36.浓缩	nóngsuō	to concentrate, to enrich
37.无关紧要	wúguān-jǐnyào	of no importance; immaterial
38.生疏	shēngshū	not familiar; not as close as before
39.客套	kètao	polite formula; polite expression
40.分寸	fēncùn	proper limits for speech or action
41.恰到好处	qiàdàohǎochù	just right (for the purpose or occasion)
42.告辞	gàocí	to take leave; farewell
43.送别	sòngbié	to see sb. off
44.挽留	wǎnliú	to persuade sb. to stay
45.挥手告别	huīshǒu gàobié	to wave farewell; to wave goodbye to sb.
46.依依惜别	yīyī xībié	reluctant to part
47.气氛	qìfen	surrounding feeling; atmosphere

48.请安	qǐng'ān	to pay respects to sb.; to make obeisance by drooping the right arm in front of oneself and bending the left knee
49.拱手	gǒngshǒu	to make an obeisance by cupping on hand in the other before the chest
50.跪拜	guìbài	to kneel down
51.长揖	chángyī	to make a bow with hands clasped
52.顿首	dùnshǒu	to kowtow
53.叉手	chāshǒu	to raise one's folded hands to one's chin to salute
54.折腰	zhéyāo	to bend one's back – to bow in obeisance
55.久别重逢	jiǔbié chóngféng	to meet again after a long separation
56.拥抱	yōngbào	to embrace, to hug
57.入乡随俗	rùxiāng suísú	Wherever you are, follow local customs; When in Rome, do as the Romans do.
58.鞠躬	jūgōng	to bow
59.遗体	yítǐ	remains (of the dead)
60.遗像	yíxiàng	a photograph of the deceased
61.团拜	tuánbài	to gather to exchange greetings
62.千里送鹅毛，礼轻情义重		qiānlǐ sòng émáo, lǐ qīng qíngyì zhòng The gift itself may be light as a goose feather, but when sent from afar, it conveys deep feelings.
63.土特产	tǔtèchǎn	local product and specialty
64.寿桃	shòutáo	peach offered as a birthday present; peach-shaped birthday cakes
65.寿面	shòumiàn	birthday noodles
66.营养品	yíngyǎngpǐn	nutriment; nutritious food
67.花圈	huāquān	(floral) wreath

语法聚焦 Notes and Examples

一、作为交流一方的中国人应该明白，这是美国人想让你做这件事

"作为"是介词，表示就人的某种身份或事物的某种性质来说，可用于句首。

Preposition 作为 means as and can be used at the beginning of a sentence indicating the nature or identity of the noun follows it. For example:

1. 作为一个领导，应该以身作则。
2. 作为一个医生，应该救死扶伤，发扬人道主义精神。
3. 作为园内主体建筑，我觉得设计很一般。
4. 作为一种新生事物，大家应该热情支持它。

二、人们相见彼此打一声招呼

"彼此"是代词。"彼"指对方，"此"指己方。用于人与人之间，指"双方"。在句中作主语，也可作定语和宾语。

Pronoun 彼此 means each other. 彼 refers to the other party, and 此 refers to oneself. 彼此 can also mean both parties. It can be used as the subject, the attribute, or the object. For example:

1. 彼此都很熟悉，就不要客气了。
2. 我们彼此虽然没见过面，但电话里是老朋友了。
3. 我们俩从来不分彼此。
4. 通过打招呼，交流了彼此的感情。

三、主人一般站在门内，向客人握手告别

"一般"是形容词，表示"普通"、"普遍"、"通常"或在多数的情况下。

一般 means generally, usually, or on most occasions. For example:

1. 在一般情况下，只要照顾得好，这些鸡会长得很快。
2. 施大爷一般是早晨去公园散步。
3. 我们一般上午有两节课，下午没课，有时加课。
4. 一般而言，这种可能不大。

四、传入中国大约有一百年左右

"左右"是名词，用在数量词或带数量词的名词后面，表示概数。

Noun 左右 is used after a numerical or a noun with a numerical to indicate a rough number. For example:

1. 今年的增长率，大概是百分之十左右。
2. 这个旅馆大约可接纳一千人左右。
3. 这种计算机大概五百元左右。
4. 修建这样的体育馆，需要一年左右的时间。

五、人们通过馈赠礼物，表达祝贺、感谢、慰问或哀悼的心情

"通过"是介词，介绍出动作或手段，因而达到某种目的。

Preposition 通过 indicates by means of or by doing something so as to reach a goal. For example:

1. 通过别人介绍，孙小姐认识了李先生。
2. 通过学习，大家了解了这种产品的性能。
3. 通过多次谈判，最后双方达成了协议。

六、送的礼物多是喜幛、艺术制品或生活中实用物品等

"多"是形容词，在这里用作状语，表示"很多"、"大多"或"更多"。

Adjective 多 in this case is used as an adverbial, meaning mostly, almost or more. For example:

1. 现在中国人家中，多是独生子女。
2. 你在这里多了解一些情况。
3. 这种树长得快，多种些吧。

想一想 Questions

1. 中国人的问候习俗是什么?
   What are the greeting customs in China?
2. 中国人的告辞和送别与你的国家有哪些不同的习俗?
   Are there any differences in China and in your country in saying goodbye?

3. 现在中国人的见面礼是什么?
What are the gestures used in greetings in China?

4. 请比较一下，中国人送礼和你的国家有哪些异同。
Compared with your country, are there any differences or similarities in giving gift in China?

超级链接 Super Links

(一) 中国全体公民放假的节日

新年 (1月1日)：庆祝新的一年开始。法定放假1天。

春节 (农历1月1日)：中国农历新年，是中国最隆重的传统节日。人们辞旧迎新，欢庆佳节。放假3天（农历除夕、正月初一、正月初二）。

清明节 (4月5日前后)：是人们祭典祖先，缅怀先人，扫墓踏青的日子。放假1天。

五一国际劳动节(5月1日)：是国际节日。放假1天。

端午节 (农历5月5日)：是中国古老的传统节日，也称“诗人节”。放假1日。

中秋节(农历8月15日)：是中国重要传统节日之一。秋高月圆，象征人间团圆，也叫“团圆节”。放假1天。

十一国庆节(10月1日)：是中华人民共和国成立的日子。放假3天（10月1日、2日、3日）。

(二) 中国部分公民放假的节日及纪念日

妇女节(3月8日)：妇女放假半天。

青年节(5月4日)：14周岁以上的青年放假半天。

儿童节(6月1日)：不满14周岁的少年儿童放假1天。

中国人民解放军建军纪念日(8月1日)：现役军人放假半天。

(三) 中国不放假的传统节日

元宵节(农历1月15日)：也叫“上元节”，是中国古老的传统节日之一。

寒食节(清明前一天)：人们不生火做饭，吃冷食。

七夕节(农历7月7日)：也叫“乞巧节”。

重阳节(农历9月9日)：人们登高赏秋，也是老人节。

腊八节(农历12月8日)：是一个古老的传统节日。

语法聚焦索引

主要参考文献

《中国汉字文化大观》	何九盈 胡双宝 张猛	北京大学出版社
《社会语言学》	陈原	学林出版社
《中国文化》	韩鉴堂 编著	国际文化出版公司
《中日文化比较》	蔡振生 编著	北京语言学院出版社
《文化撞击案例评析》	汪福祥 马登阁	石油出版社
《文化语言学中国潮》	邵敬敏 主编	语文出版社
《中英（英语国家）文化习俗比较》	杜学增	外语教学与研究出版社
《文化与交际》	胡文仲 主编	外语教学与研究出版社
《汉语言文化研究》	谢文庆 孙晖 主编	天津人民出版社

责任编辑： 任　蕾
英文编辑： 郭　辉
封面设计： 胡　湖
印刷监制： 佟汉东

图书在版编目（CIP）数据

中华文化趣谈：汉英对照／张亚军主编.—北京：华语教学出版社，2008
ISBN 978-7-80200-400-9

Ⅰ.中… Ⅱ.张… Ⅲ.汉语－对外汉语教学－语言读物
Ⅳ.H195.5

中国版本图书馆CIP数据核字（2008）第076413号

中华文化趣谈
张亚军　编著
*

华语教学出版社出版
（中国北京百万庄大街24号　邮政编码 100037）
电话：(86)10-68320585
传真：(86)10-68326333
网址：www.sinolingua.com.cn
电子信箱：hyjx@sinolingua.com.cn
北京市外文印刷厂印刷
中国国际图书贸易总公司海外发行
（中国北京车公庄西路35号）
北京邮政信箱第399号　邮政编码100044
新华书店国内发行
2008年（16开）第一版
2009年第一版第二次印刷
（汉英）
ISBN 978-7-80200-400-9
定价：68.00元

Printed in China